Andrew Boot was bo‍‍ turned to writing after a career in the music business, running his own independent record labels. He worked for a Fleet Street features agency and contributed two regular columns to *Kerrang!*, as well as writing for the *Mail on Sunday*, *Punch* and *Record Collector*. He lives in East London with his wife, Penny, and three ancient cats.

Psychic Murder Hunters

Andrew Boot

HEADLINE

First published in 1994
by HEADLINE BOOK PUBLISHING

First published in paperback in 1994
by HEADLINE BOOK PUBLISHING

10 9 8 7 6 5 4 3 2 1

ISBN 0 7472 4302 6

Typeset by Keyboard Services, Luton

Printed and bound in Great Britain by
Cox & Wyman Ltd, Reading, Berks

HEADLINE BOOK PUBLISHING
A division of Hodder Headline PLC
338 Euston Road
London NW1 3BH

Contents

Dedication

This book is dedicated to my wife Penny, my mother
Millie, but most of all to Jim Ashton (1918–91),
whose faith in me sometimes outweighed my own.

Acknowledgements

In preparing this book the following people were invaluable: Keith Hudson, of Above And Beyond, St Mary's Road, London E17, who was a powerhouse of ideas and supplied me with numerous out-of-print books needed for reference, the secretaries of the Society For Psychical Research and the College of Psychic Studies who made their libraries open to a nervous first-time researcher, and Alan Wesencraft – keeper of the Harry Price Library at the University of London – who scoured his archives for relevant material. Thank you, all of you.

Also invaluable were Ian Marshall, who edited the book, Alan Brooke who commissioned the damn thing in the first place and Linda Silverman, whose diligence found the excellent pictures.

Finally, anyone whose interest in the paranormal has been whetted could do worse than check out Colin Wilson's *Beyond The Occult*. This is the book that first re-awakened my interest in the paranormal, and its bibliography was a good starting point in my researches on the subject, setting me on a chain of fascinating reading that culminated in this book.

Introduction

Psychic phenomena *do* exist. There is more than enough evidence to prove that they do, and the sixteen cases in this book provide good examples of how those powers can help to solve baffling crimes. Science cannot, as yet, explain why these things happen; and because they are erratic in nature, it cannot quantify them. Scientists find it hard to reproduce psychic phenomena under laboratory conditions so tend to dismiss them as fraud, bunk and lies.

The purpose of this introduction is to try to explain the theories behind the different forms of psychic experience that occur in the pages of this book. Sometimes the theories of those few scientists who take such phenomena seriously may make the reader do a double take, and put the book down in bemusement. In this case, I urge you to read the murder cases first, and refer back to the relevant section in this introduction when you need an explanation of the way in which the psychic solved the crime. It will become clearer then, I promise! I

1

have also endeavoured to illustrate a theory with an example or two in this introduction, in order to try to clarify the more difficult points: difficult not because of their scientific complexity, but because we are travelling into areas that no one yet fully understands.

Most of these theories can be slotted together in a way that may possibly supply us with a clue to the ultimate answer about psychic powers and where they come from. This unifying theory will be dealt with at the end of the introduction. First, we have to understand what the other theories mean.

Psychometry

The psychic handles a personal item belonging to the victim – a piece of clothing, a possession, something that has a close association with the victim rather than just something that was found at the scene of a crime – and reads from it impressions that can tell him or her what has occurred. Psychic researchers put forward two possible explanations for this ability: the first is that the psychic is somehow able to read imprints that are left on the item, as though it were some kind of tape recorder recording impressions of events that occur around it.

This is also the theory that many researchers ascribe to the appearance of ghosts: the ghost is, in fact, a replaying of past happenings by an object. The tape recorder theory was espoused by Tom Lethbridge, an ex-archaeology don at Cambridge

University who first became interested in the paranormal after seeing a ghost near his Devon home.

Lethbridge found that most ghosts tend to appear where there is a strong electro-magnetic field, such as water (he saw his ghost beside a stream). He reasoned that a strong emotional impression could imprint itself upon the electro-magnetic field, and be replayed to anyone who was sensitive enough to pick up the recording: in the same way sound is recorded on to magnetic tape, and can only be replayed by the right equipment. A psychic has that equipment.

This theory has one flaw: many psychics psychometrise from objects that were not near the victim at the time of their disappearance or death. Gerald Croiset used Pat McAdam's Bible, which was sitting in her bedroom at the time of her abduction and murder; Suzanne Padfield used Inessa Tchurina's schoolwork, completed in another country some days before her abduction and murder.

Much more likely in these cases is the second theory: that items belonging to someone, and of great personal value to them, are likely to be tuned in to that person's own vibrations, and resonate in harmony with them. Thus, a psychic who can psychometrise an object can tune in to the vibration of the missing or dead person, and so is able to see what has happened to them. This is not perhaps as far-fetched as it may sound: a major tenet of Buddhist philosophies concerns the idea of a human being's personal vibrations, and western science has shown that all things vibrate at different frequencies, according to the atomic weights of the molecules that comprise each object.

However, Lethbridge had another idea. He spent many years experimenting with a pendulum, and found that each concept that he concentrated on had its own pendulum rate – e.g., silver made the pendulum rotate twenty-two times at twenty-two inches of pendulum length. When he thought of death, the pendulum swung forty times at forty inches (he found that the string length must be right before the pendulum would respond to the thought). Beyond the length for death (i.e. forty inches), everything was as before, except that you must add forty (so when he thought of silver, it responded at sixty-two inches at a rate of twenty-two rotations – forty plus twenty-two). But when he thought of time and had the pendulum at a length of over forty inches it would not respond. Did this mean that time did not exist after death?

Lethbridge concluded that his discovery tied in with many of the old beliefs that a person's existence worked on a series of spirals, and after dying we go on to the second spiral, where there is no time as we know it. He theorised that psychics were like people who had déjà-vu dreams: they had somehow journeyed to this second spiral, and so could see everything that has ever or will ever happen. According to Lethbridge, psychometry was a way in which an object acted as a pendulum, allowing a psychic a gateway on to another spiral, or into another dimension.

When an object is subjected to psychometry, the psychic receives impressions in the shape of sensory sensations: vision, touch, smell; and sometimes in the shape of emotional sensation. There is nothing clear-cut about this. The impressions are not a well defined and linear narrative, like a feature film. Rather, they are jumbled and confused, like a film where the reels are shown in the wrong order, and you only get a few seconds from each reel.

Therefore, a lot is left in the hands of the psychic, and those to whom he or she relays those impressions. This is vital when psychics are used in criminal cases. If they are badly interpreted, then the impressions will reveal nothing. If, on the other hand, they are placed within the context of a case, and studied in relation to the evidence that is already known, they can provide vital links, and lead investigations in new directions. Psychometry is only half the story. Interpretation is equally vital.

In this way, the use of psychics can provide a quantum leap in an investigation that seems to be going nowhere. The clues supplied by a psychic's impressions can open new avenues and lead to the solving of otherwise baffling crimes. On the other hand, it can also cause confusion and dissent. In some of the cases included here – Pat McAdam and Gerald Croiset, and Peter Hurkos and Melvin Rees – where police are sceptical, or who are dealing with the psychic through an interpreter, get their information confused, they believe that they have been given nothing of value when in fact the clues were there all the time.

Spiritualism and Ghosts

The idea of ghosts that are more than just tape recordings means that there must be survival after death: that the spirit of a dead person carries on in some way. Some people believe in reincarnation, some in a heaven or nirvana, where the spirit goes to rest for eternity. But there do seem to be some spirits that are unable to move on to the next plane. Like the spirits of Mona Tinsley and Teresita Basa, who had to tell a psychic of their terror and try to avenge their death.

Some psychics do not believe in ghosts and attribute their powers entirely to their own minds. But others believe that spirits are all around them, talking to them. The two ideas are not incompatible: if a psychic did not believe in ghosts, he or she would not be receptive to a spirit. It doesn't preclude their ability to see things through psychometry. Some psychics can do both.

In the past, psychics who talked to spirits tended to shy away from helping find murderers, as they would be sending someone to the gallows, and this was against their creed – Spiritualism, a religion with its own church.

The roots of Spiritualism lay in 1822, and the services of Edward Irving, a firebrand Scots preacher whose meetings in London's Hatton Garden were full of cries for miracles, and whose congregation soon began to speak in tongues – always a part of any medium's repertoire, whether genuine or fake.

Since the turn of the century the wave of Spiritualism and interest in the spirit world had been running high, aided by such forceful and literate proponents as Sir Arthur Conan Doyle, the journalist Hanner Swaffer and the high-profile investigation of mediums and psychic phenomena of English eccentric Harry Price. Even Edgar Wallace – at first sceptical – later became a convert.

The Spiritualist Church grew from disorganised beginnings into a loose organisation and by the 1920s was a fully fledged religion that had a well-defined creed, and a rigid set of beliefs. These included the belief that we are all surrounded by the spirits of our family, and that they are watching over us and guiding us. These spirits manifest themselves to mediums as tangible beings, and far from seeming on a higher plane, they appear to be earth-dwellers who simply have no substance – an apparent contradiction never fully explained.

There is also a rigid system through which a medium can communicate with these spirits, and through which they can communicate with the earthly world. This involves the training of a

7

medium, a code for rapping on tables, and the use of a 'control': the control is a spirit who acts as a sort of referee between the medium and those spirits who may wish to communicate with loved ones on earth via that medium.

A committed Spiritualist believed that the act of projecting a murderer from this world into the next by means of another murder – albeit that execution was a legalised killing – would not necessarily put an end to the murderer's criminal activities. The Spiritualist would hold the belief that the murderer's spirit may become earth-bound, and attempt to inhabit a person who was unbalanced, or of weak will, and having 'possessed' this person, would force them to commit acts similar to those for which it was executed.

This may be difficult to accept for those of us who are not Spiritualists, but perhaps it is easier to understand their point of view if you take into account the experience of Remy Chua when 'possessed' by Teresita Basa and the argument for discarnate spirits presented by Guy Lyon Playfair in his 1980 book, *This House Is Haunted*.

Playfair is a noted investigator of psychic phenomena, and was called in to investigate poltergeist disturbance at a house in Enfield, North London. Most poltergeist activity centres around a disturbed adolescent whose sexual energies are awakening, but it soon became obvious that this was something else.

A seance was held, and the results were recorded on tape. The medium was Dono Gmelig-Meyer, who is Dutch – but the voices captured on tape talk in tones that are pure North London. There are at least two spirits present. One identifies itself as Joe, and the other, when questioned, replied that his name was Bill Haylock and he was seventy-two years old. He claimed to have come from Durants Park and was looking for his family – who were not there. He was unhappy. When asked if he knew he was dead, the spirit told Playfair to 'fuck off', obviously disturbed at such a thought!

A subsequent investigation revealed that a Bill Haylock was buried in Durants Park Cemetery, a short walk from the house, and that a Joe Watson had lived in the house prior to the incumbent family. He hadn't moved home – he had died in the house.

The spirits were finally convinced by Dono Gmelig-Meyer that they were dead, and no longer belonged among the living. The poltergeist activity ceased. So Playfair concluded that some poltergeist activity must be attributed to earth-bound spirits who either don't realise that they are dead, or have some reason for staying behind.

Another manifestation of discarnate spirits is believed to be the appearance of hypnagogic voices.

Hypnagogic phenomena occur at the moment of waking from sleep (the word is derived from the Greek for sleep). At this point when the two spheres of the brain – the conscious and the unconscious –

overlap, strange things happen. Most of the time, the instant between waking and sleeping is so brief that it is impossible to remember what has occurred, just as you very rarely remember everything you dream. However, there are occasions when this state lasts a little longer and you can find yourself holding a conversation with someone you have never seen before.

The hypnagogic state is important in relation to discarnate spirits because it is then that our dormant psychic faculties are, for the briefest of moments, open in all of us. This is possibly the state in which Etta Smith and Remy Chua – two psychics featured in this book who had one-off psychic experiences – were approached by spirits and strange dreams.

Despite the fact that mediums and clairvoyants (those who see spirits) believe in ghosts and many of the psychics in this book differ wildly in their opinions, there is a link between them, a link that ties those who believe purely in science and those who believe only in spirits.

This dichotomy is as much a product of differing generations as anything else, as we can see by contrasting the worlds of Suzanne Padfield and Estelle Roberts, who had many similarities but wildly differing points of view.

Spirits versus Science

Suzanne Padfield first began to have psychic experiences when still young. There was a ghost who came up to her bed and touched her, and there were lights and poltergeist phenomena – a disappearing clothes horse vanished from her parents' kitchen one day without trace! As a child she believed them to be spirits, but as she grew older she tended towards the scientific theories of psychic powers: that they all come from inside, from the mind, and that nothing comes from outside. This is in direct contrast to an earlier generation, who felt that all psychic powers were gifts from the spirits, and that their world could contact us directly.

Estelle Roberts, too, had psychic experiences in her childhood. She recounted in her autobiography how she talked to spirits when she was small, and also told the story of a knight appearing at her bedroom window.

It is interesting that both women had their first experience of phenomena in their bedrooms, pre-sumably when they were trying to sleep – the state of semi-consciousness between sleeping and waking seems to provide a key. Both women were told by their parents not to make up stories when they reported what they had seen. Perhaps this made them more determined to be receptive – to prove their detractors wrong.

Padfield found herself flung out of bed on many occasions. This, too, happened to Estelle Roberts: she was flung from her bed many times on the night a fire started in her drawing room. Both women were also adept at levitating tables. Padfield reproduced this effect many times when being studied by Benson Herbert at his Paraphysical Laboratory, and Estelle Roberts recalls many such instances in her autobiography, and many other books co-authored by her.

When we get to the individual cases, the similarities become even more striking. Mona Tinsley appeared to Estelle Roberts and told her of her ordeal at the hands of Frank Nodder, during which the medium felt the intense emotions of the girl. Travelling to Nottingham after handling some dress material belonging to the girl, she was able to map out the area leading to the place where the child's body was hidden. In the Inessa Tchurina case, Suzanne Padfield felt the intense emotions of the child as she saw what happened to her, and she, too, was able to draw a map leading to the place where the girl's body was hidden.

Yet Estelle Roberts was firmly convinced that she was talking to spirits from the world of the dead, and Suzanne Padfield was convinced she was using an inherent power emerging from her own brain! How could it be that the two women could have such differing ideas on where their powers came from?

For the answer to this, we have to backtrack a little further, and mention the name of occult philosopher Allan Kardec. This was the pseudonym of Denzard-Hippolyte-Lyon Ravail, a Parisian doctor born in 1805, who became interested in mesmerism in the

1850s. At this time, the art of hypnosis was new, and still named after the man who first developed it (Anton Mesmer). To admit interest in such a thing would have been professional anathema to a doctor such as Ravail, yet he had used it several times with success, and through it came to know a Mme Plainmaison, who held seances at her home.

As time went on, Ravail began to attend more seances, and to study other forms of psychic activity such as automatic writing and telekinesis – although it was not known by that name at the time. He was the first psychic researcher to approach the subject without a firmly held belief. Gradually, he evolved a theory as to how these things occurred which encompassed the idea of spirits from beyond the grave, convinced by what he saw as the irrefutable proofs provided in seances. He expanded his theory in *Book of the Spirits*, but was warned that to publish it under his own name would cause a scandal that could ruin him, so he adopted the pseudonym of Allan Kardec. The book became one of the most influential works of its time, and was the basis for the founding precepts of the Spiritualist Church.

Such was the fervour of the Spiritualists that they would not consider the possibility that any practising medium could be a fraud. This blind acceptance hit its peak with the trials of Helen Duncan, a medium who was found to be producing fraudulent phenomena, and was tried and convicted in Scotland in both the 1930s and 1940s. Yet, despite this, some members of organisations such as the Society for Psychical Research stuck to their convictions that she was genuine!

Of course, some genuine mediums produced fraudulent effects when under great pressure, and a lot of genuine mediums and psychics slipped slowly down the long inexorable slide to obscurity. By the end of the Second World War, Spiritualism was virtually dead.

In its place came a harder, more scientific attitude as the Soviets and the CIA attempted to get to the bottom of psychic phenomena to harness them for their own ends. Some scientific groups began to acknowledge that such powers existed, even if they could not be explained. In attempting to find explanations they dropped notions of the spirit world and started to claim that these powers could emanate from areas of the brain that human beings do not appear to use. A new theory put forward the idea that we could all be psychics and that all man needed to do was find a way to unlock that part of the brain. All notions of such things as discarnate spirits went out of the window along with the Spiritualist ethos.

Unfortunately, it's not that simple: even the most cursory glance reveals that there is some proof to support both sides of the argument – and it's probable that the truth is a mixture of both ideas. But psychics who did not believe in discarnate spirits would not be receptive to them, and so their psychic activity was coloured by their own beliefs. Time and again, it can be seen in the cases in this book that each psychic has his or her own way of working, which depends very much on the emotional make-up of that particular person.

Automatic Writing

One type of phenomenon that could spring both from the brain and from spirits is that of automatic writing and drawing.

Automatic writing is something that you may have tried at school. The idea is to take a blank sheet of paper and write the first thing that comes into your head. It is called 'stream-of-consciousness' writing, and most of what is produced by school children is gibberish. Similar techniques were used by James Joyce and Virginia Woolf in their writing, and are supposed to reveal the inner thoughts of the character 'speaking' through the text. (James Joyce took medication for his eye condition that had hallucinogenic side effects – perhaps this accounts for his ability to tap into the unconscious so startlingly in his writing.)

The unconscious is the key factor here: by writing the first thing that comes into your head, you are allegedly unlocking the unconscious. But when the unconscious is unlocked, who knows what may emerge? This is where the skill of automatic writing can enter the field of psychic phenomena.

Someone who has psychic abilities and powers may be able to produce material under automatic writing that has no obvious explanation for its origins. Michael Bentine, in his book *Doors of the Mind*, recounts some interesting experiences from his youth. Bentine's father was a scientist who became interested in psychic phenomena and decided to investigate the subject. Many mediums and psychics visited the Bentine house. Several of those who practised automatic writing produced manuscripts that were full of strange prophecy packed with 'thee's' and 'thou's' – obviously emanating from the imagination, as they were very poor fakes of medieval Middle English!

However, there was one medium from their home town who obviously had something: while talking to the family about local gossip and events, she would write without looking at the paper and produce reams of manuscript that contained mathematical formulae, academic German and French, and scholarly English in a seeming variety of hands. Bentine's father had these manuscripts checked to verify their authenticity. The formulae and grammar were correct.

How did the medium know all this? The cynics would say that she was a fake, expert in languages and mathematics. If this is so, why is she assuming the part of a poor Kentish widow who lives in a small cottage? Why isn't she on the stage, or exploiting her talents legitimately for money?

So, assuming that she was genuine, we have to ask ourselves where the information that seeped through her unconscious originated from. There are several possibilities. The first is discarnate spirits: that is to say, she was communicating with the dead. The second possibility is that she was communicating with incarnate spirits: that is, those who are living – a form of ESP. The third is that she was in touch with what Jung called the collective unconscious. This theory assumes that man's spirit and mind (which can be considered much the same thing) are part of a greater universal consciousness from which they travel to be part of a human being, and to which they return after death. While we are alive, we still have this link with the greater whole, and the unconscious is able to tap into it at will. And finally, the fourth possibility: that at some time in her life, the medium had come into contact with all three languages and higher maths and had somehow absorbed them into her unconscious, only to reproduce them later. This last possibility – the one used by those who do not believe in the existence of psychic phenomena – seems the most unlikely!

An interesting proof of automatic writing was provided by a story which was suppressed by the outraged Church of England at the time it broke.

Frederick Bligh Bond and John Alleyne were friends who were interested in magic, and were also members of the Somerset Archaeological Society with a particular interest in the ruins of Glastonbury

Abbey. Alleyne practised automatic writing, and one day he began to write what purported to be messages from Abbot Beere, Brother Ambrosius and Brother Johannes. The script seemed to be monastic Latin and Middle English. On checking, Bligh Bond found that this was so. The men put this down to the unlocking of Alleyne's unconscious and its connection with the collective unconscious. At no time did they claim to be talking to discarnate spirits.

The tone of the documents was scholarly, and told them of the locations around Wells Cathedral where the old Glastonbury Abbey stood. As both men were archaeologists, they decided to try to gain permission from the Church of England to institute a dig at these sites in an attempt to uncover any remains of the old Abbey.

Permission was given by the church for excavations to begin, and using the script 'dictated' by automatic writing the Edgar Chapel was uncovered in 1908 and the Loretto Chapel in 1919. Both sites were exactly as described by the script. Nowadays they are open to visitors.

The church was only too happy to let Bligh Bond and Alleyne work on these sites, as they assumed that the information had come from some old manuscript discovered in a library or archive. However, the men co-authored a book entitled *The Gate of Remembrance*, and entrusted their script to Sir William Barrett, a fellow of Dublin University and a leading member of the Society for Psychical

Research. When the book was published, the church elders exploded: the idea of such a document being dictated from either the collective unconscious or the spirit of the dead monks was against their beliefs concerning Spiritualism and what was then still known as the occult. An attempt was made to discredit both men publicly and professionally, and Bligh Bond eventually emigrated to America in an attempt to work and rebuild a reputation shattered by the church.

The script was checked time and again, and the language used was a combination of monastic Latin and Old English and was certified genuine. Neither of them could understand it and had to have it translated. The excavations were carried out according to its directions and plan. So whatever your view – be it spirits or the collective unconscious – it's obvious that some kind of psychic insight had enabled Alleyne to see the layout of the old Abbey and locate the remains that were later unearthed by their digs. But the Church of England devoted much effort towards discrediting the archaeologists instead of trying to understand their findings.

ESP

A possible clue to mind-reading and ESP lies in the dowsing method used by Maximillien Langsner to find the murder weapon in the case of Mannville Farm. It's generally agreed that dowsing involves the muscles of the body reacting to an outside stimulus, usually some kind of electro-magnetic force in the earth. This is how water diviners usually work. But this does not account for the details that Langsner was able to supply concerning the manner in which the crime was committed: he was able to give a detailed account of what occurred by reading the suspect's mind.

A more scientific theory of dowsing leads us further: the theory of the split brain. This works on the assumption that the left brain governs our everyday lives, leaving the right brain to cope with the less strenuous and mechanical tasks, such as creative work, and the inner machinations of the unconscious. The theory maintains that we are so bound up with the mechanistic way of life that civilisation has brought us that we have lost contact with the right brain, and that, therefore, the natural reaction to electro-magnetic fields that, for instance, birds have is denied to us.

The scientist Roger Sperry experimented with a patient whose brain was obviously split by a physical disorder. By flashing green and red lights into the 'blind' eye of the patient – that connected to the right brain – and then asking him which colour he saw, Sperry was able to observe the following result: when the patient answered incorrectly (always remembering that the left brain – our everyday brain – was unable to view the colours well), he suffered from twitches and muscle spasms, almost as though his right brain was trying to alert the left brain to its error by sheer physical force. Sperry further posited that mind-reading and certain forms of ESP came not directly from the mind, but rather from an innate ability to read these twitches, and thus deduce from instinct whether or not the truth was being told.

To a certain extent, this theory was proved by Wilhelm Van Osten, a Prussian aristocrat, who decided to train a horse to 'read' a number off a card, then stamp its foot the exact number of times. The horse was able to do this, but an experiment showed it could only do it when Van Osten knew the value of the card – if he didn't look at the card before holding it up, then the horse would answer incorrectly. A careful study of Van Osten revealed that he was – quite unwittingly – telling the horse when to stop stamping its foot by a variety of twitches and spasms when the exact number had been stamped out. Without these subconscious signals, the horse did not know when to stop.

The researcher Maurice Maeterlinck worked on similar cases to that of Van Osten, and found that often animals were easy to train because of their lower level of conscious intelligence. He linked this with the manner in which many mathematical prodigies he had studied among humans had been children with a markedly low level of intelligence in every other way. He maintained that the lower the level of conscious intelligence, the greater the chance of repressed powers like those of dowsing breaking through. He cited the fact that many of the psycho-metrists and dowsers he had tested had poor results until it was realised that, instead of predicting the result of a card being held up in front of them now, they were predicting the result of a card which would be held up in two minutes, or even longer ... usually about three cards in front of the one they were studying!

To Maeterlinck, it was obvious that precognition – a form of ESP that enables someone to see into the future – was something that went hand-in-hand with dowsing.

Precognition

Nella Jones was able to see the Yorkshire Ripper committing another murder before it happened. Greta Alexander was able to describe a man who found a body before she had even located the position of the corpse on a map. This is the ability to see into the future called precognition.

But is it possible to see into the future? Certainly there are some who believe that the brain has powers far beyond those that we understand. If it is true that we can see the past in the form of ghosts via information that is recorded in the electrical fields of objects (Tom Lethbridge's theory), then it is logical to deduce that information is always recorded on objects throughout time. If that is so, then all the information ever recorded is held within an object ready to be unreeled for the receptive mind.

Why the future as well as the past? Good question: here we have to consider the nature of time. Why does time always go forward? According to Professor Stephen Hawking, the only reason time runs forward not backward is because the universe needs a build-up of entropic matter – that is to say, the stuff of decay. For example, when a cup falls from a table and is broken, it adds to the decay of the universe. But because decay is necessary, and does not run backwards, it is impossible for us to see the cup rise up on to the table and become whole. This would detract from entropy, and so is not permissible. The reason why is not really known, this just seems to be the way the universe works!

However, if time only moves forward for this reason, then it is possible for information stored on objects to leak through, as these recordings are not dependent on entropy. It could be possible for someone with a receptive mind to pick up a recording that had not yet happened in our terms. (There is another theory which claims that time does not run in a straight line but in a series of irregular loops, which could also account for the ability of this information to break through.)

Nella Jones was watching television when her vision came to her: it is, perhaps, possible that she picked up a later news broadcast in her subconscious – information recorded on the surface of everything in the room.

This does leave us with the frightening thought

that destiny is preordained. But perhaps this is not so. There are those who believe that there are several alternate universes, one for each course of action. Theoretically, time travel would only be possible if a person moved from one universe to another. In this way, a traveller would not be able to affect his own universe. So information picked up by a psychic may even possibly relate to an alternate universe close to our own but not exactly the same; which leaves the way open to the concept of free will and the multiple-branching universe.

This is getting into areas of quantum physics and philosophy which are beyond most of us. To the psychic who experiences these things almost every day, it is something that just happens – whatever your explanation or theory.

It does seem that a sudden shock, particularly to the area around the brain, can cause the right brain to unleash powers that were up to then dormant. For instance, the psychic Peter Hurkos gained his powers after he fell from a ladder and injured his head. Peter Fairley, who was for some years the Science correspondent for the ITN television news company developed second sight after a virus that attacked his brain had left him temporarily blind in 1965. He later made a programme about his experiences of second sight, which included rather mundane things such as being able to pick winners from the racing form because the names literally leapt out at him, or thinking about doing something to help blind people seconds before receiving a phone call from a charity for the blind.

This gives weight to the claim that these powers are something that we all have, and that can be used in any way – not merely for the occasional grand spectacle. How the powers manifest themselves seems to depend on the personality of the psychic: Hurkos was egocentric about his gifts, so they manifested themselves in grand ways, whereas Fairley was matter of fact about their appearance, and so they came to him in the normal course of events.

In discussing precognition – which involves the concept commonly called 'second sight' – it is useful to look at time a little more closely, and consider the point of view posited by P. D. Ouspensky.

The philosopher and mystic Ouspensky had the idea that time was four dimensional, and that we only perceived those parts of it that were right in front of us. Somehow, the brain could step outside this present and see the overall picture. He claimed to have been able to do this in moments of illumination. When he was concerned about a friend who had died, he had been able to see the whole of that person's life in one flash, and realise that there was little he could actually have done to help.

He was able to do this because time itself does not roll forward as we think – that is only the way we choose to order time. In fact, according to this idea, time is like a flat surface where everything is laid out:

like a table set for lunch. If we stand above it we can see the place settings, the cutlery and the cruet – all as one thing. This, according to Ouspensky, is the way time really is, and how he was able to observe it in those rare moments.

However, if we were to be on the table – miniaturised – and walked from one end to the other, with our eyes cast down in order to see where we were treading, it would take us all our lives, and we would encounter the place settings, cutlery and cruet only as we walked past them – they would otherwise be too far away to see, for we would be concentrating only on what was directly beside and in front of us, and would remember only what we had already passed.

Ouspensky's theory is very similar to that of the German physicist Herman Minkowski. In 1908, Minkowski posited the idea that we live in a block universe: it is four dimensional and static, with no such things as past, present and future. These are concepts introduced into the universe only by the observer – in this case, man.

His model of how this universe worked used the idea of the observer as a beam of light. This beam moves along a line: the past is where it has already shone, the present is where it now shines, and the future is where it will shine. All events are already mapped out, we merely think that there is a future because our beam of light, moving along the line, hasn't as yet touched all points.

The idea of the observer was refined a little by the

American psychologist William James, who described the observer as living in a specious present, moving from one small, finite chunk of space time to another, each chunk representing the now and being what is observed at that particular moment. If it can be established for speculative purposes that time, and the way we observe it, works in this way, then a theory of precognition can be worked towards.

The first man to try to explain precognition in this way was the psychic researcher H. F. Saltmarsh, who modified the idea of the beam of light sweeping across the block universe. Saltmarsh puts forward the idea that there are two beams of light: one represents the conscious mind and one represents the unconscious mind. The conscious mind is a strong, concentrated beam that takes in only the present moment (as we believe it) in its field of light. The unconscious mind is also a strong beam, but it is more diffuse, and covers a wider area with its field. Thus, instead of being a point travelling along a line, it still travels that line, but also spreads out into the specious future and the past, as well as crossing other lines – that is, other diffuse unconscious mind beams: the fields of other people.

Thus, by having a larger chunk of space time to observe, it is able to pick up what may happen in the future. It can also cross to other unconscious mind-fields, and so pick up things from other people's pasts and futures – this was Saltmarsh's possible theory for ESP and telepathy. The field of the unconscious spanned the whole of a person's life, and the conscious spanned only the subjective present. Thus, the unconscious was able to pick up the whole of another person's life from their unconscious: and this could perhaps explain the abilities of psychics, mediums and clairvoyants. An apparent ability to tell the future, or to talk of the dead spirits of relatives, may be no more than the picking up of someone else's unconscious.

This does not preclude the idea of discarnate spirits co-existing with this theory, it merely offers another alternative in a field where there is probably no single answer to all the questions. In many ways this is compatible with the idea of discarnate spirits and the unconscious mind on Tom Lethbridge's second spiral, where time as we know it does not exist.

Saltmarsh's notion was that precognition was the unconscious letting the conscious mind know of any forthcoming events that were either dangerous or exceptionally good. The way this usually happened was through dreams. There are many recorded examples of what could be dream precognition. The engineer and scientist J. W. Dunne, whose 1927 book *An Experiment With Time* caused a sensation in its day, believed that everybody had precognitive dreams, but that like many other dreams they were simply not remembered when the dreamer awoke. To try to demonstrate this, he began to keep a record of his dreams, attempting to note them whenever he awoke during the night. He found that most of his dreams were of a trivial precognitive nature: he would be reading a book or newspaper, and could suddenly remember it – from his dreams. This is typical of the everyday feeling of déjà vu, and perhaps it represents the unconscious scanning the future for us, in order to forewarn us. The dreams may not be all that straightforward either – they may be symbolic!

The most interesting example of this concerns the writer Wilbur Wright, who dreamt of major horse race winners in 1946, 1948 and 1954. The strange thing is that he had no interest in horse racing, and didn't bet on any of the races! Each time, a similar thing happened: he dreamt that he was standing at a racecourse watching the racing, when a well-dressed man in a hat came up to him. Each time it was the same man, although it resembled no one he knew and his attempts to describe the stranger fully ended in frustration. The man would start talking to him, and in the course of his conversation he would give the name of the winner of a forthcoming race.

The first two times it happened, Wright only noticed by accident that the horses had won. The third time, he was exasperated in his dream when the man approached him. 'Not you again!' he said, and noted that the man looked at him sharply before delivering his tip. Then, with a tilt of the hat, the man walked off.

Wright gave the name of the horse to his wife, and also to Mrs Cheesewright, with whom the Wrights were at that time staying. They didn't bother to bet, but Mrs Cheesewright phoned her bookie straight away – and came out of it £100 richer (a considerable sum in 1954!).

Interestingly enough, the man never came to see Wright again, and the writer puts it down to his reaction. He recalled the sharp look the man gave him when he said 'Not you again!' It was as though the man was a representation of Wright's unconscious self, and became annoyed at the way he was being consistently ignored and derided by his conscious counterpart!

But why does precognition happen mostly in dreams? A probable explanation is that the sleeping state allows the unconscious to seep through into the conscious mind – throughout the book, visions, premonitions and statements will be seen coming to psychics when either asleep or in a trance.

The worrying problem with all this is that it seems to assume that the future is pre-destined, and that free will does not exist. It doesn't have to be so.

The diffused beam of the unconscious and the focused beam of the conscious are travelling along a line. In the field of the unconscious are the events of the past and the events of the future, as well as those of the specious present which the conscious mind is concentrated upon. Suppose that there are junctions in time, where all possible events are laid out, and it is up to the individual to make up his or her mind. The unconscious field cannot see where these junctions are, for they do not all fall within its field. If this is so, then an event that spells danger in the future, seen by the unconscious and transmitted to the conscious via precognition, can be acted upon. There are examples of this after every great disaster. For instance, after the sinking of the *Titanic* in 1912 there was a rash of newspaper stories concerning people who had dreamt of the disaster, and themselves drowning, and so had cancelled their passages. On the other hand, the golden example of not taking your future in your hands is that of newspaper editor W. T. Stead, who dreamt of the sinking of the *Titanic*, wrote a fictionalised short story about such a disaster – then went on the voyage anyway and drowned.

Of course, all stories such as this can be put down to synchronicity, or simply to a journalist's nose for a good story and people's desire to be in the media. However, the example holds as a model for our theory. Some people acted upon their precognitive dreams, and some people did not. So obviously some people were able to change their futures. Whether or not this is free will is arguable and depends on your definition of free will.

It is, however, a perfect demonstration of physicist Hugh Everett's theory of the universe of multiple branching. In such a universe all probabilities are laid out in the field of time. At each juncture where change can occur there is a branching of probabilities, so that the four-dimensional field of time resembles a spider's web. The field of the conscious and unconscious travels along a line until it reaches a junction, then goes off along one line, leaving the other untouched. Thus every probability is possible, but only one at every juncture is actually realised. In this way it is possible for someone to act on precognition and either make this precognitive vision or dream come true, or send the conscious and unconscious fields off on another branch.

There is another theory – that which enables the possibility of time travel – which states that there are many possible futures because there are many possible universes. This is a variation on the idea of the multiple-branching universe.

This is leading us ever closer to the idea that links together all these theories of psychic activity. But first it is necessary to look at those people who have only the occasional experience, and also those who find it necessary to fake psychic experiences. Strangely enough, many fakers are also genuine psychics. Why, then, do they feel the need to fake?

Psychic Pressures

In his book *The Geller Effect*, co-authored by Guy Lyon Playfair, Uri Geller claims that faking is often the result of too much pressure. He was asked to produce results constantly, and this was just not possible. Yet, if he said this, he was immediately condemned as a fake; and if he said nothing, and continued with no result . . . yet again, the charges of fraud were laid at his door.

Standing back and looking at this attitude from a

distance, it seems absurd: do we expect footballers to play well every game? Is a chess champion expected to win every game without fail? Do we expect every novel from a Nobel-prize winner to be a classic? Of course not. We recognise that people are subject to good days and bad days. This is true also of those with psychic powers. Doris Stokes was discovered planting subjects in concert halls during her tours in order to get good results with her audience, and the researcher Harry Price found evidence of trickery by the young German medium Rudi Schneider in the 1920s. Yet Stokes was able to give a *Sunday People* reporter full details of a 'relative' invented by the journalist to try to deceive her – evidence not of fakery but of excellent ESP. And Schneider produced phenomena early in his career that had the scrupulous Price completely baffled. So why did such obviously talented mediums as Geller, Stokes and Schneider feel the need to cheat?

Perhaps because under constant pressure to deliver, the medium becomes all the more prone to the foibles of mere humanity, and the strain can sometimes cause a cessation of powers, just as a writer with a quick deadline can go blank, and a footballer faced with an open goal and thirty seconds on the clock can shoot wide. The difference is that mediums and psychics aren't given a second chance: one failure and they are dismissed as fraudulent.

Michael Bentine has a theory, evolved from years of studying mediums at work under laboratory conditions, that their abilities are partly reliant on their body chemistry. Therefore, we have to take into account not just the regular changes caused by the daily cycle (eating, defecating, sweating, etc.) but also the release of adrenalin and the effects of tensions that come with the pressure of celebrity and the repeated requests to perform phenomena. Bentine found that, during his father's tests on psychics, even something like drinking a cup of tea could affect a psychic's performance as it changed the pH level (the chemical balance of acidity and alkalinity) of the body chemistry.

Under such circumstances, the cheating of Geller *et al.* is understandable, if not condonable.

Prior to his involvement in the Son of Sam case, Geller had helped the FBI to recover some kidnap victims. He had been able to pinpoint the locations of victims, and describe kidnappers. He had used psychometric talents to trace routes on maps. Yet when it came to the Son of Sam killings, Geller wandered around the area of one of the crimes, and was able to make a description and supply background information in a manner that was different to his customary ease. On the contrary, the information came only very slowly and hazily, and at one point he thought he might draw a blank. What caused this difference?

Geller himself is convinced that the reason was two-fold. Firstly, the police are involved in the case. Murder cases are by nature more emotional than run-of-the-mill police work. Detectives want to get results, and are often under very great pressure to obtain those results quickly, which makes them anxious and on edge. This would easily communicate itself to the sensitivities of a psychic, making him or her feel under a great pressure, which would of necessity make them react differently to their surroundings, and in trying to force a result they could in fact cause the opposite. It's worth bearing in mind that some mediums and psychics – whether they are trance mediums or practising psychometry – get their best results from a great distance (Gerald Croiset's greatest 'hits' came from his living room in Utrecht), and nearly all require tranquil conditions.

The second factor to consider is that of self-preservation! This may seem a strange thing to say, but Geller's arguments are simple and convincing. Suppose a medium or psychic came along who could see where crimes were about to be committed, and could solve any number of robberies, murders, drug-smuggling operations, and so on. Would not such a person be in great danger? The massed ranks of organised crime – not to mention lone operators – would see their livelihoods threatened, and their crimes brought home to them, with long prison sentences as a result. The life of the psychic would be in danger, stalked by criminals, with contracts out for his or her assassination. It would be no way to live (even if you could survive for long!). Geller believes that his subconscious has figured this out, and puts a block on too much success in criminal cases – he stays relatively harmless, and very much alive.

The combination of self-preservation and the immense pressures surrounding cases of murder could be a very good explanation for the relative lack of psychic success in this area as opposed to that of, say, kidnapping, where psychics usually get excellent results when called upon to help. This pressure can also stunt the developing psychic powers.

The Occasional Psychic

An interesting analogy is used by Colin Wilson when describing Gerald Croiset (in the introduction to Tom Lethbridge's *The Power of the Pendulum*). He describes the Dutch psychic as being like a badly tuned TV set that can pick up signals almost at random. This seems to be very much the case with Etta Smith and Remy Chua, both of whom had a one-off psychic experience detailed in this book. Remy was concerned about her dead friend, and Etta was concerned for the safety of herself and her children after hearing of a disappearance in her neighbourhood. Suppose that, for whatever reason, these worries act on the subconscious in such a way as to open up parts of the brain not previously used. If worry was somehow able to awaken their faculties for psychic ability, then it isn't hard to suppose that their first experiences would be fuzzy, like the pictures of a badly tuned TV set – Etta first felt waves of emotion, and Remy saw an indistinct vision. It was only later that both women received full visions of crimes being committed.

Of course, this is all supposition. That is all it can be because at this point in scientific study we know little about the powers of the mind. But it would be wrong to dismiss all psychic theory out of hand simply because there are no scientific explanations. All it means is that science is not as far advanced as it would like to think. There is no such thing as the 'supernatural' – there is only the natural that science hasn't managed to explain yet. Man has discovered a lot in the last 300 years, but there is more yet to come.

The fact is that something happened to Etta Smith and Remy Chua. In both cases, the women were put under intense pressure from police and court officials who were either sceptical, or had a vested interest in proving them liars. The awakening of psychic powers brought to both women nothing but stress and trauma. After the murder cases in which they were involved were resolved, both women had no more visions, and their psychic powers – so recently awakened – never returned.

This isn't surprising: the trauma following Etta Smith's near arrest, and her finding of a body, was enough to dissuade her subconscious from breaking through again. This is not without its precedent. Remy Chua's psychic experiences stopped after the conviction of Teresita Basa's murderer, and it would also be as well to recall the sister of Estelle Roberts:

when both sisters first experienced a vision (a knight appearing at their bedroom window), Estelle welcomed it and wanted to discover more. Her sister, on the other hand, turned her face away in fear, and never had another vision.

The Information Universe

Just as Colin Wilson once compared Gerald Croiset to a TV set that wasn't working properly, with the result that it was able to pick up random signals from all around, the late Brian Inglis used a similar metaphor to describe the way in which all human beings operate. According to Wilson our brains are like TV aerials and receivers all in one, and translate messages and information we receive from all around into pictures that are assimilable by our conscious minds. But what do they cut out that cannot be easily assimilated?

Everything that has ever happened or will happen is all around us, though we only see the subjective present because that is how our conscious mind copes with space time. In this book, you will see how psychics were able to solve individual crimes: sometimes it was by psychometry, sometimes by ESP, sometimes by seemingly talking to the spirits of the dead. Each idea has been taken separately and examined in this introduction.

In some ways, though, it's totally wrong to take these occurrences as separate phenomena, as there is a theory that unifies all of these psychic powers under one umbrella – that of the information universe. And it ties in with the idea of the psychic as a TV set able to receive random signals.

What is the information universe, and how does it relate to the powers of psychics? The information universe is exactly what it says: everything that has ever happened or will happen is in the universe at all times. In fact, there is no such thing as time: what we call time is the subjective present that is spoken of when referring to theories of linear time. We only see time as moving forwards because the build-up of entropic matter precludes us from seeing it run any other way. But the actual information about what is happening in our subjective present and past and future is already there – always has been and always will be.

This is why a psychic can see into what we call the past or the future. It is also how they can see things that happen vast distances away as well as those close to them. For if time is static and we only perceive it as moving, then the same is true of space: in quantum physics, the two are taken as one concept – space time.

If this seems a little hard to grasp, consider the words of Tom Lethbridge that everything we see around us is illusory to a certain extent. If you look at a table it seems a good, solid piece of wood. But it isn't: for the wood is made up of atoms that move in their own electrical fields without touching, at an incredibly rapid rate. The solidity is an illusion. So isn't it possible that, in order to make sense of the world in which we live, and enable us to survive in it, our brain (the TV receiver) tunes in only to certain signals? And that by doing this it enables us to go about the mechanical tasks we need to perform to survive instead of just sitting around unable to do anything because we are overloaded with information? If we can admit this is possible, then it is not too much to presume that psychics are just that bit more random in their ability to filter the signals reaching them, and that some things break through – like static, or pirate channels that overlap the ordinary signal.

Psychometry, dowsing, trances, even the ability one medium showed the researcher Dr Gustav Pagenstecher of tasting the food and drink that passed his lips ... these are not separate powers, but different ways of crossing the circuits and turning the random selector of the brain so that we can pick up signals other than our subjective reality. And if this is really the case, does it not explain the reason why psychic powers are somewhat erratic?

The problem with these ideas is that the closer we come to understanding them, the further away we get. Scientists have discovered what they call the experimenter effect, whereby a molecule that is observed appears to behave differently to when it is not observed!

All that can be said is that psychic phenomena do exist. They occur with the erratic brilliance of lightning, but when they do, they can illuminate a situation to such an extent that they can supply a solution – even in cases of murder.

Red Cloud for a
Murdered Child

Mona Tinsley was ten years old, tall for her age, and skinny; she was a quiet, reserved child who didn't have many friends. Her parents had been arguing a lot since Uncle Fred had moved out of their Newark house. She liked Uncle Fred, the tall man whose eyes bulged when he looked at you. She didn't know why he had had to go, only that the amount of money coming in to the house was less without a lodger, and her parents found it hard to cope. Uncle Fred had always been a happy and laughing presence, always joking with her – even if his breath did smell of drink most of the time.

As she came out of the school building on the first day after the Christmas holiday and crossed the small playground, one of her friends tapped her on the arm. 'There's someone waiting for you,' she said, indicating the tall man standing just across the road. Mona followed the direction of her friend's pointing finger. It was Uncle Fred!

With a quick goodbye, she rushed excitedly across the road. She was full of questions: why was here?

When had he come back? Where was he staying?
Was he back at home? She hoped so – the arguments might stop if he was bringing in extra
cash.

Uncle Fred answered evasively, looking around
nervously. Mona could see that there were very
few people about – only the mother of a boy whose
name she couldn't recall. The woman was staring
at them strangely. Mona wondered why. Uncle
Fred was looking at the woman. He seemed worried.
Seizing her by the hand, he almost dragged her
down the road, towards the bus station. She asked
where they were going, but he again evaded answering, muttering something about a cottage he was
renting. Mona was confused: why weren't they
going home? Uncle Fred replied that he had her
parents' permission to take Mona away for a few
days.

Mona was puzzled as they sat on the bus that took
them out of town. Why had her parents said she could
go away when school had only just started?

The newspapers reported the case over the next few
days.

Mona Tinsley had just started the winter 1937
school term, five days after the new year, when she
disappeared. She failed to return from school in the
afternoon and her parents, after searching among
her friends, became worried and contacted the police.
Police questioning of neighbours and householders

on her usual route home produced a clue: a man had been seen loitering near the school. Fortunately for the police, the witness was able to identify the man: he was Frederick Nodder, who until recently had been a lodger at the Tinsley home. At the time, the witness had thought nothing of it – after all, it was obvious the man knew the girl and he may well have been picking her up from school for her parents.

There was another sighting of Mona – at the local bus station, with a middle-aged man who fitted the description of Nodder. The police had enough to act upon.

At that time, Nodder lived in the village of Hayton, some twenty miles from Newark. When the police called to interview him, he denied all knowledge of the child, claiming that he hadn't been back to Newark since before Christmas.

Frederick Nodder stood in the centre of the grimy room at the front of the house. There were a few chairs and a table strewn about, and the smell of alcohol hung heavy in the air. Nodder was dishevelled but sober as he answered the barrage of questions from the uniformed constable and the plainclothes man.

'Why should I want to go back there?' he shouted. 'They chucked me out – I want nothing to with 'em.'

The plainclothes man spoke sombrely, 'You've got a record, we know that.'

Nodder waved dismissively, and turned his back on them. 'Get out of my bloody 'ouse.'

'We know you also use the name Frank Hudson, and as such you've a nice little record for assault and petty thieving.'

'What's that got to do with the kid?' snarled Nodder.

'Nothing directly. It gives us a chance to bring you in, though,' said the plaincothes man. He gestured to the uniformed officer, who grabbed Nodder and handcuffed him.

'We'll have to use the back door,' said the plainclothes man as he tugged and pushed at the weather-beaten front door. 'This won't open.'

Frederick Nodder, aka Frank Hudson, was taken into custody on a bastardy warrant, which covered a myriad of possible charges. The very name of the warrant caused newspapers and local gossips to speculate about the relationship between Nodder and Mona. It was a well-known fact that Nodder had become the Tinsleys' lodger after being introduced to the family by Mrs Tinsley's sister, with whom he had been conducting a long-running affair. Rumours abounded that the child was, in fact, their daughter.

If this was so, then Nodder would have a very good reason for abducting the girl. His relationship with the sister had deteriorated, and since being thrown out the Tinsley home he had moved to another town. Perhaps he was frightened of losing contact with his child?

The police were sure that Nodder was their man, despite his protestations, and they investigated the matter carefully. They traced Mrs Tinsley's sister to a boarding house in Blackpool, but she denied having any contact with the family for some time. She confirmed the rumours that she and Nodder had had a relationship, but was vehement when questioned about Mona's parentage: the child was not hers.

The accusations proved to be nothing more than idle gossip, but none the less kept the case in the public eye. Speculation was rife in Fleet Street. A kidnapped child was always a good story, particularly for the tabloid press. In those days, little could be stated, but much hinted; and as the rumour about Nodder's parentage of the missing girl was squashed, so a new and more sinister note crept into the press reporting. What if he had kidnapped the child for other purposes?

The gossips in Newark picked up on this, and before long the area was awash with rumour concerning Nodder's reasons for taking Mona. Attempts to find the missing girl had been fruitless, and many believed that this was because she was dead: Nodder had killed her and hidden the body. But what had he done to her first?

All this reached the ears of the police, and through them the prisoner. If he was released, there would be gangs waiting for him. The lynch mob was fuelled by rumour, not fact. The world grew black around him, and the thought of what would happen if he was released preyed on his mind.

Soon he changed his story. In his second statement,

he claimed that he had, indeed, met Mona outside
school, and taken her home with him. From there he
had put her on a bus to Sheffield, where his girlfriend
would collect the girl and look after her. The police
were not convinced. There was still no apparent
motive for snatching the child – she was not his, and
there was no reason why she should be taken from
her natural parents. Nodder hinted vaguely that his
girlfriend was unable to have children, but beyond
that he resumed a policy of silence. This, in essence,
was to remain his story.

Nodder refused to aid police further; he would not
reveal the name of his girlfriend, or indeed any
address where the police might find her. The
Sheffield police were contacted by the Notts force,
and began a systematic search in the city. But no
trace was found of the mysterious girlfriend ... nor
was there any trace of Mona Tinsley.

By this time it was obvious to the police that
Nodder was hiding something, and they strongly
suspected that he had killed the child and hidden the
body. However, a thorough search of Nodder's home,
and the countryside around Hayton revealed nothing. Without evidence, the police grimly accepted
they could only charge him with abduction.

All this had taken place in the space of two months.
Yet three days after Mona had disappeared, something strange happened.

Estelle Roberts was sitting alone in her study, late

one evening, replying to the mail she received by the sackload. Estelle was a famous medium and received many cries for help from people who had lost their loved ones. It was some of these letters she was attempting to answer. Estelle put down her pen and rubbed her eyes. She was exhausted, and couldn't go on for much longer. She promised herself a rest after one more letter.

Suddenly, she heard a voice: a faint, whistling voice, as though from a great distance. It was little girl's voice, and it wasn't calling her by name. Rather, it was crying pitifully, and asking for help. It seemed to be behind her, and was growing in intensity. Estelle spun around in her chair to see a little girl in tears, reaching out to her. Estelle, a mother herself, longed to reach out and touch the distressed child.

Estelle knew this was a spirit visitation, because she was used to seeing such things, and instead of the fear most people would feel, she experienced only an overwhelming love and sympathy for the disconsolate child.

Gently, she asked the little girl her name, and what she wanted from her. The child replied that her name was Mona, and she wanted help. She wasn't sure what had happened to her, she only knew that she was wandering in a void that was strange to her. A man had taken her, done terrible things to her, and then strangled her. She remembered everything going dark before a great light had come towards her

– and now she didn't know where she was, and she was frightened.

Then, as suddenly as she had appeared, the child began to fade. Estelle begged her to stay; she couldn't help if the child would not stay to talk and listen... But it was too late: Mona had gone.

Over the next week, Mona appeared to Estelle every day; she would not leave Estelle alone. Each time she was able to tell the medium more about what had happened to her, and how she felt held back from progressing further: she wanted to go on, but was being prevented by ties to the earthly plane. She was miserable at being trapped, and asked Estelle to help her take the step from this world to the next.

It soon became obvious to the medium that the spirit's progress into the after-life was impeded by the violent manner of Mona's death and the conflicting emotions and thoughts of her earthly surroundings. It was as if the anguish of her parents, not knowing whether she was alive or not, kept pulling her back.

Estelle could not decide what to do. If she could help the police to find the body, and find the murderer, then she would be sending a man to the gallows. And the aiding of a death was against the Spiritualist creed. She believed that the spirit of someone who had been murdered – and capital punishment was included in this – would not be able to move on to the next plane easily. A criminal who had been executed might even try to possess someone and commit further crimes. Estelle was torn between her beliefs and her compassion for the dead girl.

Whenever there was to be a communication from the spirits Estelle would be contacted via her control, Red Cloud (a native American, and the spirit deputed to act as her link between this world and the next). The fact that Mona had been able to come directly to Estelle proved that the poor girl was still earthbound. She would be trapped until her killer was caught, and her parents' minds could rest easily.

For a week, Estelle agonised over the matter: should she go to the police about this? Should she try and contact the parents directly? She asked Red Cloud for his help in assisting Mona to the next world, but he replied that there was nothing he could do while the child's spirit was still earthbound.

Estelle's mind was made up when the BBC broadcast a message about the disappearance, requesting help and detailing the anguish of the parents. This, combined with the distress of the spirit visitation, convinced Estelle that she must do something. Through the *Daily Express* journalist Hannen Swaffer, a great exponent of Spiritualism who had already asked her to help the parents, she established contact with the Tinsleys. She told them that Mona had been to see her, and that the girl had been strangled and 'outraged' – a delicate term she used to avoid revealing to the distraught parents the full details of the assaults suffered by their daughter before her death and which Mona had recounted to her.

She then approached the police. Unlike today,

Spiritualism was a respected and popular movement in Britain between the wars, and Estelle Roberts was one of the country's most famous mediums, whose meetings at the Kingsway Hall in Holborn were always packed. She was as respected as any medium or clairvoyant could hope to be, and was not without her devotees in the police force. The police were delighted when she offered to help.

Estelle asked Scotland Yard for something of the child's to hold: from this she hoped to pick up vibrations and see more clearly what had happened to the girl. Estelle understood why the spirit of Mona had been too confused and distressed to tell her anything that would be of use to the police in building a case, yet she needed something concrete she could present to the officers, something that would enable them to convict Frederick Nodder.

Scotland Yard detectives relayed her request to the Notts force and eventually a pink silk party dress arrived. It was taken to Estelle's home, where she sat in a darkened room, running her hands over it. A baffled Yard officer sat quietly in the corner, notebook open, ready to record what happened.

Closing her eyes, Estelle asked Red Cloud to come and help her. She was about to psychometrise the dress, and believed that her ability to see events and pictures from an object was a gift that was given to her by the spirits to enable her to help them. She could feel Red Cloud near her, guiding her towards a clear picture of events. Sometimes she would see things as though they were a film, or as though she herself was walking through them. Sometimes Red Cloud would introduce her to a spirit who would talk to her. She had no idea in advance of what would happen. Red Cloud appeared to her, and to her astonishment, with him was Mona!

Under the guiding hand of Red Cloud, Mona was now able to address Estelle in a clearer manner. She told her of her feelings as she was strangled. Because this experience was still at the forefront of her mind, at times she became incoherent and hysterical, and the statements she made to Estelle had to be sifted by Red Cloud in order to be explained. There was plenty of information coming through, but it was – at the moment – mixed up and confused; Mona was confusing her last earthly experiences with her emergence on the 'other side'. There were several sittings over the whole day, each following the same pattern: Estelle would run her hands over the pink dress, eyes closed, and Red Cloud would appear to her.

The man from Scotland Yard recorded everything Estelle said. To him, she was just a woman sitting across a darkened room, talking to herself. Yet Estelle was in a vibrant world of colour, seeing things through Mona's eyes as the story unfolded, and conversing with the dead girl and Red Cloud, both of whom she could see as clearly as the man from the Yard could see his notepad.

The first clear thing to emerge was that Mona had

been taken from her family to a house some distance away. She had travelled there in a vehicle with wheels, possibly a bus. (Reading the account later, the police were interested to see this as they already had Nodder under suspicion for Mona's disappearance and possible murder, but had not let this be generally known. At this point – it was not yet the end of January – he had not been taken into custody.)

Mona gave Estelle details, which the police were surprised to find remarkably accurate, of the clothes she had been wearing, and also spoke of water pipes being nearby. The water pipes reference caused Estelle some confusion – every time Estelle asked her about how she got to the house, Mona was keen to mention the pipes. Only later would Estelle understand their significance.

The spirit of the dead child then went on to tell Estelle how her body had been carried from the house in a sack or blanket of some kind. Estelle questioned her as to how her body could be found.

She was then given a picture of events as the spirit of Mona Tinsley could remember them. This part of the vision was clairvoyant rather than a question of talking to the spirit: Estelle later compared it to the kind of visions she received in psychometry, where things seemed simply to be 'known'. It unrolled before her like a dark film, with everything confused and moving at a rapid speed.

Mona's body was taken past a row of trees as far as a bridge that ran over some water – possibly a small stream, but certainly not a full-sized river; it was carried over the bridge, along a muddy lane, through some fields, and was thrown into a larger stretch of water.

Throughout the vision, the spirit of Mona carried on a running commentary, in an attempt to supply Estelle with more details. She told the medium that she had passed some carts, and could hear the cartwheels turning. She was also able to say that the route taken passed by a church, which was bordered on one side by a high hedge: the other side opened out on to a field. Very near there was a public house, or possibly a small brewery: she wasn't sure. The vision was too dark for Estelle to make the distinction.

As suddenly as this description had begun, it was over. Mona disappeared. Red Cloud told Estelle that the child was exhausted and distraught by what she had told her. Estelle felt frustrated by this: she was sure that one more session would fix things in her own mind. The whole vision had spun by at such a speed that she wasn't quite sure of what she had seen. If only she could get a clearer picture for herself, she was sure she could find the body for the police.

The man from the Yard reassured her that the description of events she had given would be of help; they would be able to make progress with the case. But Estelle was unsatisfied; she was still distracted. To get her to relax, the Yard man asked her how she became a medium. Estelle ordered tea and told her story.

* * *

Her first psychic experience had been at the age of eight, when she had seen a knight in shining armour outside her bedroom window. Her sister, who had also seen it, was scared, but Estelle was not: to her it was a wondrous vision. When she told her father, she was punished for telling lies, and assured that such things did not exist. Her sister had no more visions – but for Estelle, that was only the beginning. As she grew up she saw spirit forms around her, and conversed with them.

She married as a young woman, but it was not long into the marriage before her husband grew ill and died. She claimed to have been told by the spirits that he would die on his sick bed, and she said she watched his spirit body rise from his earthly one. The next time she saw him, he was standing in the crowd at his own funeral, smiling at her. It was then that she determined to become a medium and help others in their attempts to contact those who had died.

She became a member of the established Spiritualist Church, and accepted their rigid system for contacting the spirits, including a code for rapping on tables and the control method, whereby all messages from the spirits had to be passed via the one spirit who had been selected for them – their control.

Early in her second marriage, and encouraged by her new husband, Estelle developed her psychic skills and was able to levitate a table which followed her around the room. She was alerted to the danger of fire in the home by being transported from her bed to the upstairs hall floor; her husband awoke to find her in mid-air. Opening the study door to investigate a plume of smoke coming from a downstairs room, he was faced by a roaring explosion of fire. Without her levitational warning, Estelle and her family would most likely have suffocated in the smoke.

But it was in her healings and her meetings that Estelle was happiest: she could cure or ease minor ailments, and most important to her she was able to relay messages to the bereaved from those that had passed on to the other side. The comfort this brought to people was something from which she derived a great satisfaction.

Estelle heard nothing more from the police. Their efforts to break down Nodder in interrogation had come to nought: the most they could charge him with was abduction. Despite Mona's story passed on by the medium, no concrete evidence had been gathered.

The next month, by which time Nodder was ready to stand trial, Estelle Roberts decided to visit the scene of the crime, and see if she could help the police any further. She contacted the Notts police for permission, and they were only too pleased, as conventional means of detection had thus far drawn a complete blank. They hoped that Estelle would perhaps have another meeting with Red Cloud and Mona.

She travelled with a party of fellow Spiritualists,

who were keen to see the great medium at work.
Taking the train from St Pancras Station in London,
they travelled first to Newark, where they were met
by an officer from the local force, who knew the
Tinsleys, and had been involved in the investigation.
Estelle asked him if she could meet the family, as her
only previous contact had been through a third
person, Hannen Swaffer.

At first he was unsure. It would be an emotional
occasion, and his duty was to help Estelle follow the
tracks of the child in an attempt to find the body. But
the medium's fellow Spiritualists badgered the poor
officer until he was forced to give in.

The Tinsleys lived in a small terraced house. When
the policeman knocked on the door, surrounded by
the gaggle of well-dressed Spiritualists, the neighbours peered from behind curtains, or paused in mid-
conversation on doorsteps; children playing in the
street stopped in mid-cry and mid-game.

To the embarrassed police officer it seemed like an
eternity before the door was opened, and Mona's
father invited them in. The house was small but neat,
and the visitors were crowded together in the front
parlour while Mr Tinsley went to fetch his wife.
When she entered, Estelle could see that she had once
been pretty, but the last month had exacted a terrible
toll on her: her face was drawn, pale and haggard,
and she walked with a sagging, stooped demeanour.
Her eyes were dull and lifeless. Mr Tinsley looked
nervous at the number of people in the room.

'Is it about our Mona?' asked Mrs Tinsley in a flat voice. The policeman shook his head: there was no news. He introduced Estelle, but before he could attempt to explain, Estelle was on her knees in front of the seated woman. She held her tightly, and tried to explain that Mona was now safe, and that her passage into the next world would be assured once the man who had killed her was captured.

The Tinsleys were not surprised to learn that Mona was dead: it was the natural assumption to make when no trace of her had been found despite such a concerted search. Estelle told them how Mona had come to her, asking for help, and how Red Cloud was assisting her into the next world. She tried to reassure the weeping Mrs Tinsley that Mona would be happy there and that she had sent her love, and would always be looking over them. The other Spiritualists stood in the room with beatific smiles; only the police officer looked in the slightest uncomfortable. He ran his handkerchief around his neck, reflecting on these strange London folk he had been put in charge of.

After leaving Mona's parents, the policeman put the Spiritualists and Estelle on a train for Hayton. They were to go to Nodder's cottage to see if the medium could pick up any impressions from the building itself.

In many ways it was a standard cottage of its type: it had a living room, kitchen, and three upstairs rooms. There were small gardens at the front and rear. These had already been dug up by the police, and the house was clear of furniture and spotlessly clean: everything had been removed by the police in the course of their search, and the landlord (who had no intention of letting Nodder return even if he was acquitted) had the place cleaned and ready for a new tenant.

This caused Estelle some problems. The disruption of the cleaning and search had disturbed the vibrations and impressions left in the house by Mona Tinsley which Estelle needed in order to see what had happened. However, the feelings attached to the events that took place there were so powerful that Estelle Roberts was soon able to pick up psychic messages.

The policeman accompanying Estelle asked her in which room Mona had slept and Estelle took him to an upstairs back room – the one Mona had described during some of her earlier visitations, and which was recognisable by the position of the window and the colour of the wall. She had been put in there as it contained the only bed in the house. (This had been intended by the police as a test, since they already knew from evidence gathered earlier that this was the room Mona had been kept in.)

But the policeman was a little taken aback at what Estelle told him next. Looking around, she exclaimed that there should be water pipes of some kind, as these had clearly imprinted themselves on the memory of the dead girl to such an extent that she had repeatedly referred to them. Estelle had good reason to recall the pipes, for had she not spent so much effort trying to coax other details from the child's spirit, only to be told yet again of the pipes?

The startled policeman went to a small cupboard set into the corner of the room, near where the bed had stood: opening the cupboard door, he revealed a small water tank surrounded by piping. The only thing that puzzled Estelle was how Mona could have seen them, hidden as they were by the door. Perhaps she had found them when searching for some means of escape?

There was still one more test: taking Estelle back into the main room, the policeman asked her through which door Nodder and Mona had entered and left the house. Without hesitation, Estelle led him to the back door, through which she also had entered. She ignored the front door, in the main room itself. The policeman asked her why she felt so sure and Estelle confessed that she had no idea, merely that Mona had told her that the back door was the only one used.

Then the officer led her into the living room, and asked her to open the front door: she could not, even when given the key. The policeman revealed to her that the door had been secured to the jamb by screws at the top and bottom; it would be impossible for anyone to use it.

Standing in the middle of the room, Estelle told him that Mona had eaten and spent most of her time in there. She then told him that the child had spent some time copying something from a book – and, more chillingly, that this was the room in which she had been strangled. Walking to one corner she shivered as an indefinable sense of cold terror overwhelmed her.

The policeman revealed that the search of the house had produced two important clues which confirmed Estelle's evidence so far: a child's handkerchief had been found in the water tank, and some scraps of paper in handwriting identified as that of Mona Tinsley had been uncovered during the search of the main room.

Estelle decided to try to trace the route that Nodder had taken with the body in his attempt to dispose of it. She led the party of policeman and Spiritualists from the house, and crossed the back garden. Instead of taking the footpath that wound around the house, she pushed her way through a thick hedge, and crossed two muddy fields until she came to a church. This was immediately identifiable as the church Mona had shown her in her vision. Following the medium, who felt that Mona's spirit – although no longer visible to her – was none the less leading the way, the party kept to the left-hand side of the church and walked along a muddy lane until they came to a small bridge traversing a canal.

The party went over the bridge: the lane continued on the other side. On one side was a high hedgerow, and the other opened on to fields which stretched into the distance. A road ran parallel to the lane for a short distance before branching away. At the bend of the road, some three or four hundred yards from the bridge itself stood a small inn – the public house or brewery described by Mona.

Greatly encouraged, the policeman asked Estelle to take them further. They continued down the lane until it ran into the fields and dwindled away. It soon proved impossible to continue across the fields, turned by the constant rain into seas of mud, which sucked at them like quicksand, making progress impossible.

The Spiritualists, muddy and dishevelled, were struck by the ease with which they had recognised the land around Hayton from the description Estelle had given them before they had left London, a description directly received from her clairvoyant experience with Mona Tinsley.

Back at the bridge, the officer gave Estelle a map of the area, on which she traced their path until she arrived at the River Idle. She indicated one small section of the river on the map; she was certain that the body of Mona Tinsley would be found there.

A search of the River Idle was soon organised. Unfortunately, the heavy rains of January and February had made the river swell almost to the level of bursting its banks. The police search was conducted under nearly impossible conditions, hampered by the rapidly flowing torrent and at great risk to the men involved. Despite all their efforts, they found nothing and reluctantly had to conclude that the swollen river had carried the body away. There was little chance of it ever being found. Though Estelle Roberts was convinced they were wrong, no further search was undertaken.

Shortly afterwards, Frederick Nodder stood trial on the abduction charge, and was sentenced to seven years' imprisonment. He was silent throughout the trial, despite the jeers and threats from the public gallery. It seemed as though the case would reach an unsatisfactory conclusion.

But the story was far from over . . .

The summer of 1937 was warm, and there was little rain in the Midlands during May or June, with the result that the River Idle was lower than usual, and the flow was gentle. It was perfect boating weather. In June, a party of holidaymakers boating on the river spotted an object in the water, by the bank, and decided to take a closer look. To their horror, they found that the object was, in fact, a heavily decayed corpse. It was the body of a young girl.

The police were called, and the body was recovered. In an attempt to stop the body from floating, the head had been stuffed into a drain that emptied into the river, and it was surrounded by some sacking which smelled strongly of decomposing flesh. A few months earlier the high water level would have made it difficult to find the body in its hiding place.

The police suspected that this must be the body of Mona Tinsley: the decomposition indicated that it had been in the water between four and six months, and the drain was near the spot that Estelle Roberts had marked on the policeman's map some four months earlier. A series of forensic tests soon confirmed this – Mona Tinsley had been found at last.

Frederick Nodder was taken from prison to Newark police station for further questioning. He stuck to his original story, despite the weight of evidence against him. His denials were to no avail: he was charged with murder.

At his trial, Nodder strenuously protested his innocence. However, a clearer picture of the man began to emerge. Nodder was a heavy drinker who was never in work for long: his continual drunkenness led to the loss of every job he ever had. His wife had left him, partly because of this and partly because of his fondness for little girls: a lot of circumstantial evidence pointed to a tendency to paedophilia.

During his time at the Tinsley house, his relationship with Mrs Tinsley's sister had broken up. He had lost the latest in a long line of jobs, and he was again drinking heavily. The prosecution claimed that it was then that he had developed an obsessive interest in Mona – something he denied.

His drinking and unemployment led to his being asked to leave the Tinsley home, and he left owing three weeks' rent. From there he had gone to Hayton, perhaps hoping to start over. Despite this, he had been unable to gain work, and had kept drinking. The prosecution suggested that he was drunk when he decided, on impulse, to go and see Mona on 5 January. Still under the influence of alcohol, he had taken her home with him and kept her prisoner while he abused her. Mona's pleasure at seeing Uncle Fred again had been short-lived.

Around midday on 6 January, a neighbour recalled seeing a child standing in the back doorway of Nodder's house. By nightfall, Mona was dead: perhaps she had been trying to escape, perhaps Nodder had realised the neighbour had seen her, and had panicked. For whatever reason, he must have known he couldn't keep her prisoner for much longer, nor could he allow her to return home. For Nodder, the choice at that dark hour must have seemed simple: allow Mona to leave, and face certain imprisonment; or kill her, and take the risk of being caught.

To his fevered and sick mind, the second option at least offered a chance of escape. He strangled the child and put her body into a sack before heading over the fields and hiding her in the drain he knew to be beneath the level of the swollen river, which he hoped would preclude all possibility of a search.

He then walked to the inn past which he had carried the dead child and drank heavily before returning home. The police were waiting for him there, armed with evidence suggesting his abduction of the child. They missed Mona by a few short hours.

Frederick Nodder was convicted of murder and was

sentenced to death. He walked to the gallows on 14 September 1937, still spuriously protesting his innocence.

The execution of Nodder gave Estelle Roberts no satisfaction: to her, Nodder was now just another troubled spirit who would suffer for his sin by the laws of the spirit world – something in which the Spiritualist Church had a great belief. But at least the spirit of Mona Tinsley was now able to rest in peace.

Too Clever By Half

It's a rather strange, but indisputable, fact that many murderers have an uncanny knack of trapping themselves. Often the crime has been committed with the greatest care paid to detail: all evidence will be removed, strong alibis will be established, and sometimes the killer will take great care to point the finger of suspicion at a third party by the careful placement of fake clues.

Sometimes the killer won't go this far, but will just make sure that no thought of murder ever enters the minds of the police. A good example was the infamous John Reginald Halliday Christie, who simply stated to police that women last seen in his company had gone away – all the while assiduously secreting their corpses about his house and garden.

Teenager Owen Etheridge adopted a similar approach, but came up against American psychic and clairvoyant Dixie Yetelerian, and in so doing pinpointed another area in which the murderer who has planned 'the perfect crime' can go so very wrong . . .

Dixie Yetelerian lives in the small town of Lompoc, California, just down the coast from Los Angeles. By English standards it's a small city, with its own infrastructure and network for the media. On one of the local radio stations, Dixie has held a phone-in show once a week for many years, enabling people to call her with any problems they may have. As she is a big, blonde middle-aged woman who looks and sounds like the archetypal American Mom, people respond readily to her. However, the questions she is asked have little in common with the average phone-in: there are no recipes and political points of view. Instead, Dixie answers people's questions concerning their recently dead loved ones, and their hopes of finding missing children or other relatives.

Dixie Yetelerian is one of the most gifted psychics working in the USA at present, and her success rate is phenomenal. She has often been called in by police to help trace missing persons, and assist in cases of abduction. Many of Dixie's callers go from her show greatly comforted, or with new hope for the future. But just occasionally she gets a caller who is so obviously distraught that she feels the need to meet them face to face to help them with their problem. Such a caller was Owen Etheridge.

The studio was its usual bustle of activity on 7 April 1978. Dixie was in the middle of her show, and technicians moved around her, checking connections, because there had been some trouble with the phone lines. As she came on air again after the 8 p.m. news and weather, Dixie was hoping to get her first call free of technical trouble of the show.

The producer sat across a cluttered table from her, cigarette drooping from his lips, earphones in place. Dixie had her earphones around her neck: they played hell with her immaculately styled hair, and were hot and uncomfortable. The drooping cigarette nodded at her, and she put the headphones back on.

'Hello caller?' she said brightly. There was a moment's silence, and she glared at the producer. Were the phone lines down again?

'Hi. Is that Dixie?' The voice was hesitant, but clear. Dixie answered, and the voice continued, 'I'm Owen, and I'm calling about my dad. He went away on business about a week ago, and I haven't heard from him since. I'm real worried.'

'What do you want me to do about it, hon?'

'I don't know... I just thought that maybe you could tell me if he is all right.'

'I can't do that right here and now. If you wait on the line for a second—' she gestured at the producer, who knew what she wanted '—I'll arrange something for you.'

The producer slotted in an ads cartridge, and Dixie was temporarily off the air. She talked some more to Owen, found out that his name was Etheridge, and that he was only in his late teens.

'If you bring something of your dad's down to the station as soon as possible, I'll see if I can feel anything from it.'

'Like what?' asked the baffled teenager.

'Anything that was his, hon, anything personal. It'll be all right, you'll see.'

Dixie was concerned by the call. She hadn't felt anything psychically, but as a mother she knew pain when she heard it: young Owen was in some distress, and she wanted to do all that she could to help him.

After the show, she waited in the lobby of the radio station until she was approached by a teenager. Owen Etheridge was eighteen; a tall, thin youth who looked on the point of tears. He introduced himself, and explained to Dixie that he and his father lived alone; his mother was dead, and he had been an only child. A fortnight ago his father had told him he would be going away on business for a few days, leaving a forwarding address. When the old man had not returned after five days, Owen had called the hotel where his father was supposed to be staying, only to discover that he had never been there! There had been no hotel reservation, no business appointment. His father had simply disappeared into thin air. Of course, the youth had reported this to the police, but they could do nothing: there were no clues as to his father's fate, and no way he could be easily traced. And now Owen was desperate, and willing to try any method to get a lead.

Dixie was taken aback at this statement, but Owen blushed and apologised. He hadn't meant to imply that he didn't believe in psychics, only that the first thing anybody thought of was the police.

Dixie felt for the young man, who seemed afraid that his *faux pas* would affect her willingness to help him, and reassured him that she would do her best to help find his father.

'Have you brought anything of your dad's with you?' she asked. Owen reached into his pocket and withdrew an old pocket watch on a gold chain. It was slightly tarnished with age, and obviously a much loved family heirloom.

'This was his favourite watch,' said Owen quietly. 'It belonged to his dad, and his dad before him. I guess you'd call it our family treasure.' The boy smiled wanly. 'He takes it with him everywhere he goes, so when I found it the other day I got real worried. I don't know why he'd go off without it.'

Owen handed the watch to Dixie, who smiled at him. 'I'll see what I can do, hon,' she said. Holding the watch in her hands, in the darkened lobby of the radio station, Dixie felt herself transported to another place. She had a sudden rush of emotion: it was anger mixed with a great disappointment. Then came the pictures.

The pictures were clear: it was like watching a silent movie. A middle-aged man burst into Owen's bedroom, and started to shout at him. She wished she could hear what it was all about, but the only sound was a rushing of static.

Owen leapt from his bed, shouting back. They were so much alike: both tall and skinny, with the same shock of wiry hair, Owen's blond, and the older man's

light-brown speckled with grey. It had to be Owen's
father.

They were toe to toe in the bedroom, shouting into
each other's faces. Then Owen ducked out from in
front of his father and ran from the room. Dixie
followed them, almost as though she were walking in
their footsteps. Owen was in the spacious sitting
room of the house, staring out of the window. His
father came up to him, spun him around and
continued to yell at him. Owen yelled back. Then
with an impetuous toss of the head he ran from his
father.

The argument raged on as the father followed his
son to a small room at the back of the house. Owen
was fumbling in a drawer. Then, his father's yelling
ringing in his ears, Owen turned around. In his hand
was a small, snub-nosed gun. He was crying as he
shouted something at his father. The middle-aged
man moved forward, and Dixie saw three flashes
from the gun; still there was no sound. Owen's father
seemed to fall to the floor in slow motion.

The boy flung the gun on to the body and fled from
the room. Dixie stayed with the dead body. For dead
he must be: one of the shots had ripped a hole in his
chest, another had taken a bloody chunk of flesh from
one arm. The third bullet had ripped away the side of
his head, and a mixture of grey brain cells and blood
oozed on to the carpet.

For a moment Dixie felt sick, as she returned to the
darkened lobby of the radio station and looked at

Owen Etheridge standing in front of her, watching her intently. She couldn't believe that this apparently distraught youth was the same boy she had just seen shoot down his father! She tried not to let the horror and fear she felt show on her face, concentrating on the watch. She needed to relax in order to find out more.

Within a few seconds she was again in the Etheridges' back room. Owen was crouched over the body of his father, crying. It was obvious to Dixie that the murder had been committed in the heat of the moment, when, blinded by fear and rage, Owen had shot his father as their argument got out of hand. Now he was sorry beyond words; she could feel an aching void. She was torn between a mixture of horror and sorrow but realised that these were not her emotions but Owen's which she was picking up along with the pictures.

Owen seemed to weep over his father for a long time – yet Dixie knew that, in real terms, she had only been watching for a fraction of a second. Finally, he decided to act.

While she watched, Owen brought a large green canvas groundsheet into the room, and wrapped the body in it. He tied it firmly with a thick green rope that looked like the kind used to secure tents, then dragged the body through the house and into the garage. With great difficulty, he heaved it into the boot of the car before returning to the house and taking up the carpet in the small back room. This he disposed of in the furnace in the basement.

Returning to the garage, he calmly got into the car and drove out of his suburban neighbourhood. He headed for the outskirts and stopped when he got to a piece of waste ground, ready for development. Scattered about the rubble-covered site were the remnants of the building that had once stood there.

Owen took a spade from the boot of the car, and in the shelter of one semi-demolished wall began to dig. The area was deserted, and there was nothing to interrupt him. When he had dug deep enough, he returned to the car and dragged from the boot the green canvas sheet containing his father's corpse. He heaved it over the rubble until he was able to roll it into the grave.

As he began to fill in the hole, the vision started to fade. Dixie found herself back in the lobby of the radio station, facing an innocent-looking Owen Etheridge: either he was a wonderful actor, or she was imagining things. Trying hard to disguise the confusion and horror caused by her vision, she explained to Owen that it had been a little hard to concentrate in the crowded and busy lobby and asked him if it would be all right to take the watch back to her house to attempt a further reading there. Owen agreed, and accompanied her home.

Uneasy at having this possible killer sitting in her kitchen, Dixie made coffee and tried to engage him in small talk about his father before attempting to psychometrise the watch, but Owen had little to say.

When Dixie took up the watch, she knew that she must be careful to hide her feelings, whatever she saw: if Owen Etheridge was a murderer, there was nothing to stop him striking again.

Once again the events leading up to the murder, and its sordid aftermath, unfolded in front of Dixie's eyes as she held the watch in her hands. She asked Owen if it would be all right to hang on to the watch for a few days. She explained that sometimes she could see things that had little bearing on the questions she was asked, and that she needed time to filter through the superfluous information and arrive at a reading that might be of some help. Certainly this was generally true; but in this case, she was purely playing for time.

Owen agreed to let Dixie keep the watch and attempt further readings. He left the house claiming to be happy that she could help. Dixie was appalled at his callousness. Owen Etheridge had come to her thinking that she was a fraud. His plan was obviously to build an elaborate cover story as the dutiful son, trying every avenue open to him in the search for his missing father. She felt sick at having let him into her house.

As soon as Owen was on his way, Dixie contacted Mel Ramos, a detective on the Lompoc force with whom she had collaborated before in the search for missing people. Mel did not claim to understand how Dixie worked, but he knew that her results were consistently good, and he trusted her judgement. She

told him how Owen had spoken to her on the radio
show, and how she had invited him to meet her
afterwards; then she went on to explain about the
watch, and how she had twice seen the murder
committed.

Dixie wasn't sure how Ramos would take this: after
all, it was the unsubstantiated word of someone who
claimed to be psychic, and from this alone she was
asking him to institute an investigation. However,
Ramos had seen Dixie achieve results that he would
otherwise have dismissed as impossible, and he was
sure that she was on to something. He asked her to
come down to the station the next day.

Dixie was ill at ease in the interview room of the
Lompoc police headquarters. But Ramos, a slim,
handsome man in his mid thirties, did all he could to
make her feel comfortable. He brought her coffee, and
told her to take as long as she liked. From past
experience, he knew that he could not expect instant
results.

Dixie took the watch in her hand for the third time
and began to concentrate. The film of the murder
played itself in front of her eyes again. As she made
her statement, Mel Ramos had the records checked:
Owen Etheridge had reported his father missing a
week before.

Less than an hour later, a car containing Ramos
and his partner arrived outside Owen Etheridge's
house. The boy let them in and while Ramos was

ostensibly checking details about Owen's father's disappearance, the other detective was taking the opportunity to look around the house.

Neither policeman had been there before, and they were relying on Dixie's description of the layout of the rooms. Ramos' partner was therefore impressed to find the small back room with ease. There was no carpet on the floor.

Ramos was still talking to Owen Etheridge when his partner appeared in the doorway. He shook his head. Ramos turned to Owen, 'Are you sure your father went away on business?'

'Yes, of course I am,' said Owen indignantly. But there was tremor in his voice that betrayed his real emotions.

'If you've got anything you should tell me, boy, I'd say it now,' said Ramos quietly.

Owen said nothing. Ramos had no hesitation in detaining Etheridge.

During questioning, Owen stuck to his story: his father had supposedly gone away on business, but had not returned. Worried, Owen had checked up and found that his father had not been where he had said he would be. Owen had notified the police, and had then turned to Dixie in desperation. He had given her his father's watch in an attempt to help her locate him. Why didn't they go and see her instead of harassing him?

It was then that Ramos dropped his bombshell: Dixie had indeed been able to see something, and that was why Owen was sitting in that room. Describing Dixie's findings in great detail, and stressing that she had seen the events three times, Ramos didn't accuse Owen of any crime, but simply asked him what he thought about it.

Owen replied equally simply: he would take them to where the body was buried.

Owen took them to the eastern outskirts of the town to a derelict and deserted area where few people lived – the perfect place for the discreet burial of a body. Owen led them through the ruins to a secluded spot and indicated that this was where they should dig.

After the police had dug down only a few feet, they struck something soft in the earth. A fuller excavation revealed a bundle wrapped in a green sheet, tied with a green rope. The bundle was unwrapped – it was Owen's father. He had been shot three times.

Back at the station, Owen told them what had happened: in many ways it was a story that is as old as time. Owen had been going out with a girl of whom his father did not approve. In an attempt to stop his son seeing the girl, the old man had been keeping Owen short of money. This annoyed the son intensely, and he had begun to row frequently with his father, which was unusual as they had been close since the death of Owen's mother. Perhaps it was this that made their arguments all the more intense.

Owen had a gun: it was a revolver he had bought by mail order, and which he used mainly for target practice. During one highly charged row he threatened the old man with the gun. He hadn't actually meant to use it, but his father had driven him to the point of blind rage: he threatened to send Owen away from home, anything to stop him seeing the girl.

As he sat in the quiet of the interview room, Owen laughed softly to himself. The girl hadn't even meant that much to him. The whole thing had blown up out of all proportion. Before he realised what was happening, he had fired three times. His father was so close that death was inevitable.

Owen was genuinely distraught by what was, in effect, an accidental killing. However, his next reaction was to sit down and try calmly to think of a way out of trouble. He methodically set about removing and disposing of the body. Then he returned home to plan how to lay a false trail. A few days later, he telephoned a hotel his father often used for business, asking if his father was still there. When the baffled receptionist replied that his father hadn't even made a reservation, Owen had established the first part of his story. From here it was an easy step to bring the police in, and act the part of the distraught son: indeed, he was very upset, as he had not intended to kill his father.

Unfortunately for Owen, he went too far when he contacted Dixie Yetelerian. He had presumed that all psychics were practised fakers, intent on telling people only what they wanted to hear, and thought Dixie would simply help him to set in place another brick in the wall of his disguise as a dutiful son.

To him it was a minor detail: but many killers slip up on minor details, and this was Owen's undoing.

Dixie wasn't called to the stand when Owen stood trial. There was no need: he had made a full confession. Owen was charged with murder. He tried to claim it was manslaughter, but the jury distrusted the calculating way in which he covered his tracks. It seemed too strongly to suggest premeditation. He was found guilty, and sentenced to life.

This was a strange case: the murderer approached Dixie in order to establish his alibi. Yet all he did was lead her to his crime. In turn, she was able to inform the police of a murder they knew nothing about, and present them with the murderer.

A Voice from Beyond
the Grave

Teresita Basa was forty-eight-year-old nurse at the Edgewater Hospital, in Evanston, Illinois. She was of Filipino extraction, and had worked at the hospital for a number of years specialising in physical therapy. A small, heavy-set woman, she was unmarried and lived alone in an apartment near the hospital. Because of the nature of her job, and the unsociable hours and shiftwork that it entailed, she had little in the way of social life. Apart from a number of acquaintances at work, she had few close friends, but she enjoyed her job, and was generally well-liked by her colleagues. This made what happened to her all the much harder to comprehend.

On 21 February 1977, Teresita Basa was murdered in her apartment. The police had no leads, and what seemed like a random killing was set to join the ranks of other such slayings in the unsolved files. At a time when Evanston was in the grip of a mini crime wave, this was enough of a problem, but what followed was cause for sheer amazement in the police department.

* * *

It was early evening. Teresita Basa was glad to be home from yet another long shift at the hospital. Even though she liked her work, she found the hours exhausting. She would have been happy to relax in front of the TV before retiring for the night, but the set was broken. Instead, she was sitting quietly, reading a medical journal. Teresita had ambition, and wanted to progress in her work.

The doorbell rang. She wanted to ignore it, as she wasn't expecting any visitors, and was in no mood to see anybody. But her caller was insistent, and the bell rang again. Teresita pulled herself up from her chair and warily went to the door, calling out as she reached the hall. The whole of Evanston was in terror over the recent crime wave, particularly because there was a rapist at large, attacking single women in their homes.

Her visitor must have heard the fear in her voice, as he laughingly reassured her of his identity. She knew him and so Teresita opened the door. 'What are you doing here?'

A tall, muscular black man entered the hall, claiming that he had arranged to visit her that evening to mend her TV set: surely she remembered? Teresita was at a loss to recall the arrangement. But the TV was broken, and she would appreciate not paying some extortionate charge to a repair man. She told him as much as she turned into her lounge.

Turning her back was a grave mistake . . . Before

she knew what had happened, the man was on her. The room became a blur of colour and light as he wrestled her to the ground. But Teresita was strong – her job demanded strength – and she tried to fight back, struggling as hard as she could. The man began to tear her clothes off rapidly.

Was he the rapist? Had she unwittingly let a maniac into her home? Rape was the one thing Teresita was terrified of more than anything else. She was a virgin, and had remained so through choice. The thought of someone violating her body held more horror for her than the thought of death. She fought back harder, using all her strength to try and break the hold this maniac had on her.

But all her efforts were to no avail. The man she had thought of as a friend was behind her, pinning her to the floor in a wrestling hold, which was draining the blood from her head. She felt the colours start to fade as consciousness slipped from her. Each attempt to struggle seemed to bring her closer to the black abyss – and if she passed out, then she knew that her life was over.

He was holding her down, pulling off her clothes as he waited for her to pass out, with seemingly all the time in the world in which to accomplish his evil intent. She had to make one last effort. Marshalling all her strength, she tried to free herself: but the hold was too tight, the man's grip too strong, and the effort too much ... Blackness descended.

With Teresita unconscious, her assailant set about

his task with calm precision. Firstly he stripped her of the rest of her clothes. He wanted it to look like a sexual assault, although he had no intention of actually carrying this out: he had other motives.

He placed the naked body on the floor, and took a large knife from his jacket. Picking a spot over her ribs, he thrust down with all the strength he could muster: he had to reproduce a frenzied attack, like those of the rapist currently sought by the police. The knife blow was so hard that it went right through her body, sticking in the floor beneath. It had splintered two ribs completely, and punctured a lung. It was hard to withdraw the weapon and he found himself sweating. When the knife was free, he wiped the blood from it with Teresita's dress, and put it back in his jacket, intending to dispose of it later.

The killer then searched the flat, looking for his real prize. He knew what he was looking for, and he had an idea of where it could be hidden; there was no need to disturb many of Teresita's belongings. He stood in each room before beginning the search, calmly working out possible hiding places. It wasn't long before he had located it: jewellery, some of which had been in Teresita's family for several generations. He pocketed the jewellery, and set about his task of hiding the real crime. He placed a mattress on the body of Teresita Basa and set fire to it: he wanted to damage the body as much as possible, and also ruin the apartment. The fewer the traceable clues for the police, the better his chances of escaping detection.

He left the apartment burning and made good his escape.

Unfortunately for him, a quick-witted neighbour spotted the flames and called the fire department. They were quickly on the scene and there was relatively little damage. The lounge was charred, but the mattress had not been completely burned. One fireman, turning it over to investigate a possible cause of the fire, found himself confronted by the burned and naked body of Teresita Basa.

Forensic evidence showed that Teresita had not been sexually assaulted. The police were forced to conclude that the killer had wanted them to believe she had, but were at a loss to explain why. If it was not rape, then what was his motive? They could find little evidence of robbery and no sign of a forced entry. The killer must have been someone Teresita knew, with a motive only he or she could explain. Find the killer, and you'd find the motive.

But the police had no leads. Interviews with Teresita's few close friends and the people she worked with had drawn a blank. All those questioned had been able to produce convincing alibis for the night in question. It seemed as though yet another random killing was to go unsolved.

It was at this point that fate took a hand.

Two weeks after the killing, Remy Chua was discussing the matter with a colleague in the restroom at work. Like Teresita, she was a Filipino nurse, employed as a respiratory therapist by the Edgewater Hospital. Unlike the dead woman, she was slim and pretty, married to a doctor. She was barely acquainted with Teresita, as their shifts did not often overlap, but like most of the staff at the hospital, she felt appalled by the murder.

'Teresita must be turning in her grave. Too bad she can't tell the police who did it,' said Remy's friend.

Remy replied: 'I'm not afraid of her. She can come to me in a dream.'

Later, Remy returned to the staff restroom during her break. It was nearly two in the afternoon when she began to doze. Through the darkness of her sleep, something stirred, made her want to open her eyes and look: but at what? She shifted in her chair and gradually became conscious. She felt the presence of someone else in the room. She opened her eyes fully and saw that there was indeed someone else, standing by the doorway.

She was about to greet the newcomer when she saw, to her horror, that it was Teresita Basa! She tried to speak, but found herself unable to utter a sound. At the far end of the room, the figure of Teresita raised a finger and beckoned to her. Remy was terrified.

Mustering all her strength, she ran screaming from the room and didn't stop until she was outside the hospital. She sat on a wall by the green that fronted the building, gasping for breath, shocked by the apparition and exhausted from running.

When she had calmed down, she returned to the restroom, but the figure was gone and Remy decided it had been nothing but a dream. After all, hadn't she been talking about Teresita that morning and saying that she could come to her in a dream? Her subconscious had obviously been playing tricks on her. Relieved that she could put the whole thing down to her imagination, she got on with her shift and forgot about the figure. And so things remained for a couple of days.

However, her fellow staff at the hospital noticed a change in Remy. They thought her face had in some way altered, and her voice seemed different... It reminded them of Teresita Basa. It was nothing they could pin down if asked: just certain inflections, certain ways of holding herself. But it was too absurd! Surely they were only noticing these things because of Teresita's sudden and violent death, and her racial similarity to Remy. Nobody mentioned the apparent resemblances.

A few nights later, the dreams began...

At first it was like a film in slow motion, seen through a mist. Remy was Teresita, sitting in her apartment. The doorbell sounded, and she went to answer, calling out. There was a reply – muffled, indistinct. And yet there was something familiar about the voice of the visitor. She let him in: his face was indistinct, but she knew that she was acquainted with him, and felt no fear. And then the terrible part of the nightmare began. As she turned her back, she was thrown to the floor: she struggled, but could not escape, and felt her clothes being torn off. She was Teresita, she felt her pain and fear. She felt the blackness descend . . .

Suddenly she was looking down on the scene. She watched as the assailant stabbed Teresita, then went off to another room, returning with jewellery which he stuffed into his jacket pocket before setting fire to the mattress and the body.

She awoke with a start, her heart pounding. Had she really just seen the death of Teresita Basa?

Her husband, Joseph, was concerned about these sudden nightmares. He wondered if she should take time off work until they stopped. Remy told him not to be silly: she was a bit disturbed at knowing someone who had been murdered. It was preying on her mind, that was all. Just give it a few days, and she would soon calm down. It was nothing more than imagination.

But the dreams continued over the next three nights, each one becoming more awful in its clarity. On the third night, the face of the killer became clear. Remy awoke, covered in sweat, her heart pounding even harder. Teresita's fear had become all the more real to her, for she had seen the face of the killer – and it was someone she knew!

Still Remy kept quiet about her dreams. She had never had any experience of psychic phenomena, and had never given any thought to the matter. The world of the paranormal was a closed book to her, and she would rather keep it that way.

At work, Remy came into contact with the man she now knew to be the killer, and was terrified by his presence: yet it was not just the fear that came with knowing he was a killer – it was deeper than that. Remy felt as though she herself was the murder victim: she felt as she believed Teresita Basa would feel!

Still she did nothing about the dreams – and then they went one step further.

It was a warmish night for the time of year, and Joseph Chua was finding it hard to sleep. He was worried about his wife. Since the death of Teresita Basa, she hadn't been the same. Her manner towards him had changed in almost imperceptible ways. He was worried about the continuing nightmares, and had wanted to consult a colleague at work – a psychiatrist, who might be able to help in some way. But Remy had refused to co-operate; she wanted nothing to do with it.

As he lay on his back in the half-light filtering through the blinds, he could see and feel his wife twist and turn in her sleep. He could only presume that she was having another nightmare. In her disturbed restlessness small whimpering noises escaped from her.

He was about to wake her when she was suddenly still. In the dim light he could see that she had opened her eyes. He was going to ask her if she wanted anything when she began to speak. Joseph Chua was struck by a strange mixture of cold fear and sheer amazement – for it was not his wife's voice that emerged! Instead, it was a harder, older voice that came from her sleeping lips: a voice that spoke of pain and the cold urge for revenge.

'I am Teresita Basa. I want you to tell the police who murdered me . . .' The voice went on to describe in detail the events of that night, but strangely did not name the killer.

When the voice had finished speaking, Remy awoke. She remembered nothing, and when her shocked husband told her what had occurred, she was both astounded and scared. The voice had spoken in Tagalog, the native language of the Philippines: yet it was in a dialect unfamiliar to Remy – but a dialect known to Joseph Chua, who came from the same part of the islands as Teresita Basa!

They were both scared, but reasoned that if they went to the police, they were unlikely to be believed; at best they would be ridiculed, at worst arraigned for wasting police time. But the voice of Teresita did not want them to remain silent.

Two nights later, the voice returned. Once again, Remy was in the midst of a troubled sleep when, suddenly, she opened her eyes. Joseph Chua was frightened, but prepared for what was to happen.

'I am the voice of Teresita Basa. I want you to tell the police who murdered me . . .'

'How can we if you won't name him?' asked the

exasperated Joseph. 'We'll do it, if only you'll leave my wife alone.'

'The man who killed me was called Alan.'

'Alan who? The police will just laugh unless I can give them a full name!'

The spirit was silent for some time, and Chua looked anxiously at his wife. What was going on inside her head? Where was this all coming from? Finally, she began to speak again with the voice of Teresita. 'His name is Alan Showery. He came to repair my TV set, but instead he killed me...'

In a dull, monotonous voice, the spirit of Teresita again told how Alan Showery had agreed to visit her to fix her TV set, but how instead he had attacked her and killed her before stealing her jewellery. She also explained how he had then set the apartment on fire before leaving, in an attempt to destroy the evidence. The jewellery could be identified by members of her family, Teresita said, giving the names of Ron Somera and Ken Basa. The voice intoned a telephone number, which Joseph wrote down. Then, as suddenly as it had arrived, the voice departed and Remy awoke. As she sobbed in his arms, her husband told her what she had said in this 'trance voice'. The whole experience was getting to be too much for her.

The Chuas decided that they could no longer keep quiet about this: if nothing else, Remy was too frightened by the appearance of the voice, and wanted to stop it. So the following day they went to the police, and told them the full story – from the first apparition to the telephone number. The officer they spoke to was Joseph Stachula, who had no direct part in the Basa investigation. He listened to them with an open mind and took their statements.

So far, police investigations had concentrated on the theory that the murder was the work of the Evanston rapist, but officers attempting to tie it in with the rapist's other attacks had been getting nowhere. Then the medical evidence had proved that Teresita had not been raped. Their entire investigation had been on the wrong lines.

Now the police were convinced that the case was a straightforward random robbery and murder and the last thing they needed was a couple of cranks with a ghost story.

As the Chuas left the police station their statements seemed destined to be filed away and forgotten. The officers in charge of the Basa case had other, more pressing, crimes to attend to: they were disinclined to take any notice of what seemed to be just another wild story told by well-meaning lunatics; the sort of thing that happened every day. As one detective joked to his colleagues, at least they didn't confess to the crime!

Stachula, however, had an intuition that the Chuas were not the sort of people to make up such a story. He pressed for their statement to be followed up.

Some months passed before more officers were

assigned to the Basa case; it was in August 1977: six months since Teresita was murdered, and some four months after the Chuas had made their statements.

The officers called at the Chuas' apartment to question Remy about her statement, and her husband about the voice, but they found the story a little hard to stomach.

'You mean to tell me that you were visited by a ghost?' The detectives looked at each other with a grin.

Joseph Chua nodded. 'You don't have to believe me,' he said simply, 'but I know that my wife was haunted for weeks before we got the truth out of this ghost.'

The detectives were frankly disbelieving, but with little else to go on, they resigned themselves to questioning Alan Showery again, in spite of the fact that a previous interview with him as part of the general interrogation of everyone associated with Teresita Basa had yielded no results.

Showery was a black hospital orderly. His pay was low and there were little prospects in the job. He had been there for some time and knew all the staff. He knew Teresita Basa and had been quite friendly with her. Perhaps significantly, he lived only a few blocks from Teresita's apartment.

His alibi rested on the fact that he had been with his girlfriend Yanka on that evening. She, however, freely confessed that she was a bit hazy on the date. 'Jeez, I don't know, really. It's a long time back, right?

I can't remember the date, they all get to be the same thing, y'know? I remember it was the night there was a fire a few blocks away, 'cause I remember a fire engine going by while I was waiting for Al to get home. I had to look out the window, see where it was going, y'know?' She giggled at the thought of acting like a child.

The detectives exchanged glances. So Showery had been out when a fire engine had passed by, heading for the area where the dead woman lived? Things were beginning to fall into place.

Showery arrived home while Yanka was being interviewed. A tall, muscular black man, he was shocked at finding the two detectives in his home, and asked them what they were doing with barely disguised hostility. They explained that they were following up on the case of Teresita Basa, and that they wanted to go over his statement again.

'Why me?' he asked suspiciously.

'We're interviewing everybody whose statement we took before,' said one of the detectives, noting that Showery was decidedly nervous. He was fidgeting with a string of beads Yanka had left on the coffee table, and seemed ill at ease. It was time to play a long shot. 'We're also taking the fingerprints of everybody involved,' he added softly.

Showery's reaction was electric. He rose from his seat, and dashed towards the door. Before he could reach it, one of the detectives had brought him down.

'I think you may have a few questions to answer,

my friend,' he said as he handcuffed the hospital orderly .

Down at the precinct house, under questioning, Showery admitted that he had agreed with Teresita to go over to her place and fix her TV; but he claimed to have totally forgotten about the arrangement, and had not turned up. Perhaps she had opened the door to the murderer believing it to be him? He was now more confident, sure that his supposed honesty was helping him. As he didn't know about Remy Chua's trance voices, he had no idea that he was digging himself deeper and deeper...

Two things that hadn't been known at the time of the first interview now seemed relevant: the first was that Alan Showery's apartment was near to Teresita Basa's; the second was that Showery had a police record. He had twice been convicted of rape, and had served a prison sentence. Yet this didn't quite fit: Teresita hadn't been raped. Her body had only been undressed to suggest rape. There was still something missing that could make the connection from Showery to Teresita.

The detectives returned to Showery's apartment to question Yanka. This time she was hostile. One of the detectives suddenly turned around and asked her if she had any jewellery. She replied that Showery had given her some as a late Christmas present. She left the room, and returned with a ring that fitted the description of one of Teresita Basa's stolen pieces.

This was enough for the police to obtain a search

warrant. In Alan Showery's apartment were found several other pieces of jewellery, hidden in separate rooms. All of these fitted the descriptions of items that Teresita had insured, and which were missing from her apartment after the robbery. When questioned, Showery was unable to produce receipts, or proof of purchase for any of the jewellery. Showery was taken into custody.

The police now decided to ring the phone number that Remy Chua had given to her husband through the trance voice. 'Do you know a Ron Somera, or a Ken Basa?' the detective asked the woman who answered the telephone.

'Ron is my husband,' she replied.

When asked if either of the men were related to Teresita Basa, she revealed that they were both cousins of the dead woman.

Glad to help the detectives in any way they could, both men travelled from out of state to Evanston, and positively identified the jewellery as belonging to Teresita Basa.

Faced with overwhelming evidence, Alan Showery confessed to the crime. He had arranged to visit Teresita Basa's apartment to fix her TV. He was aware that she had some jewellery, and he was short of cash. He had overpowered Teresita, and stabbed her. He had stripped her to suggest a sexual assault, and had then ransacked the apartment in search of the jewellery. He claimed the robbery and murder hadn't been planned: he just took advantage of the opportunity presented by the broken TV set.

This account contradicted certain aspects of Remy's dreams: to her, it had been obvious that Showery had intended the robbery and murder, and that was his sole reason for calling. He had killed Teresita with chilling calm, and had methodically searched the apartment. There was no wild ransacking in her dream visions.

Anyway, though Showery's job was poorly paid, Yanka also worked and there was no reason why he should be so desperately in need of money. The police suspected that he was a gambler, but never managed to turn up any evidence to support this theory. It was just another part of the strange jigsaw that didn't quite fit. More importantly, there was no murder weapon: the knife with which he had seemingly stabbed Teresita hadn't turned up in the search of Showery's apartment and was nowhere to be found. Six months had passed since the murder and the police had little hope of finding it.

Despite this, detectives were satisfied that they had a strong enough case to prosecute. Alan Showery was arraigned on charges of robbery and murder, and finally came before judge and jury on 21 January 1979. It was when the trial started that the police realised things wouldn't be as straightforward as they had hoped. Showery had withdrawn his confession, claiming that it had been forced out of him by a combination of mental and physical pressure.

This left the officers with a big problem: their

entire case was now based on the dreams and trance voices of Remy Chua.

Though psychics are now used quite commonly in the USA by the police, the big problem is still the perceived image of the great fakers of yesteryear, which has led to a general scepticism about the quality of any evidence that may be presented by a psychic. Even a psychic who has a long track record of results that have been proved correct is still looked at with a jaundiced eye by the press and public. In this case, the psychic wasn't even a generally accredited medium who had helped police before: Remy Chua was a Filipino nurse in her mid thirties who had never experienced psychic phenomena before, and was frankly scared by her experiences. Even worse for the police was the fact that Remy Chua had been an acquaintance of Teresita Basa and could be considered to hold a grudge against Alan Showery, a man with whom she had also worked. But surely Showery's possession of the jewellery at the very least pointed towards his involvement in the robbery of Teresita Basa, if not her actual murder?

The defence lawyers had a field day with what had originally seemed a strong case. Without the confession, the burden of proof rested on Remy Chua's statement, and how it fitted the facts the police had collated.

The biggest thing in Remy's favour was that she had said, through the trance voice, that Al Showery had visited Teresita to fix the TV set – something he had stated freely to the police was his intent. How would Remy know of this unless the ghost of Teresita had visited her? On the stand, Remy did her best to keep calm. When she was asked about the trances, she tried to describe all that she could remember, but the defence was keen to press home the point that she could not actually remember saying anything: all the statements had been heard solely by her husband. As for the dreams – everybody has nightmares.

Joseph Chua was also called to testify. He stated firmly and clearly all that he had heard from his wife. He reiterated that she had spoken in a dialect of Tagalog that she did not know. However, the defence was quick to point out that she may have picked it up through being married to him.

'Ghost' is a loaded word with all the connotations that years of fiction and bad movies have given it. Calling the trance voice the 'spirit' of Teresita is more acceptable than calling it the 'ghost', but the defence kept hammering home the point about Remy's trance voice being the 'ghost' of Teresita.

'How can we take seriously the evidence of a ghost?' asked Showery's attorney. 'Is the evidence of a ghost trustworthy?'

The jury, obviously confused by all this, found themselves unable to agree on the question of Alan Showery's guilt: the overwhelming weight of circumstantial evidence pointed towards his guilt, but only Teresita Basa's words, through the medium of Remy Chua, put the knife in his hand. There was no murder weapon, no eye-witnesses who could place Showery at Teresita's apartment building; and Showery's girlfriend Yanka seemed genuine in her uncertainty about the date. His alibi was shaky, but not unproven. A hung jury was unable to come to a decision.

So the case of Illinois vs. Alan Showery was to go to a second round. The odds were very much on Showery being freed, as any case not strong enough to result in a conviction first time around is unlikely to do so at the second time of asking. But even as police intensified their search for the murder weapon, suddenly, for no apparent reason, Showery changed his plea to guilty. He gave no explanation. Did he perhaps feel the 'ghost' of Teresita Basa would not rest until he was convicted? Alan Showery was sentenced to fourteen years' imprisonment.

Legal history had been made: it was the first time that a police case had gone to court supported almost entirely by the statement of a dead woman. And Alan Showery became the first killer to be convicted in a court of law by the evidence of his victim!

The Sleeping Prophet
and the National Hero

Trenton Penitentiary, New Jersey, 3 April 1936.
Bruno Hauptmann, a mild-mannered carpenter and
German émigré – intelligent, but with a recent
arrival's sometimes tenuous grasp of English – is
executed in the electric chair. His crime? The
kidnapping and murder in 1932 of Charles A.
Lindbergh Jnr, the son of the famous airman and
national hero who, three years before, had become
the first man to fly the Atlantic solo in his plane
'Spirit of St Louis'.

Many reporters who had covered the kidnapping
and trial were convinced that Hauptmann was not
the perpetrator of the crime. It seemed as though he
was being made a scapegoat at the altar of public
opinion, and evidence and statements were changed
and contradicted at will in order to ensure this man's
conviction.

Why a scapegoat? Because Lindbergh was a
national hero, and even the subsequent revelations
that he had far-right leanings and urged America to
side with the Nazis as war approached (something he

made amends for, to his credit, with his excellent work for intelligence during the immediate pre-war period), and that – as an idol – he had feet of clay, with his lack of personality and pawky temperament, could not deter the American people from demanding a sacrifice. The Lindberghs were the perfect American family, and the desecration of this family by kidnap and murder at the height of the Depression, with America insecure about its national character, seemed a symbolic attack on the American way.

Why Hauptmann? Simply because he had been caught in possession of some of the ransom money. He had a feasible explanation for why he had the marked notes, but the press were out for blood. Hearst newspapers, keen as ever to make money by selling controversial stories and, if necessary, inventing news, conducted a war against the lone carpenter, and even paid for a defence lawyer famed for his incompetence. This ploy worked, as chance after chance to poke holes in the prosecution story was passed by, and Hauptmann was left with no defence that any jury would believe.

Hauptmann, the outsider, was a perfect aunt sally...

In the middle of this maelstrom of emotions sat Edgar Cayce, the man known as the Sleeping Prophet. Cayce's involvement in the Lindbergh case has been downplayed by his followers and also by his son, who wrote in a biography of his father that the

Lindbergh case was one of his few failures. But this is not so: Cayce pinpointed the whereabouts of the Lindbergh baby – and also identified the killers of the child mistaken for Lindbergh Jnr!

In the seventies, Theon Wright, a journalist and author who had covered the kidnapping and the trial of Bruno Hauptmann, wrote a book about the case expressing his conviction that the wrong man had been executed. Wright believed that the full story had never emerged due to the inefficiency and incompetence of the New Jersey police, who had later lied to secure a conviction and save face. Wright was sure many witnesses – including Lindbergh himself, for reasons that had nothing to do with corruption, and everything to do with misplaced anger – had colluded with the police.

Events took a bizarre turn when Wright was introduced to a man named Harold Olsen, who had spent his entire life trying to discover his real parents. He had been told by his adopted mother and several members of his family that he was either the son of Al Capone or of Charles Lindbergh – they didn't know which one for sure, only that they had taken him in as a favour to a gangland member. Many odd happenings had convinced Olsen that one or other of these propositions was true, as strangers had sometimes approached him with the same story – strangers who, on Wright's investigation, proved to be associated with the Capone gang.

Olsen has never been able to prove his claim, but the fact that he signed a document waiving all rights to the Lindbergh estate seems proof that he just wants to find the truth. Olsen appeared to fit into the jigsaw Wright was slowly putting together, for his 1980 book *In Search of the Lindbergh Baby*, but he does not concern us here. Edgar Cayce does. He is mentioned only briefly in the book, but startlingly! If his trance visions had been taken notice of by the FBI and Lindbergh at the time, the whole case might have ended differently, and the baby might have been recovered. Instead, Lindbergh chose to believe his son dead and an innocent man was eventually electrocuted.

So what happened to Charles A. Lindbergh Jnr? The story is long and convoluted...

Sourland Mountain, near Hopewell, New Jersey. The first day of March 1932. The Lindberghs had planned to spend the week with Mrs Lindbergh's family, a short distance away at Englewood. At the last minute, however, plans were changed as the baby had a cold.

It was a cold night, with a strong blustering wind. The child's nurse, Betty Gow, was in her room above the nursery, and the Lindberghs were in their drawing room. At about nine o'clock, Lindbergh heard a noise like breaking glass; he remarked on it to his wife Anne, but she had heard nothing.

Approximately an hour later Betty Gow entered

the nursery to attend to the child. But he wasn't in his crib. Anxious about his whereabouts, Betty went down to the drawing room, where Anne Lindbergh was reading, but the baby was not with his mother. Together, they looked for Colonel Lindbergh, but he didn't have the child either.

They returned to the nursery, led by the Colonel. They found the window had been opened by force, and left open a crack. An envelope rested on the window-sill, propped on a radiator. There was no sign of the child. Lindbergh told the nurse to take care of his wife, and went down to his study, where he called Colonel Harry C. Breckenridge, a friend and attorney. He then told his butler Oliver Whately to call the chief of police to notify him that the child had been kidnapped and set off with a rifle to search the grounds.

In a short while, the grounds of the house were swarming with state troopers. There's little doubt that they destroyed more evidence than they found, but there *was* the discovery of the ladder: this flimsy, home-made structure, constructed from old floor-boards and shelving, which hung together very loosely, had been used to climb up to the window of the nursery. Footprints in the nursery showed traces of the same clay that was round the house. A fingerprint expert was called in to dust everything in the room for prints. The prints of the Lindberghs, Whately, his wife Elsie (a maid at the house), and Betty Gow were taken to eliminate them.

(These prints – containing the only known ones of

the Lindbergh child – went missing from the case files, in the late seventies, when Harold Olsen won a court battle to have his prints compared with them. Was this more New Jersey police inefficiency, or was there a conspiracy going on?)

The police turned up very few clues – this was a professional job. The ransom note, written in very poor English and signed with a symbol and three holes in the paper, asked for $50,000 in small bills. It reassured the Lindberghs that the child would be well looked after, and that they would be contacted in two to four days and told where to leave the money.

The letter seemed to echo the way a German immigrant would speak English. It said the child would be in 'gut' care, and later notes claimed the child was being held on a 'boad'. At Hauptmann's trial the prosecution used this phonetic spelling of English with a German accent to 'prove' Hauptmann was the kidnapper. If his English was poor, wasn't he more likely to spell boat as 'boot', the German word for it? It seemed far more likely that this was just an attempt to disguise the identity of the kidnappers.

These are the only totally verified facts. The rest is a welter of rumours and confusion fuelled by a hostile press and angry public. Only by looking at the whole situation from a distance of over sixty years is it possible to try to reach the truth. It begins with Edgar Cayce . . .

Edgar Cayce lived from 1877 to 1945. He was born in

Kentucky, and spent his early years on a farm. As an only child he was lonely, and he was also a poor scholar, which made his family despair of his progress in the world. One night a voice told Edgar that help would come as he slept, so he began to put his schoolbooks under his pillow every night and when he awoke he found that he had absorbed the contents. By the age of nine he was at the level of a genius. However, he was still maladjusted, and left school at fifteen to drift into a series of short-lived jobs.

Just before he left school, something happened that signalled the way ahead: while playing baseball, he was struck on the base of the spine. This left him in great pain, and he returned home to lie on his bed. In a dazed state, he asked his mother to prepare a poultice containing ingredients that he reeled off as though reading them. She did as he asked, and the application of the poultice eased his pain enormously. He had no idea how he got the idea for the poultice, as he knew little about medicines.

Cayce became a salesman. In 1900 he approached a travelling hypnotist to help relieve him of terrible headaches that he was convinced were being caused by his continued failures in his work. Having tried all kinds of medicines to no avail, he had sought out the hypnotist Al Layne as a last resort. Layne attempted to hypnotise Cayce, but found that he was immune to post-hypnotic suggestion. Layne pondered over this, and suggested to Cayce that he should try to hypnotise himself and use post-hypnotic suggestion that way. Cayce agreed: it would change his life! He found that not only was he able to hypnotise himself easily, but also it unleashed some kind of energy within him. Before long, he was able to cure Layne of a long-standing back complaint that the hypnotist had been unable to do anything about.

Cayce discovered he could slip into a trance at will. While in this state, he was unsure of what he was saying, and his wife acted as a recorder, writing down all he said in order to go over it later. He found he was able to prescribe medicines for people's illnesses and complaints, and that many of the medicines were of a type unheard of for many years. On one occasion he prescribed balsam of sulphur to someone and it took a pharmacist some weeks to find the drug – in a fifty-year-old pharmaceutical catalogue!

Cayce was a heavily committed Christian, and felt that these messages came directly from God: an impression that was strengthened when he found that blinding headaches would result if he failed to give readings for more than a couple of days.

As time went on, Cayce discovered that his powers extended beyond the mere prescribing of medicines; much to his surprise he found that he was beginning to delve back into the distant past and focus on the past lives of both himself and those for whom he was prescribing. This greatly disturbed him: as a Christian, the idea of reincarnation was anathema. He believed in the everlasting soul that reposed in heaven – something that the concept of constant rebirth was not quite in tune with ... However, ever resourceful, Cayce worked out his own philosophy, in which these past lives became part of a universal unconscious that people came from and returned to in order to learn, each life taking them that much closer to a final resting place in God. So Cayce gradually moved away from the idea of Christianity towards his own ideals, which were realised in 1931 when he founded ARE, the Association of Research and Enlightenment. The Association is kept active today by members of the Cayce family and is the repository of all Cayce's visions – both medicinal and of the past.

Cayce had sometimes worked with the police: as far back as 1906 he had helped Canadian detectives to solve a murder case, by psychometrically finding the hidden murder weapon that helped convict a killer. Generally, though, he preferred to help individuals in need.

Cayce was recommended to Lindbergh by Major Thomas Lamphier, a friend of the Lindberghs, and David Kahn, friend of Lamphier's and a wealthy furniture manufacturer, who lived in New York City. He was also a member of Cayce's Virginia Beach circle – the group of devotees who would sit with Cayce while he went into a trance and began to reel off histories of past lives and medical cures, spurred on by the letters and supplications that were read to him. Lindbergh was keen on the idea of using Cayce –

at this point he was eager to pursue any route that might lead to the recovery of his child.

The first meetings took place on 8 and 9 March at Cayce's home. He was asked to try to trace the movements of the child and its present whereabouts. He was also asked to suggest the best possible way in which the child could safely be recovered. Cayce sat in a well-lit room, facing his garden – not for him the need for the traditional darkened room! Despite this apparent everyday atmosphere, Lamphier, who was also present with Kahn, still felt uncomfortable.

Cayce, in a trance, told of the baby being removed through the window, and carried by a man. There were other men waiting. The child was driven away in a car. But then a switch occurred, and the child was taken in the opposite direction in another car, through the tunnel leading to New Jersey, and across New York city into the Cordova region of Connecticut.

Cayce's account was rambling and confused. As they sat listening to his droning 'in-trance' voice, Lamphier and Kahn found it hard to follow the thread of his speech. It took the two men several readings of Mrs Cayce's notes to sort out which direction led where, and which group of men Cayce was referring to at any one time.

The second sitting produced the additional information that the child was on the east side of New Haven: the FBI should follow a route along Adams Street, turn right at a shingled house two-tenths of a mile from the end of the street at number 473. The baby was held in a brown house, formerly painted green, on Scharter Street. It was the third house from the corner, with red dirt alongside the paving.

On 10 March, FBI agent E. J. Connelly reported to J. Edgar Hoover that the 'alleged soothsayer' Kahn of Virginia Beach said that the baby was being held in Connecticut. An investigation had proved this to be of no value. Not only had Connelly confused Kahn with Cayce, but the so-called investigation had consisted of a perfunctory look at street maps!

Cayce was consulted again on 12 March: and a problem with his readings was revealed. Mrs Cayce had a tendency to mishear her husband's speech, and in recording his trance mumblings, she spelled Cordova as Cardova.

The psychic became testy when asked by Lamphier to explain how to find the street he had spoken of; he replied: 'You find a street by going out on the streets and looking!'

He referred again to three people he claimed were looking after the baby. One was a woman named Madge Beliance, and the other was a man named Meglo – which was later spelt as Megleo. He was asked about the return of the child, and replied that negotiations should secure its release. He again referred to Megleo...

The FBI agents should have taken the erratic spellings of Cayce's wife into account: Megleo was too similar to Maglio to be ignored. Paul Maglio was a

Capone gang lieutenant who was resident in New Haven, Connecticut! This was significant, as Al Capone, at this time in prison on tax evasion charges, had offered his services as a negotiator when the Lindbergh child was kidnapped – on condition that he be released and pardoned if the child were found safe. This was instantly dismissed by the New Jersey police and also by Lindbergh, which may have been a terrible mistake. If Theon Wright's theories are correct, the child was then being held by Capone's gang!

The FBI investigated Megleo – Special Agent Merrick even spelt it as Magleo in one report (how much closer can you get to Maglio!) – by combing the New York phone directory for the name and coming up with a blank!

Cayce was asked if Betty Gow, the nurse, had been involved. He replied that she had indirectly been implicated through Red Johnson, her boyfriend, a small-time hustler who was associated with Maglio. Cayce reasserted his conviction that Megleo was the one to deal with: he was the leader of the group. He also said that a gangland go-between was being used. At this time, one of the leads Lindbergh was pursuing involved one Mickey Rosner, a bootlegger and small-time racketeer who had approached the Colonel.

In the seventies, Wright checked out Cayce's description of the place where the baby was said to be held. Working on the assumption that Cayce's pronunciation and his wife's erratic spelling were partly to blame for the confusion, he talked to James Kilmartin, who ran a service station in East Haven. Kilmartin told him that there was no Cordova or Cardova, but there was a Dover section of town... It was across the river, where Lindbergh had spent so much time following up one of his leads. There was no Adams Street, but there was a Chartham (pronounced Chat-ham) Street.

There Wright found a shingled house numbered 73. Turning right at a point two-tenths of a mile from the waterfront, he came face to face with a store building. Scharter Street did not exist any more – nor had it in 1932. However, it had been called that once, in the last century, later being renamed Maltby Street. The store building was a recent addition to the street.

Asking around, Wright found that the resident of 73 Chartham Street in 1932 had been someone called Maglearo! He was then directed to a woman who had lived in the area for many years. Her son recognised their former home (now the storefront in Maltby Street) from the description Cayce had given, and told Wright that a woman named Herkler had lived there, and had at that time looked after a child. Her apartment was above them at 109 Maltby, and a local rumour at the time was that she was looking after the Lindbergh child!

This floored Wright: not only was it amazing that the FBI had failed to follow this up, but Harold Olsen (the man who believed he was either the son of

Lindbergh or of Capone) had once been stopped while on holiday in the area by a woman answering Herkler's description: she had told him he was the son of Lindbergh, and that she had looked after him as a baby!

(Both Wright and Olsen later followed up on Mrs Herkler: she was dead, but her daughter was still alive. She remembered her mother telling her that she had looked after the Lindbergh child for Maglio...)

There is little doubt that Cayce had supplied the FBI with all that they needed to crack the case. The child had been abducted as a way of getting Capone legally pardoned. When the plan fell through, the little boy was handed over to the Olsens, who were looking for a child to adopt and lived near one of Capone's many homes – this would also account for the rumour that Olsen was Capone's son.

Meanwhile, on 6 March, supposed psychic Mary Cerrita, accompanied by Peter Biritella, a Spiritualist preacher, gave a press conference at the Princetown Junction Hotel in Hopewell, where she informed reporters that a man initialled JFC would intervene in the case, and that the Mafia were involved. The ransom money would change hands, but the child would not be returned.

Two days later, a retired headmaster named J. F. Condon (known as Jafsie) put an advertisement in the *Bronx Home News* offering a $1,000 reward for information leading to a conclusion to the case, and also offering his services as a go-between. He was contacted, and the marks on the note he was sent tallied with those on the note left at the Lindbergh house.

Lindbergh trusted Condon. They went together to meet a man named 'John', who had a Scandinavian accent. (This was the man that both later identified as Hauptmann – who had a strong German accent . . .)

The ransom was set at $50,000, and was paid at Van Courtland Park on 13 March. Another man seemed to be acting as lookout when 'John' collected the money from Jafsie. This second man fitted the description of a certain Isidor Fisch, a business associate and friend of Hauptmann. But Fisch, and any possible part he might have had in the proceedings, was ignored at Hauptmann's trial, and expunged from the evidence.

After this, a note was sent to Lindbergh telling him the child was being kept on a boat off Elizabeth Island, near New Haven. Lindbergh scoured the area without success.

At this point, John Hughes Curtis enters the picture. Curtis lived in the New Haven area and was approached to act as a go-between. He met with a man called Sam and also a Scandinavian named 'Dynamite', and arranged a rendezvous at Cape Mary. This proved to be unsuccessful (Lindbergh spent the day on his yacht waiting for a contact that failed to show), and Lindbergh did not trust Curtis after this.

A strange twist to the story was the suicide of Violet Sharpe, a maid at the Morrow house (Lindbergh's in-laws). She had telephoned someone on the evening the child disappeared, but when the police questioned her about this, she reacted hysterically, then killed herself by taking poison. It was never established who Sharpe telephoned. However, a bizarre coincidence was that Sharpe and Oliver Whately, the butler at the Lindbergh house, attended a Spiritualist church on East 127th Street, New York, where the minister was Peter Biritella, and the resident psychic was Mary Cerrita. Other regular attenders were Jafsie Condon and Isidor Fisch. The apartment house where Hauptmann and Fisch lived was across the street from the church.

Wright proffers the interesting theory that, as soon as it was known the child had been kidnapped, the small group at the church came up with an extortion plan to take advantage of the kidnapping, but succeeded only in muddying the waters further. This doesn't explain how they knew the child was in New Haven ... unless Mary Cerrita wasn't quite the fake Wright assumed her to be when he interviewed her in 1932! Hauptmann, who did not attend the church, was an innocent bystander but was sucked in by the death of Isidor Fisch.

Meanwhile, Curtis was put under pressure by the police who were already tending towards the idea that a gang was not involved: either he signed a statement saying that he had lied about his contact with a so-called kidnap gang, or he would be charged with complicity. Curtis signed.

This is appallingly ironic, as there is a strong possibility that the people Curtis met with were members of the Maglio–Capone faction who were attempting to cut their losses on the deal and extract some money from Lindbergh. It was when Curtis was arrested and his contact with them ignored, that they lost interest and farmed the child out to the Olsens.

Enter Mrs Evelyn Walsh, estranged wife of the publisher of the *Washington Post*, and owner of the famous Hope diamond. A society hostess who knew both the Morrows and the Lindberghs, and a wealthy woman in her own right, she was determined to help the Lindberghs get their child back. She engaged the services of Gaston B. Means, an ex-FBI agent who now worked as a private investigator and also as a bootlegger. He straddled both sides of the law with ease, and as such seemed the perfect man to make contact with the kidnappers. Mrs Walsh authorised him to track down the kidnappers and offer to pay their ransom demand. (This seems like giving Means a licence to print money!)

Means claimed to have contacted the gang and agreed a ransom sum of $100,000, to be handed over at a bridge, whereupon he would be told where to pick up the child. He took the money to the appointed rendezvous but claimed that the gang had driven off before telling him where the child was being kept... Mrs Walsh was, obviously, far from pleased, and Means was charged with robbery, tried, and convicted.

During the Hauptmann trial he told a reporter that he was convinced that Hauptmann was innocent, and that the gang involved were connected with Capone. He also swore that he had not kept Mrs Walsh's money. Where did he get the idea of Capone being involved? With his underworld connections and ex-tenure as a G-man for the FBI, Means would have come across most prominent members of the Capone gang during his chequered career. If, as he claimed, the money was taken from him on the bridge, then it's likely that he recognised the men who took it. Certainly, the money was never recovered and Means, not a well man, died in prison in 1937.

Seventy-two days after the kidnapping, it turned into a murder hunt...

A truck driver named William Hunt found the body while making a delivery near Mount Rose Heights – less than two miles from the Lindbergh estate. As he walked towards some bushes to answer the call of nature, he came across a mound of recently disturbed earth. Like most people in the United States, he was aware of the Lindbergh case and he knew the Lindberghs lived in that area. He moved some earth, and found the remains of a child buried near to the surface.

The State Police were called to remove the body to

the mortuary, where it was examined. Cause of death was given as strangulation.

The corpse has been the subject of controversy ever since. Why hadn't the police found it earlier in their supposed searches of the area? Had it been only recently interred? Certainly the child had been dead for about a month, and the body was quite badly decomposed but it was possible that it had been buried fairly recently in this spot, perhaps put there to deflect attention once the ransom had been paid. If so, who had put it there? The group centred around the Spiritualist church? Gaston B. Means? Or the Capone gang led by Maglio?

And there is little doubt that it wasn't the Lindbergh child...

When the body was found, Lindbergh was out near Elizabeth Island pursuing the search for the boat on which the mysterious 'John' had said his son was being kept. He wasn't told that a body was discovered and that it needed identification; he was told that his son had been found dead. Thus he travelled to the mortuary convinced that it was indeed his child. At the mortuary Lindbergh took one look at the body – highly decomposed, with much of the flesh gone and one leg missing – and confirmed that it was his son. This was something that he clung to for the rest of his life. But was it really Charles Jnr on the slab?

Charles Lindbergh Jnr suffered from rickets as a result of a milk allergy, and his diet was supplemented with bonemeal to compensate for this. He was twenty months old, and had been measured a fortnight before his abduction: he was 29 inches long. He also had a toe deformity: the little toe on each foot overlapped the two toes next to it.

The corpse that lay on the slab was 33½ inches long. He did not have rickets. He did have a toe deformity; however, in his case the big toe on the remaining foot overlapped the two toes next to it. If it was not the Lindbergh child, who was it?

The same day as the Lindbergh abduction, a child of about two years was snatched from St Michael's Orphanage at Hopewell – where the Morrow family lived, and where the Lindberghs normally spent their week – probably by one of the gangs involved in either the kidnapping of the Lindbergh baby and/or the extortion attempt. The idea was probably to provide a decoy by planting a corpse, and to buy time before upping the demand with proof that the real child was still alive.

So why did Lindbergh identify it as his son? Because he was in a grief-stricken state, and had been told by the FBI that the child was his. He saw what he expected to see. Why did he stick to this identification, even when it became obvious in later years that the child was not his son? Partly because it was in his character to stick by what he said – he was a stubborn man. And partly because he felt that his wife Anne had already suffered enough heartache: her diaries, later published in book form, reveal the hell she was going through at this time, and she had a nervous breakdown. Why give her hope that the child was alive, only to – perhaps – have it dashed again? The Lindberghs later had five other children: but Charles Jnr was the first born, and his loss must have affected his mother deeply.

Certainly, at the time of Hauptmann's trial Lindbergh was still sure in his own mind that it was his child, and that may explain his willingness to perjure himself in order to convict the man he was convinced was guilty. His right-wing beliefs precluded considering the possibility that the State was doctoring evidence, as now seems likely.

One thing is for sure. The child found in the shallow grave had been dead no more than a month. Cayce was consulted only a few days after the kidnapping. If his visions had been properly followed up, the murdered child might have been saved...

It was to be two years before anyone was arrested.

The breakthrough the State Police had been waiting for came on 18 September 1934 – over two and a half years after the initial kidnapping. There had been sporadic reports of some of the marked ransom money handed over by Lindbergh and Jafsie (mainly low denomination bills and gold certificates – legal tender at this time) being spent in various places. Mostly the reports were of shadowy men, and once a woman driving a large car changed a gold certificate in a bakery. There was also the mysterious account opened with some of the money in an uptown bank –

the payee was never traced, and the money never claimed. The description was of a tall, thin man with a pointed nose.

On 18 September, a man used one of the gold certificates to pay for petrol at a service station. He had a fairly large bundle of them, and joked that he would have to get rid of them quickly as Roosevelt had put a time limit on their use as legal tender. The sharp-eyed station attendant noted down the licence number of the man's car, and handed this over to FBI agents when it was ascertained that the gold certificate was indeed from the Lindbergh ransom.

The car was traced to Bruno Hauptmann, a carpenter who lived quietly with his wife in a rooming house near East 127th Street. Hauptmann was arrested, and after cursory questioning was charged with the kidnapping and murder of Charles Lindbergh Jnr.

Hauptmann protested his innocence right up to his execution, and there's every reason to believe that he was guiltless: his only crime was to spend the money that had been left in his care by Isidor Fisch. Fisch and Hauptmann had been in business together, dabbling in stocks and shares with their spare cash. Hauptmann was intelligent and shrewd, and this was reflected in the profits they made from their tiny investments. Fisch had owed Hauptmann some money when he returned to Germany; after his death, Hauptmann took the money left by Fisch as payment of the debt and began to spend it.

* * *

The public were overjoyed that someone had finally been captured for this heinous crime: and it was the public's lust for blood that led to Hauptmann's conviction. Hauptmann was a foreigner who couldn't speak English, and had taken work from Americans in his trade as a carpenter. On the other hand, Lindbergh was the blue-eyed All-American boy who could do no wrong, and whose only son had been slaughtered (doubts about the identity of the child were hushed up for many years). Fanned by the yellow press of Hearst, the flames of public xenophobia raged. Hauptmann was a dead man before he even reached the courthouse.

State Prosecutor Dave Wilentz was planning to run for governor, and knew that a conviction would secure his election. So he devised a theory of the kidnapping that ensured Hauptmann would be convicted – the 'Lone Kidnapper Theory' took shape. According to this, Hauptmann had travelled to the house on his own, and had scaled the home-made ladder in order to abduct the child. When Hauptmann got in the nursery, the little boy had tried to cry out, and Hauptmann had strangled him. He then took him down the ladder and buried the body in the woods before starting his extortion campaign. He was 'John' from the cemetery.

In order to accommodate this theory, a number of facts had to be changed. Firstly, there were the multiple prints in the nursery; none of these matched the Lindberghs' or their staff's prints. Neither did they match Hauptmann's. Therefore, Hauptmann must have been wearing gloves. The mysterious prints were filed away. As too was the fact that the corpse of the child, on closer examination by a pathologist, did not match the Lindbergh child.

Witnesses were found to testify that Hauptmann had driven around the area with the ladder on his car, among them a man who was claiming two amounts of social security from separate addresses and was officially classed as blind, and another man who changed his story at the last minute, and many years later claimed to have been paid by the prosecutor's office to swear to Hauptmann's presence in the vicinity, though he himself had been miles away at the time!

Ignored was the evidence of the petrol station attendant who had served a man who was in a car that did not answer the description of Hauptmann's, together with two other men: it also had the ladder attached...

John Hughes Curtis and Edgar Cayce were brushed aside – they talked of gangs, and this was not a gang affair. Forgotten was the strange suicide of Violet Sharpe, and Betty Gow's petty gangster boyfriend.

The next problem was the description Lindbergh and Jafsie Condon had given of 'John', as a tall, thin man with a pointed face and a Scandinavian accent (a description also fitting the man who had opened a bank account with some of the marked money). Hauptmann was tall, but stocky, with a square face and a flat nose; his accent was unmistakably German. Jafsie Condon had no problem in changing his story – after all, he was probably part of the extortion gang, if not the kidnappers ... (He stuck to his changed story in the book he later wrote on his part in the case.)

Lindbergh was a different problem altogether; he was an honest man, for all his faults, and not the kind to lie on the witness stand. He had secretly been taken by the FBI to see Hauptmann shortly after the German's arrest. He hadn't recognised him. However, the prosecutor worked on Lindbergh's trusted friends, who convinced him that Hauptmann was the man – after all, it was nearly three years since he had met 'John' ... He could be mistaken, couldn't he? And wouldn't he like the man who killed his son to pay for it? Wouldn't he like his wife to be relieved of all the suffering she had been through? Lindbergh was convinced by this argument to the point where he – probably unwittingly – perjured himself in the belief that he was doing the right thing.

One other problem about the cemetery meetings was disposed of easily; the lookout who had dropped his handkerchief as a signal when the money was handed over to 'John' – the lookout who fitted the description of Isidor Fisch – was simply expunged from the statements of Lindbergh and Jafsie Condon. FBI agent J. E. Seykora, who had accompanied the two men on this expedition also thought better of mentioning it – but not to the extent of erasing it from his report, which is still available in the FBI files.

Hauptmann's fate was sealed by his wife's choice of defence attorney. On her way to hire the services of James M. Fawcett, a man known for his ability to win tough cases, she was suckered. Outside Fawcett's office, she was greeted by a reporter who persuaded her that he knew of a much better attorney, and that his newspaper would pay for him... The confused woman, troubled by money worries (all Hauptmann's money, such as it was, was frozen – and with her husband gone, there was no source of income), agreed to go along with the suggestion.

The reporter worked for a Hearst paper that had been condemning Hauptmann since the day of his arrest, and had a vested interest in seeing him executed. The man he led her to was Thomas Reilly, the Bull of Brooklyn, an idiot known in the criminal fraternity as the man who could land you in jail even if you were innocent.

The trial itself was pure farce. Reilly's handling of the case, with no evidence put forward to defend Hauptmann and the appalling falsifications of the State Prosecutor's Office never challenged, had his deputies speechless in court.

Hauptmann's main chance of acquittal lay in the identification of the body; if it were possible to prove that the dead child *wasn't* Lindbergh, then the entire prosecution case would collapse. However, at the beginning of the trial, Prosecutor Wilentz and Judge

Thomas W. Trenchard offered Reilly the opportunity of examining the records of St Michael's Orphanage, to determine the possibility of the child being anyone other than the Lindbergh baby. Reilly, who knew who was paying him and in private often referred to his 'obligations' in this respect, declined – much to the amazement of his deputies, who were then powerless to pursue their own lines of questioning. Hauptmann was also speechless when told, but by then it was far too late...

The evidence at the trial consisted of a series of lies and contradictions: firstly, there was the hand-writing on the ransom notes. A series of experts called by the prosecution were unable to identify it conclusively as being Hauptmann's.

Then there was the hiding place of the money. Mrs Hauptmann swore that she hadn't seen the parcel of money left by Isidor Fisch. Hauptmann agreed, claiming that he had hidden it on a high shelf as his wife didn't approve of Fisch, and wouldn't like him to have the money. The jury were taken to the Hauptmanns' apartment, where the shelf was seen to be in plain sight. Quite what this was supposed to prove, I don't know – but it none the less became clear after the trial that the shelf had been lowered by FBI agents searching the apartment. There was also the matter of the number written in the cupboard, the number of a sequence of notes in the Lindbergh ransom. It was taken as proof of Hauptmann's complicity, despite the fact that a reporter claimed he had written it in there some days before, while interviewing Mrs Hauptmann!

The matter of the money was never fully explored; Hauptmann had only a fraction of the ransom. Nothing was ever done to investigate the woman in the expensive car, or the mysterious bank account, and all this was ignored at the trial ...

The most serious matter was the ladder. The jury were asked to believe that this ridiculous contraption of pieces of floorboard had been made by Hauptmann, a man who was a skilled carpenter. They relied solely on the evidence of wood expert Arthur Koehler, who told the court that one rung of the ladder matched a piece of floorboard taken from Hauptmann's attic. Koehler knew this was where the board had come from because an FBI agent had told him so! Koehler had never seen its original resting place.

Hauptmann was found guilty and sentenced to death in the electric chair. After the trial two separate investigations by Mrs Walsh and Theon Wright, both of whom believed that a gang was involved, convinced them Hauptmann had been framed. However, the insistence of Prosecutor Wilentz that a lone man had been responsible made any efforts to prove Hauptmann's innocence very difficult.

Did Wilentz really believe his own theory, or did he do it merely to further his career? It's hard to say for sure, but when Hauptmann spoke to his wife for the last time, he told her that something greatly bothered him. Wilentz and representatives from his office had called to see him on a regular basis. Each time they had asked him the same question: what happened to the child? Hauptmann was confused; they had convicted him of murdering Lindbergh Jnr. So why were they asking him what had happened to the child? Could it be that they really believed the child was alive?

After several stays of execution, Hauptmann was electrocuted on 3 April 1936.

Meanwhile, the real criminals – identified by Edgar Cayce – went free...

The Little Boy
Who Was Late

13 June 1972 – it was a warm summer evening, as the sun started to fade over the town of Freeport, Maine. John A. Nasson, a sturdy eight-year-old, had been out playing with his friends near the run-down apartment block where he lived. Just before half-past seven, John said goodbye to the others and began to make his way home, about a block and a half away. His parents had told him that he would have to be home by seven, and although he didn't have a watch he recognised the theme tune of one of his favourite TV shows blaring through an open window. He knew he was going to be late, and that his mother would be cross with him. As usual, his father would tell her not to go on so, and remind her that they did the same themselves when they were children.

John was dragging his feet. Nothing bad ever happened to him when he was late, but still he was afraid that one day his mother would get *really* mad.

'Hey John, what's happening?'

The boy looked up from his intense study of the

gutter. He wasn't only worrying about his parents; sometimes people dropped money in the gutter, and if you were really lucky you'd find it. He didn't get much of an allowance – even at eight he had picked up that money was tight in the Nasson household.

'Oh, hi!' he said, shading his eyes against the sinking sun. It was behind the old building on the corner, and the man who had spoken to him was only a dark outline in the light. 'I'm just going home.' His voice was whining and weary.

'You don't sound too keen!' said the dark shadow. John's parents had always told him not to speak to strangers, but John knew this man by his voice. He was always hanging around when the kids played on the street corners, and his mother and father knew him. It must be all right to talk to him.

'I'm late,' he said. 'Mom and dad aren't going to be happy with me. They told me to get home by seven, and I know it's more than half past 'cause I heard the "All in the Family" song through the window down there.' He gestured behind him to an apartment block at the end of the street, from where canned laughter came through an open window.

The dark shadow moved towards John. 'That's too bad, John. We can't have your mom and dad get real angry with you, can we?' He held out his hand. 'I'll tell you what. You come home with me 'cause I got some real nice games last week when I got paid, and you know I don't really have anyone to play them with. You have a look at them, then I'll tell your mom it was my fault you were late, and ask if you can drop by at the weekend when I'm not at work. How's that sound?'

'Sure.' John shrugged, and took the man's proffered hand. He didn't know why a grown-up bought games – no one his mother or father knew did that – but if this man told his mother it was his fault John was late, at least he wouldn't get shouted at.

No one saw these exchanges: the mainly residential streets were empty. Most people were eating and watching TV after a hard day, before going out later. Only a few groups of children were still around, and they were engrossed in their own games.

'I'm going to give that boy such a telling-off!'

John's mother paced up and down the small apartment. It was nearly half-past eight, and she had sent the boy's father out to look for him. Despite her words, the first thing she would do when he brought the boy home was smother him in kisses and embraces. She was terrified that something had happened to him.

She spun around sharply as she heard the key turn in the lock. Her whole body tensed as the door opened and her husband walked through. Then her muscles sagged as she saw he was alone.

Her distraught husband sat on the sofa and ran his hands through his hair. He'd looked everywhere for the child: in all the places where he knew John and

135

his gang of friends had played, and even a few places where they weren't supposed to go. There was a building site nearby that John had been warned time and again against playing in; he had searched the entire area, but there was no sign of the boy having had an accident there.

In desperation, he had even visited the parents of several of John's friends whose addresses he knew: maybe the boy had been afraid of coming home because he was late. As soon as he spoke the words, he regretted them when he saw the pain in his wife's eyes. He reassured her that he wasn't blaming her for what had happened. None of the parents he had spoken to had seen anything of John. According to his friends John had left at about half past seven to go straight home. On his way back to the apartment John's father had even stopped a few children still out playing on the streets, asking if they had seen his son; something he had to stop when he noticed a patrolman looking at him askance. After that he had come straight home.

'I think we'd better call the police, honey,' he said, holding his weeping wife.

Chief Herman Boudreau sat in his Freeport office, looking at the report filed by the Nassons. It was coming up to election time for the post of police chief, and he was in a precarious position. The last few years hadn't been too prosperous for the small town, and petty crime had increased. Any chief would have

The Dutch psychic Gerald Croiset, whose insights helped capture the killer of Edith Kiecorius and unravel the mystery of Pat McAdam. (*Topham Picture Source*)

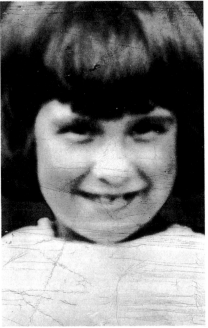

(Above) The old car and wheelbarrow at Broom Cottage. During the search for Pat McAdam, Croiset's description of this scene led a journalist to uncover a likely murder site. (*Syndication International*)

(Left) Mona Tinsley, the Nottinghamshire schoolgirl whose murder in 1937 was solved by the psychic Estelle Roberts. (*Syndication International*)

(Right) Frederick Nodder, the murderer of Mona Tinsley. (*Topham Picture Source*)

(Below) Digging at Ordsall Gravel Pits for Mona's body. Estelle Roberts was to point the police in right direction. (*Syndication International*)

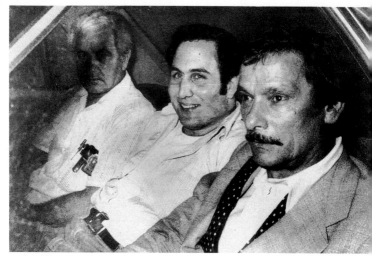

David Berkowitz (centre) – the 'Son Of Sam' – pictured shortly after his arrest with Detective Edward Zigo (right), the arresting officer. (*Hulton Deutsch Collection Limited*)

Uri Geller (left), whose insights helped trap Berkowitz, pictured that same year demonstrating his talents to fellow Miss Universe judges. (*Hulton Deutsch Collection Limited*)

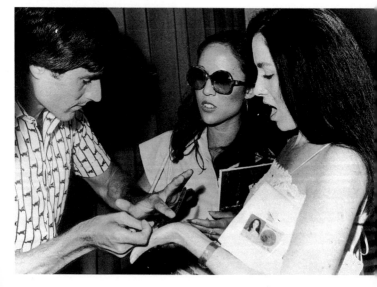

Detective Edward Zigo holds aloft a .44 calibre revolver, used by Berkowitz, at a press conference. New York mayor Abraham Beame stands at his shoulder. (*Hulton Deutsch Collection Limited*)

(Above) Officers in charge of the hunt for the Yorkshire Ripper gather at the site where the thirteenth victim, Jacqueline Hill, was murdered. (*Syndication International*)

(Left) The photofit picture of the wanted man. In many respects this tallies with the man Nella Jones described – and with the appearance of Peter Sutcliffe. (*Hulton Deutsch Collection Limited*)

The psychic Nella Jones seen here helping the police during the search for a missing baby. Her evidence, which could have trapped Sutcliffe earlier, was lost in files by the police. (*Psychic News*)

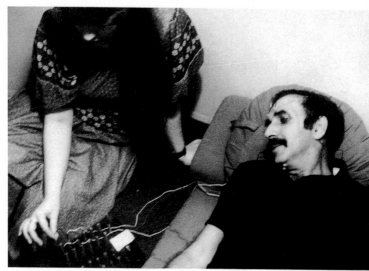

Alex Tanous traced the body of missing child John Nasson to its hiding place. Here he is seen undergoing scientific tests on his powers. (*Psychic News*)

The body of John Nasson is removed from the Freeport, Maine, building where it was hidden. (*Hulton Deutsch Collection Limited*)

had trouble getting on top of it – it was just his luck to be in charge!

He ran a handkerchief over his forehead and read the report through again. There was little to go on; the father had done all he could, searching immediately for the child, and questioning his friends. Either the boy was a runaway, or he had been abducted, either by a woman who longed for a child, or by a pervert. The first option was bad enough, but the way things were at the moment, it would be just his luck if it was some kind of pervert.

Boudreau was only in his forties, too young to retire; he wanted to win the election, and to do that he knew he had to recover the child. He took personal charge of the operation. With as many men as he could spare, armed with photographs of the boy, he led a house-to-house search of the area, interviewing everyone in the apartment blocks around downtown Freeport. The results were discouraging: no one could remember seeing John Nasson that evening.

Boudreau was forced to consider the second option: if the child had vanished without trace, then it had to be abduction. Again the police drew a complete blank; no one had seen a stranger hanging around. Appeals in the local papers produced no results.

Things were not only looking bad for poor little John, they were also looking pretty bad for Chief Boudreau. Apart from his natural desire to find the boy, he feared the ammunition a missing child would give his opponents in the forthcoming election battle.

Boudreau was desperate. There had to be *something* he could do.

It was then that chance took a hand. One evening, as Boudreau relaxed at home looking through the latest *National Enquirer*, among the usual stories of aliens and two-headed cows he came across a piece on a psychic who had been using his powers to help police in San Francisco trace missing children.

That's what I need, thought Boudreau. Someone like him. He brooded for a while; bringing in a psychic could backfire nastily on him if there was no result. On the other hand, things looked bad anyway. Was there anything to lose? Herman Boudreau talked it over with his wife; she agreed with him. There was nothing to lose at all.

'But where the hell am I going to get a psychic?' he finally said to her in exasperation.

She pointed to the photograph of the psychic in the newspaper. 'Why not him?'

The name of the psychic was Alex Tanous.

Alex Tanous was a strange and complex character: part hippy mystic, part academic, he re-invented his image in the seventies in order to use his talents to make a living.

Several years before Tanous was born, his parents (who were both involved in publishing in New York) had attended a party, where they chatted to the seer Kahlil Gibran, author of *The Prophet*, one of the most influential texts in what we now call 'new age'.

Gibran told the couple they would have a son within the next five years, and that this son would be possessed of psychic powers.

Tanous was born in New York three years later, in 1926. This story became part of the myth he built around himself.

The young Tanous soon showed himself to be gifted in many fields. After high school he attended college and did a PhD in philosophy, following this with post-graduate studies that led to him becoming a Doctor of Divinity. It seemed as though he would settle down to the life of an academic. This was not to be the case.

He did begin an academic career as a college professor, but soon started to dabble in a variety of other fields as well. He was a newspaper stringer, supplying stories to reporters on a regular basis. He worked as a disc jockey for a number of stations, playing all kinds of music. Soon he turned to creating music himself, spending some time working as a composer of both orchestral music and song. In between, there were brief periods spent teaching at colleges across the USA, particularly in California, where he found the climate – both meteorologically and socially – more agreeable.

During this time he was also developing his psychic powers, working in conjunction with scientists in a series of tests designed to push his clairvoyance and ESP to the limit. He did not agree with the claims of mediums and clairvoyants in the USA at this time – most were still of the Spiritualist and mystical persuasion – preferring to think of his talents in a scientific way, as something that everyone could develop. This set him somewhat apart.

In the late sixties, though, the hippy philosophy that embraced eastern mysticism, and led to the birth of what is now called 'new age', appealed greatly to Tanous. He was looking for a new career, again tired of academia, and was keen to break into that fringe of showbusiness reserved for the psychic and the medium. He grew his hair past his collar, and his dark complexion was enhanced by a moustache that seemed to define his whole extrovert and mystic personality.

When Boudreau contacted him, Tanous immediately agreed to come to Freeport.

While waiting Tanous' arrival, Boudreau was not idle. Even though there was, as yet, no proof of a crime, Boudreau had his men search through their files for possible suspects noting down any previously convicted child sex offenders who lived in the locality. There were four – one of whom lived in the same building as the Nassons. It seemed unlikely that such a crime would be committed so close to home, but on the other hand it did give that suspect plenty of opportunity to get to know the child.

All four suspects were placed under surveillance. This was time-consuming and costly, but there were no real leads and Boudreau had do *something*. The child's parents were desperate, and the local press was on his back. What was worse, he couldn't reveal that he had any suspects at all for fear of putting the possible criminal on his guard, and so had to sit back and take abuse from a press and public that believed he was not trying.

When Tanous arrived in Freeport, he wanted to be told nothing of the investigation so far, so it would not influence his thinking; rather, he wanted to let his psychic powers pick up influences from the vibrations around.

On the day of his first meeting with Boudreau, Tanous was driven to the apartment building where John Nasson's parents lived. Boudreau introduced the psychic to the bewildered couple and awkwardly tried to explain why he had felt it necessary to call in a psychic. He could see the boy's father looking at him with something approaching contempt.

Tanous, on the other hand, seemed blissfully unaware of all this: with the supreme self-confidence of someone who knows their powers, he assured them that he would, given time, be able to find their son. First, he wanted to look around the flat.

He spent some time in the child's bedroom, trying to absorb something of John from the room. Then he walked through every room in the apartment, trying to pick up something that would trigger his psychic senses. There was only the vaguest feeling of something amiss.

Afterwards, with Boudreau in close attendance,

Tanous walked down every corridor in the ram-
shackle apartment building, up and down every
staircase, and down into the basement. He could tell
that the child had lived here, could sense him in the
building, but the drab whitewashed plaster, cracked
in places and with peeling paint, seemed unwilling to
yield its secrets to him.

Boudreau was not discouraged, but a little appre-
hensive. Had this been a mistake after all? Was his
risk-taking going to backfire on him?

Finished in the building, Tanous asked Boudreau
if it would be possible to drive around the area,
perhaps to get a feeling of the district and the places
where the child would have played. Boudreau
assented and got in behind the wheel while Tanous
sat in the back of the chief's car.

It was during this drive that the first strange thing
happened. As the car got within a couple of hundred
yards of the Nassons' apartment building, Tanous
began to shake his head, and say repeatedly 'No, no'.
This happened several times; Boudreau would take
each road around the building, in every direction.
Each time they got within a few hundred yards of the
building, Tanous would start to shake his head. Chief
Boudreau became excited: it was obvious that Tanous
was picking up something, the psychic was on to a
lead! He asked Tanous if this was the case but all he
got was a noncommittal shrug.

Boudreau asked Tanous what he meant by saying
'no' each time they drove off. Tanous was unwilling to

commit himself at this stage, but he did explain that though he could pick up no definite impressions of the missing child, he was sure each time they drove away from the building the trail went cold. It was as if the child had never left the building, or had returned without anyone knowing. But he was unable to tell whereabouts in the building the child could be as he had not picked up anything definite in his search throughout the apartment house.

Tanous went quiet in the back seat. It was as though he was having to brace himself before saying anything else.

'Well what is it, for Chrissakes!' said the exasperated Boudreau.

Tanous shook his head. 'I think the child is dead. That's why I'm not getting anything clearly.'

Boudreau felt his blood run cold: this was just what he didn't want to hear. An abduction was one thing; a child murder was quite another.

Boudreau and Tanous sat in the car in front of the apartment building. Outside, the world went on as usual. Inside the car, each man was wrapped in his own thoughts, Boudreau wondering how he could catch a child killer and Tanous trying to pick up anything that might be in the ether.

He surprised himself when he suddenly began to speak. It was as though the words came straight from somewhere outside of him: he was speaking without thinking, or even being conscious of receiving any impressions. The child's body was wrapped up and hidden beneath something, he was not sure what. But it was not that well hidden.

As Tanous spoke, tears began to run down his face. The sadness and sheer futility of such a death touched something inside him. He wanted to be able to see more, but there was nothing: only the feeling of John's death. He became more and more upset – he had never been involved in a murder before, and he told Boudreau that he could not carry on any longer, but would be able to resume helping the investigation the next day.

Boudreau drove back to his office in silence. Why was Tanous able to tell the child was dead, and the body wrapped and hidden, but not where it was? If Tanous was picking up the thoughts of the murderer, who presumably lived in the building, why would he not know who this person was?

Tanous drove back to his motel on the outskirts of Freeport less than satisfied. He had been able to suggest something to Boudreau, but not able to give him anything concrete. The only thing he had really done was confirm the worst fears of the police chief. In the missing persons' cases that he had previously been called in to help with, he had been able to give more positive results almost straight away. Perhaps this was because he could pick up the thoughts and feelings of the abductees. Perhaps it was that the impressions of sudden, violent death were too much for him to cope with. Tanous felt under a great pressure to get results.

The next morning he awoke feeling better than the previous evening. He was refreshed, but at the same time there was something nagging at him – like a dream that you can't quite recall. It bothered him as he showered and dressed, but despite all his efforts he couldn't bring it to the front of his mind.

Tanous left the motel to drive into Freeport. On the road something quite remarkable happened. Tanous later described it as the most amazing feeling he had ever experienced: at the time it was baffling and confusing.

While driving along, Tanous began to feel an irresistible urge to pull over. There was a picture forming inside his head; he had to stop and draw it. This was strange, as despite his many accomplishments Alex Tanous was no artist, a fact he himself acknowledged. By now the compulsion was so strong that the road began to disappear in front of him: his immediate field of vision was taken up entirely by the face he felt he had to draw. He had to pull over, and quickly. All he could see was the face: any traffic coming towards him would most likely run him off the road.

Tanous pulled over to the side of the highway, slithering to a halt in a shallow ditch. Without even bothering to turn off the engine, he began to search frantically in the glove compartment for a pen and paper. The compulsion was overwhelming him. The face filled his entire consciousness, and unless he drew it quickly he was sure that his overloaded brain would burn out. Finding a sheet that was blank on one side, and a pen, he began to draw.

Something which he later described as an unknown force, seemed to be guiding his hand. The sketch was rapid, his hand moving faster than if he had attempted to draw under his own steam. He felt detached from his actions, as though he was above his body, watching himself draw. A detailed portrait of a male face took shape. When it was finished, Tanous felt drained, as though his energy had been sucked from him to make the portrait possible.

He rested for a short while, then resumed his drive to police headquarters. His vision was back to normal, although his hands trembled on the steering wheel. Once he arrived, he hurried in to see Herman Boudreau, and showed him the drawing, explaining the circumstances under which it was created. Boudreau was astounded, and repeatedly asked Tanous about the portrait: was it of someone he knew? Someone he had seen, perhaps? Tanous replied in the negative, confused by Boudreau's insistence. He told Boudreau that he was sure this was the man who had kidnapped John Nasson.

It was then that Boudreau decided to level with Tanous. Asking him to sit down, he began to explain his reasons for concern over the portrait. He revealed to Tanous that he hadn't been quite as clueless in the case as he had led the psychic to believe. There were, in fact, four suspects under surveillance, each one living within a few miles of the child's home – one in the building itself. It was vitally important that Tanous was clear on this point: had he seen anyone during the past few days who resembled the face in the portrait?

Tanous was as certain as he could be: he could recall seeing no one who in any way resembled the portrait, but wanting to be scrupulously fair, he could not preclude the fact that he might have caught sight of someone in the street. There was no way he could guarantee that – any more than Boudreau could... Boudreau smiled to himself and shook his head. The police chief was satisfied. He took down a file that contained shots of all the subjects, and pulled one photograph from it. Laying this down on the desk next to Tanous' sketch, he let the psychic compare the two: the sketch was an almost perfect replica of the photograph. Boudreau watched as amazement spread over Tanous' face. He was overawed at his own power: he was aware of the phenomenon of automatic writing, but automatic drawing was a new one on him. It was startlingly obvious that something had communicated this man's identity to Tanous.

'You sure you've never seen that face before?' the police chief asked.

Tanous shook his head. 'Never.'

Boudreau had enough circumstantial evidence to enforce a search warrant. Admittedly, the law is not geared towards accepting psychic insights, but when added to the facts already known about the suspect – the man who was more than a suspect now, in the eyes of Herman Boudreau – they made a convincing case.

The suspect's name was Milton I. Wallace, and he lived in the Nassons' apartment house – in fact, just down the hall from them. Wallace had a record: he had been imprisoned for a sexual assault on a seven-year-old boy some years before. In prison he had undergone psychiatric tests which had not indicated the need for treatment. He had been a model prisoner, and had been released early. He was now thirty-three years old, and worked in a shoe factory.

Wallace had an alibi for the evening that John Nasson had disappeared – he claimed to have been at a friend's house, and the friend had backed him up, though there was a dispute about what time Wallace had arrived. There was another problem of timing: Wallace worked shifts in the factory, and punched in at a time clock. The clock showed that on 13 June he had left a little before the end of the shift, which could, in theory, have allowed him enough time to abduct John Nasson. Wallace could have enticed him into his apartment as the boy walked down the hall; or he could have met him on his way home. No one had reported seeing them together, but as Wallace was a neighbour perhaps no one would have thought it suspicious even if they had.

All this proved was that it was possible for Wallace to have committed the crime. The alibis of the other three suspects were far from solid – they too had had the opportunity to abduct the boy. So, despite his gut feeling that Wallace was his man, Boudreau had allocated equal time to the investigation of all four. Under surveillance, none had yet stepped out of line.

The crucial fact was that it had been Milton Wallace whom Alex Tanous had drawn. Boudreau got his search warrant.

The next morning was another bright day. Chief Herman Boudreau rapped hard on Milton I. Wallace's apartment door with several men behind him and a search warrant in his hand.

'Who is it?' came a whining voice from behind the door.

'Police. Open up,' barked Boudreau.

There was a shuffling in the apartment, and the sound of a security chain being removed. Wallace opened the door: he was dishevelled and unshaven, obviously just out of bed. But more than that: he appeared to be on edge. His eyes darted back and forth from Boudreau to the other officers.

'Whaddaya want?' he slurred.

'Search your apartment, boy,' said Boudreau.

There was a pause as Wallace tried to weigh up the forces against him. Suddenly, he tried to slam the door in Boudreau's face, but the chief thrust his foot into the gap, and backed by his men forced the door open. Wallace was swept aside, and sat nervously but submissively on his couch.

A close eye was kept on Wallace, while a search was conducted. It was only a matter of moments before a grisly discovery was made. Entering the bedroom, a police officer was repulsed by a stench emanating from beneath the bed. Calling Boudreau into the room, he pulled a blanket-wrapped bundle out from under the bed: inside the blanket was the decomposing body of John Nasson.

Down at the station, Wallace told Boudreau the whole story. It was a sordid and sorry affair. Wallace had returned home early from work, and had met Nasson in the street. He hadn't planned anything, but found his old urges coming back. He had enticed the boy with the promise to keep him out trouble for being late. John had felt safe with Wallace because he was a neighbour.

Once inside his apartment, Wallace overpowered John and assaulted him. The child was distressed and upset, telling Wallace that he would go straight to his parents to tell them what had happened. Wallace had visions of prison: he couldn't face going there again, and pleaded with the child to keep silent. He had to use force to stop him from leaving, and before he knew what had happened, John Nasson was dead – strangled.

Milton I. Wallace was tried for murder on 15 December 1972. The trial was short, as he pleaded guilty. He was sentenced to life imprisonment.

There is little doubt that it was the evidence supplied by Alex Tanous that allowed Herman Boudreau to arrest Milton Wallace. When the *National Enquirer* got hold of the story in April 1973, they proclaimed Tanous a hero, and quoted Chief Boudreau as saying that Tanous had solved the case.

Herman Boudreau won the election because of Wallace's capture, and he believed he owed it to the psychic.

As far as Alex Tanous was concerned, he would rather have found John A. Nasson alive...

The Son of Sam
and the Spoon Bender

Uri Geller was one of the world's best known psychics when he travelled to New York in 1977 to help trap one of the most dangerous serial killers of recent times.

The reign of terror of the man who came to be known as 'The Son of Sam' began on 29 July 1976, when he attacked Donna Lauria and Jody Valenti as they sat talking in the front seat of Donna's car, in her parents' driveway on Buhre Avenue, New York City.

It was a warm summer evening, and the two girls had enjoyed a night out. Both were conscientious students who came from families keen to see them get on, but it was the summer holiday, and they deserved a chance to relax after a hard term's work. Donna was a medical technician and Jody a student nurse. Both were concerned about their studies, and as Jody had a summer placement in a hospital, they had become involved in a discussion about work. Jody kept looking at her watch, thinking it was time to leave, but the conversation dragged on.

'Hi! You two kids still talking about work?' Donna's father stuck his head through the open window of the car. He and her mother had been out for the evening, and had just arrived home.

'Oh, hi!' said Jody, 'What time is it now?' She looked at her watch. It was just past 1 a.m. She was shocked at how time had flown by, and told Donna she really should be getting home soon.

'That's okay, I'll drive you,' said Donna easily. Her father followed his wife into the house; Donna and Jody resumed their conversation. They didn't notice the figure lurking in the shadows.

'Tasty meat.' His voice was low and slurred. 'I know, I know.' Checking the gun pushed into a brown paper bag, he walked out of cover, and headed straight for the car. The two girls were so engrossed that they didn't notice him until he was standing in front of the car.

'Who the hell...' began Donna, looking up. It looked like a drunk holding a bottle of liquor in a paper bag was swaying in front of them. She didn't finish her question. He pulled the gun from the paper bag, and cackled with glee as he fired wildly at the windscreen of the car. The explosions of the shots sounded huge in the still night air, and the glass shattered over the two girls.

Donna's parents were about to settle down to coffee before going to bed when they heard the screams and shots outside: they rushed from the house to find Donna dead in the front seat, a bullet having taken out most of her chest. Jody was halfway into the back seat, sobbing hysterically with fear and pain, blood flowing freely from a wound to her thigh. Their attacker had vanished into the night.

When Jody was settled in hospital (ironically, the same one in which she was a student), the police took a statement from her. She was able to describe the events and give a description of their assailant. But she had no idea who he was, and the police were baffled; this seemed to be a man who killed for no other motive than purely for pleasure.

As the months passed, the shootings appeared to have been just an isolated incident. All this changed on 26 November, in the Floral Park area of New York's Queens district. Donna De Masi and Joanne Lomino, two young girls, were sitting on the verandah in front of their house at half-past midnight.

It was a chilly night but both girls were glad to be out of the house where the family could not overhear their conversation. That was the problem with belonging to a large family, Donna always said, there's always someone around the corner trying to listen to you before you listen to them!

As they chatted a man came up to them. He appeared from nowhere, it seemed. Tall, overweight, and with slicked-back black hair, he shuffled and twitched as he looked at them.

Joanne broke off in mid-sentence as she noticed

him. 'Yeah? What are you looking at, pal?'

'Directions, that's what I want.' His voice was soft, with a slight Brooklyn accent. 'I need to get to Queens.'

'This is Queens,' said Donna. 'Whereabouts do you want to go?'

'Here.' He drew his gun from under his loose shirt and started to fire wildly. In the sudden explosion of activity and noise, both girls tried to dive for some kind of cover. But there was nowhere to hide.

'Oh sweet Jesus, I don't want to die,' screamed Donna as a bullet ripped through her calf. She heard Joanne scream.

And then there was silence – only broken by the pattering footsteps of the fat man as he ran away.

Donna looked across at Joanne. She was horribly still and seemed to be dead. Then Donna passed out with the shock and pain.

It was by sheer luck that neither girl was killed. Donna was wounded, and Joanne was paralysed by a bullet which lodged in her spinal column, but most of the shots fired wildly by the mystery man had been off the mark.

Bullets were later removed from the front door of the house and from the mail box. A subsequent analysis of these revealed that they had been fired from the same gun – a .44 – that had been used in the murder of Donna Lauria.

An alert lab technician remembered that a similar wounding had occurred a month before the Floral Park shooting and told the police. Rosemary Keenan had been sitting with her boyfriend Carl Denaro in his car in front of a tavern in the Flushing district when they were surprised by several large explosions. Before they had time to realise what was happening, the rear windows of the car were shattered and Denaro fell forward, struck by a bullet. Rosemary sheltered low in the car, and their unseen assailant ran off.

Carl spent three weeks in hospital, and emerged with little evidence of his ordeal except for a damaged finger. The car had yielded a bullet which proved to be a .44. It too came from the same gun.

But there was no pattern to the attacks and while baffled police tried to get inside the mind of this mystery gunman, another murder took place. On 30 January 1977 Christine Freund and John Diel were in his car in the Ridgewood district, kissing goodbye after a night out when a deafening explosion and crashing glass shattered the air. Christine slumped in John's arms. There was no sign of the gunman, and John wasn't stopping to look for him. He rushed Christine to hospital, but her wounds were too severe, and she died a few hours later.

About six weeks later, another murder was committed only a few hundred yards from where Christine Freund had been shot.

Virginia Voskerichian was an Armenian student whose mother lived in the Forest Hills district of New York. Once a week, Virginia visited her mother, usually in the daylight. But this week she was a little later than usual, and darkness had descended. Normally, she didn't feel afraid of the walk. It was a busy district, and there was no danger of being attacked. But tonight it was different. The city was full of people talking about the mystery killer, who shot at random. Nobody was safe, as he could turn up anywhere, at any time. Virginia remembered the folk tales her grandmother had told her when she was a child, old stories from Armenia about devils and ghosts. She smiled to herself. This tale of the random killer had obviously just got out of hand.

All the same, she wished that there was someone else about. It was unusual for it to be this quiet. She was relieved when a man turned out of a side street about a hundred yards ahead of her and started to walk towards her. At least there was human life here. He was quite tall, but fat, and receding, with his hair slicked back; he was talking to himself, muttering away without even noticing her.

When they were almost level, he looked up. 'Excuse me,' he said in a quiet voice, 'are you tasty meat?'

Before the confused Virginia had a chance to reply, he produced a gun from beneath his shirt. She froze in total fear: should she run, should she try to tackle him, should she cry for help? Before she had a chance to do anything, he calmly raised the gun up to her head and fired three times before running off.

Virginia didn't even hear the first shot die away. At a range of only two yards, her front teeth were shattered by the first bullet which flew into her mouth, killing her instantly. The second removed one eye socket, and the third went over her head, embedding itself in the wall behind her.

The tally for the police now read three dead, four wounded; there was no doubt that it was the same man, as the same gun had been used on all five occasions. The description they had was of a man around five feet ten in height, with hair combed straight back and well groomed. He was overweight, and looked shorter than his height. There were no other clues, and the random pattern indicated the kind of homicidal psychopath who would continue to kill until he was caught. With no clues to go on, the police could see little prospect of this; their only hope was to catch him in the act, and the chances of this were pretty remote.

'We have a savage killer on the loose,' stated Mayor Beam in a news conference. He didn't add that the police were currently powerless.

A city that was now living in fear became more and more terrified as the frequency of attacks grew: 17 April saw two more killings, only a few blocks from where the first murder occurred, in Buhre Avenue. The victims were Valentina Suriani and Alexander Esau. Again it was the early hours of the morning, and the couple had enjoyed a night out. Alexander had driven to quiet spot and they sat in the parked car, talking, failing to notice the odd-looking fat man approaching them, holding a paper bag.

'Who's that?' Valentina asked as a sudden movement caught the corner of her eye. Then she screamed as the man produced a gun from his paper bag and began to fire wildly at the car. The first shot caused a large, dull thud and a scraping sound as it carved into the paintwork on the roof of the car. The second shot shattered the windscreen and ripped a hole through Valentina's throat. The screaming stopped with a harsh bubbling as she died instantly. Three more shots through the broken gaping hole of the windscreen caught Alexander in the head. He slumped to the floor of the car, unconscious.

The noise attracted a passer-by, who watched the tall fat man run away before approaching the car. Suppressing the urge to vomit, he found a public phone and called the police. Within minutes they were on the scene.

Valentina was dead, but miraculously Alexander was still alive! There was only a slim chance of saving him, but it was worth taking. As far as the police were concerned, any survivor might be able to give them vital information; and so far they had so little to go on that they needed all the help they could get.

Alexander was rushed to hospital, but he remained alive for only three hours – an hour for each bullet in his head.

* * *

If there was any pattern at all, it was merely that the killer seemed to frequent the same two or three areas of the city. However, these were densely populated suburbs, and a city close to bankruptcy was having problems keeping them fully patrolled.

However, the police now had their first real clue. A letter had been found in the road near the scene of the last killings. The envelope was addressed to the man leading the investigation, Captain Joseph Borelli, and it purported to be from the killer. In a strange, child-like hand, it contained details that only the killer could have known, and made continual reference to the press conferences that Borelli had held following the attacks.

Part of the note read: 'I am deeply hurt by your calling me a woman-hater. I am not. But I am a monster. I am a little brat. I am the Son of Sam...' He claimed his father Sam beat the family and told him to kill when he got drunk, and that he was just acting under orders, and could not be held responsible for his actions. Then he contradicted himself: 'I love to hunt. Prowling the streets looking for fair game – tasty meat. The women of Queens are the prettiest of all...'

At the same time a similar note was sent to Jimmy Breslin, the humorist and *New York Times* columnist. He seemed an unlikely recipient for such a letter, but was presumably selected by the killer as a well-known figure in New York life. Breslin printed part of the incoherent letter in his column after gaining police permission. The aim was to try to find someone who knew this 'Son of Sam', and could identify him from his pronouncements.

There was no response. All it did was give the publicity-hungry killer the attention he so obviously craved.

The police were out on a limb: either the killer was a total loner, with no friends or family, or else he was leading a double life, and was adept at hiding the darker side of his nature. With only the calibre of the gun and a vague description to go on, detectives braced themselves for the probability of further killings.

As if this wasn't enough for Borelli to contend with, the FBI were beginning to take an interest in the case, spurred on by the massive amount of publicity it was attracting. The FBI and other law enforcement agencies have a stormy relationship at the best of times. Over the man now known as the Son of Sam, it was going to get worse.

As for the killer, all the publicity seemed to do was spur him on: the next attack took place on 26 June, eleven months after the first murder. It followed what was becoming a pattern: Salvatore Lupo and Judy Placido were seated in their car in front of a house on 211th Street, in the Bayside area of the Queens district. It was the early hours of Sunday morning, and they had just returned from a date. Once again, a couple found themselves shocked by loud explosions and shattering glass as the gunman came out of nowhere and opened fire. After four shots, he ran away without waiting to see if he had been successful. Fortunately, in his hurry his aim had not been good; both youngsters were only wounded superficially and were soon out of hospital.

There were no other shootings before 29 July, the first anniversary of the killing of Donna Lauria, and police assumed that the murderer would want to mark the occasion with another killing. The districts of Queens and the Bronx were filled with officers. Frustratingly, the hope of catching Son of Sam in the act on the anniversary of his first strike came to nothing; the day passed peacefully, much to Captain Borelli's disappointment.

Things had become relaxed when, two days later, Son of Sam struck again.

Robert Violante and Stacy Moscowitz were seated in Robert's car near the Brooklyn shore, at half-past one on a Sunday morning. Like the other couples before them they were surprised by violent explosions and shattering glass as the killer came out of nowhere and opened fire. Once again four shots were fired before the killer made his escape. Again the firing was wildly erratic: only two of the bullets hit home, the other two bouncing off the paintwork of the car, leaving deep grooves. This time both victims were hit in the head. Robert Violante eventually recovered, although he was blinded; Stacy Moscowitz died in hospital a few hours after admission.

It was at this point that Uri Geller was introduced

to the case by his FBI contact, a man he will only identify as Carl. (Geller had on several occasions been called upon for help, by both the FBI and the CIA, with some success.) This move by the FBI did not go down well at police headquarters. Borelli took it as a personal slight on his abilities from the Bureau. For this reason, it received very little attention from the media, which suited Geller at the time.

Uri Geller was born in 1949 in the area of Palestine that later became the Israeli city of Tel Aviv. His parents were Jewish refugees from Hungary, and the young Geller was brought up initially on a kibbutz before his parents separated, and he went with his mother to Cyprus, where he spent the majority of his childhood. On reaching eighteen, he returned to Israel to serve in the Israeli Army, and spent his service as a paratrooper, being wounded in the Six Day War of 1967. Invalided out and excused the remainder of his national service, he spent time as an instructor at a youth camp. He already knew he had strange talents, and had spent time practising tricks like spoon and fork bending, and affecting the mechanisms of clocks.

It was in the youth camp that his life changed. Here he met the fourteen-year-old Shipi Shtrang. Shtrang was impressed by Uri's powers, and asked him why he was a youth camp instructor instead of a performer on the stage. When the baffled Geller replied that there was no reason, Shtrang set himself up as Geller's mentor, beginning with a show at the camp. Within a year the enterprising proto-tycoon had built Geller into a national star in Israel, and became his manager and agent – and even his brother-in-law!

Geller, who also became a male model, appearing in several advertisements in his home country, was looked on at this stage as a kind of magician. He was such a well-known figure that when a reporter asked prime minister Golda Meir what the future of the country would be, she replied that perhaps she should consult Geller!

In 1970, the assembled magic circle of Israel went all out to prove Geller a cheat – mass banner headlines in national magazines proclaimed their aim as though it had already been proved. It was as life in his native land was becoming too much of a pressure cooker, that a chance of respite arrived. Doctor Andrija Puharich flew to Israel after hearing about Uri from an Israeli friend. He was interested in studying the powers of mediums and psychics, and offered Uri a chance to travel to the States, where he would be studied scientifically, to try to determine the truth of his powers.

Geller accepted and was soon ensconced in the Stanford Research Institute in California, where he underwent two series of rigorous tests. Then, in between travelling around the world to earn money and promote himself on tours arranged by Shtrang,

Geller also submitted to tests at Kent State University, Ohio, and the Naval Surface Weapons Center in Maryland. These latter tests were conducted by Eldon Byrd, a high-ranking Navy physicist whose report to the US government was the first document on parascience to be taken seriously by that body.

Yet at the same time, Geller was creating controversy wherever he went for the simple reason that he was, occasionally, cheating. The reasons for this were simple: Geller felt under a great pressure to produce results all the time, and not just under experimental conditions – chat shows and magic shows on TV all required him to bend metal. Sometimes the stress was too much, and his powers would not respond. Faced with this and the loss of prestige and credibility it would involve, he was prepared to bend the truth as easily as metal.

In 1977, when Carl called Geller and asked him to go to New York, he was keen to help find the killer who was terrorising the city. The lack of publicity suited him well. He had just been asked by the Customs Office to help pinpoint the delivery of a drugs shipment by the Mafia, and even though he hadn't been able to do this – no doubt for reasons of self-preservation – he was none the less nervous of any publicity of his work with the bodies of the law, for fear of reprisals.

Carl introduced Geller to Inspector Dowd, one of the detectives on the case, who expressed his interest in Geller's help: he told him frankly that they needed any leads they could get. Dowd showed Geller some photographs of the victims, both those who had died and those who had been injured. Unlike in the previous cases that Geller had been involved with, where there were no fatalities and little in the way of violence, he now found himself up against the everyday realities of police work, and later admitted that the photographs made him feel ill for some time afterwards. They did, however, also make him all the more determined to help.

Together with Carl and Inspector Dowd, Geller drove to the Veranzzo Bridge in Brooklyn, the scene of the last murder. They travelled in silence, each man hoping that Geller's presence could help trap the maniacal killer. For Dowd, it would be an opportunity to rid himself of a case where there were no rewards, only constant tension and pressure – when and where would the Son of Sam strike next? For Carl, the pressure was different: his superiors wanted a result on this one. It would please them to get one up on the NYPD, and prove once again that the Bureau was a better body for law enforcement. For Geller, the pressure was of a totally different nature: the pictures had sickened him, and the thought of a lunatic on the loose, killing people at random, was more than he could bear.

Once they arrived at the scene, Carl and Dowd left Geller alone. He wandered around the area, trying to pick up some kind of impression. He states in his book

The Geller Effect that he was 'concentrating hard – perhaps too hard'. Certainly, it was not easy for him to put together images that made much sense. There was one word that kept coming to him: Yonkers, which is upstate in New York, and is a large district of the city. Geller was sure that the man they were looking for would be found there, but was frustrated because he could not be more specific. Everything came in little snatches: split-seconds of pictures, words and feelings. Unlike before, where things were laid out in front of him, this time it was as though he were on the edge of awakening from a nightmare – at that point where you can still taste the fear, but remember none of the detail.

Then he felt able to attempt a description of the man: he was about five ten, and had slicked-back hair which was receding. (Geller, of course, knew nothing of the description the police had been given by several of the intended victims.) Geller added that the man was quite chubby, probably lived alone and had arrived by car. There was nothing else he could add at that time, and he left the scene of the murder frustrated and disappointed, feeling that he had done little to aid the investigation.

He was not to know that he had contributed the vital link between the killer and a man seen running to a car in the area that night...

A woman walking her dog had responded to police calls for witnesses by coming forward and stating that she had seen a man running to his car and driving off at about half-past one on the Sunday morning – around the time of the shooting. This had been near a hydrant on Bay 16th Street, only five minutes' walk from the Veranzzo Bridge. She had been in the area for some time and had seen two policemen place a parking ticket on the car a short while before.

This could be it, reasoned Dowd. A check run on parking tickets in the Coney Island area for that day revealed that there had been only four – and one of them was issued to a vehicle licensed in the name of David Berkowitz.

Berkowitz lived in Yonkers.

The following Wednesday morning a team of detectives led by Dowd went to the address in Pine Street where the vehicle was registered. They saw the car – a Ford Galaxie – standing in front of an apartment building. There was no sign of the driver, but when they examined the car they saw a note which had been left on top of the dash – the note was immediately identifiable as being in the same hand as the notes from the Son of Sam.

They were about to enter the building when a smiling man came up to them. He was five feet ten, with slicked-back receding hair, and was quite chubby. This was the twenty-four-year-old David Berkowitz.

Dowd stared at the man, and said: 'Hello, David.'

'Inspector Dowd! You finally got me!' replied the amiable young man before being handcuffed.

After the enormous tension, the way in which Berkowitz had simply walked up to them on the street and surrendered left a feeling of anti-climax and unease among many of the men. Could it really be this easy in the final analysis?

Back at the station, Dowd found it hard to believe that the killer they had searched for could possibly turn out to be a sweetly smiling young man who looked like a cretinous schoolboy. He showed no indication that he really understood why he was being held in the police station, and seemed ridiculously pleased to have been caught. This strange reaction is not uncommon among random serial killers, who sometimes seem driven to give themselves away. Berkowitz hadn't gone that far, but did seem happy to be in a cell.

Meanwhile, his apartment was searched, and gradually a picture of the man who had terrorised New York began to emerge. His home was mess: the floor was littered with empty cartons and bottles, and the only furnishings were a bare mattress and a naked bulb. Written on the walls in his scrawling hand were little epigrams like 'In this hole lives the wicked king', 'I turn children into killers', and 'Kill for my master.'

Berkowitz was born illegitimately, and his mother had offered him for adoption. His adopted father, Nat Berkowitz, had owned a hardware store in Yonkers but had sold up and retired to Florida a few years earlier after a spate of robberies. He left David alone in the city, and the young man whose feelings of rejection had led to him developing schizophrenia moved from apartment to apartment, living in filth and solitude. He was lonely and insecure, and in all likelihood still a virgin when arrested, yet boasted to the police of his conquests and power over women.

He claimed demonic voices had first told him to kill in 1974, and that as he lived alone they began to speak to him more and more, during the night when he was kept awake by trucks passing by and barking dogs.

Berkowitz had actually begun assaulting people on Christmas Eve 1975, when he attacked two women with a knife in separate incidents. The first woman screamed so loudly that he ran away before inflicting any wounds, and the second – a fifteen-year-old schoolgirl – received cuts and a punctured lung before Berkowitz left her.

Seven months later, he bought a gun and began in earnest.

He wrote sporadically to his father, and told him that people would spit on him as he walked down the street, and that everybody hated him: 'The girls call me ugly, and that bothers me the most.' He was also in the habit of writing letters to people he believed to be persecuting him. There were several reports about him on police files, but he was generally thought to be 'a nut', and not worthy of police time.

The Sam Berkowitz he claimed to be the son of was,

in fact, a large black dog belonging to one of his neighbours, Sam Carr. He had received several letters from Berkowitz making threats to the dog, and in April that year Berkowitz had even shot at it – although his aim was so bad that the dog was only injured.

One psychiatrist who examined Berkowitz claimed that he was trying to deceive everyone merely to set up a defence. The prosecutor tended to believe Berkowitz *was* a paranoid schizophrenic and this was taken into account at his arraignment. The judge, however, dismissed it, and pronounced that Berkowitz – who pleaded guilty – should be dealt with as a sane man. His sentences ran to 365 years – virtually a year for every day he had held the city in terror.

Since his imprisonment, Berkowitz has become a cult figure in the same way as Charles Manson. Despite the desperate landlord changing the name of the apartment building, Berkowitz's old flat is still visited by sightseers, some of whom take doorknobs and pieces of wood, carpet and brick as souvenirs. Some even stand outside calling for him, believing he will be there. Berkowitz himself seems to be unaware of this cult, and is content to serve out his time in prison, where he is now acknowledged to be ill and is receiving treatment for schizophrenia.

Uri Geller is now a multi-millionaire, having used his skills in psychometry and dowsing as a consultant to mining companies searching for oil, minerals and precious metals. He has retired almost completely from the public eye.

The Killer
Played Jazz

On 11 January 1959, Carrol Jackson and his wife
Mildred were driving not far from their home in
East Virginia. They were an attractive young couple:
Carrol, a good-looking man in his late twenties,
was a non-smoker and teetotaller, in a good job
with bright prospects. He first met his wife Mildred
at the Baptist Church they both attended. She
was a pretty young woman and the president of
the missionary society. It was not long before
they married, and soon they had two children.
Both daughters, five-year-old Susan and eighteen-
month-old Janet were with their parents in the
car.

They were the picture-book family of small-town
America, and embodied all that was good about the
American dream: a dream that was still potent in the
late fifties. This is what made their fate all the more
shocking.

The Jacksons were driving along the road that ran
through the small town of Apple Grove. It was one of
Carrol's favourite drives, as it took in some of the

most picturesque scenery in their part of East Virginia. Susan was kneeling on the back seat, looking out of the window and ignoring her mother's instructions to sit down properly. Mildred cradled toddler Janet on her lap.

Carrol laughed as his wife grew more heated and flustered in her attempts to make the child sit down. Finally, she turned to him: 'Do something!' Mildred exclaimed. 'If we had an accident something awful could happen to that child!'

'What's going to happen?' Carrol replied easily, without taking his eyes from the road. 'It's empty for as far as I can see.'

But even as he said it, he was aware of a car behind them in the distance. It must have turned out of a dirt track. In his rear view mirror he saw an old blue Chevrolet coming up hard on them and he could hear the gunning of the engine as it increased its speed.

Mildred tried to look behind her. 'What's that all about?'

Carrol shook his head. 'Some kind of maniac, honey. I'm going to let him pass.'

He pulled over slightly to allow the other car to overtake; as the Chevrolet roared by, he could see that it was a lone driver. 'Probably a drunk,' he muttered under his breath.

The car seemed to be past them: it receded into the distance. Carrol looked round to speak to his wife, but her scream made him turn back; the Chevrolet was reversing towards them at speed, weaving across the road. Carrol tried to second-guess the driver, and began zig-zagging across the highway in an attempt to make room to get by the rapidly approaching car. It seemed as though the other driver wanted to run him off the road, as he changed direction whenever Carrol did, successfully blocking the road. Susan was flung to the floor screaming as she hurt herself. Mildred clutched Janet to her, and Carrol swore softly under his breath – something he only did under great stress – as he attempted to keep control of his vehicle.

He was about to cut around the Chevrolet on the inside, when the old blue car skidded sharply, leaving no room for Carrol to manoeuvre past. The Jacksons' car slewed off the road and into the undergrowth where it came to rest with a violent jolt.

Carrol Jackson lifted his head from the wheel. Susan was crying in the back, and Janet was wailing loudly as his sobbing wife held the infant to her tightly. He looked round, and could see that the Chevrolet had stopped. There was no movement inside the vehicle.

'Hell!' he hissed, banging the wheel. 'I'm gonna ask that lunatic what in God's name he was doing!'

Janet held out her hand to stop him, but Carrol was too angry to pay any attention. He slammed the door of his car, and strode over to the Chevrolet.

'What the hell do you think you're doing, mister,' he yelled. 'You could have killed us back there. What are you, some kind of damn—'

He was cut off mid-sentence as a man climbed out of the Chevrolet. He pointed a gun at Carrol Jackson and grinned amiably.

'What were you saying?' he muttered through the grin.

Later that afternoon, Mildred's aunt was driving along the same stretch of road when she saw the Jacksons' car. Recognising it, she stopped and called out for her niece and family, but there was no response. She drove back to town and alerted the police.

The area was searched, but nothing was found. However, a couple driving by stopped to inquire what was going on. When the circumstances were explained to them, they told the police that earlier that afternoon, they had been forced off the road by a blue Chevrolet. They had stopped, but as the driver of the Chevrolet approached them something about him frightened them, and they had reversed their car at speed and made off in the opposite direction.

This was no longer just a missing persons' search – it was a possible abduction.

Carrol Jackson walked back to his car with the armed stranger only feet behind him. Mildred got out as he approached, holding the infant.

'What's going on?' she asked, staring bewildered from her husband to the man with the gun.

'We'd better do as he says,' Carrol's voice was

reduced to a husk by his fear for his family.

The stranger ushered the Jackson family from their car. He made Carrol take off his tie and forced Mildred to bind his wrists with it. She pulled whimpering Susan from the back seat when the child refused to come out. Better to be hard on the child now than let the maniac shoot her.

With the armed man behind them, Carrol Jackson opened the boot of the Chevrolet on command, and climbed in. Mildred followed, pulling Susan and Janet in with her. Everything went black as the boot was slammed on them. In the dark, the children wept and screamed, while Carrol and Mildred held hands and exchanged frightened words: where were they going? What was going to happen?

After they had been driving for only a few minutes, the car stopped. They felt the door slam, and the boot was opened, making them blink and squint in the bright light.

'You, out,' said the man with the gun. He was of medium height, with greasy black hair and tattoos along his ape-like arms. He was wearing a shirt with the sleeves rolled up, and it hung outside his pants. Carrol got out of the boot, and Mildred made to follow. The man stopped her. 'Not you,' he said, a gleam in his eye making her quail, as he plucked the infant from her and slammed the boot down.

In the darkness, she tried to hear what was going on over the screams and sobs of Susan. She held the child close to her, and prayed.

The ape-like man waddled towards Carrol, still pointing the gun at him, and dangling the infant Janet by one arm, ignoring her kicks and screams. He gestured Carrol over towards a ditch. The frightened Jackson edged towards it, all the time searching for some way in which he could fight back.

The ape-man threw Janet across the dusty ground. Carrol watched open-mouthed as the screaming child flew through the air and into the ditch, landing with a bone-jarring thud. She whimpered.

Carrol turned around to see that the ape-man was laughing. Anger rose in him. 'You son of a bitch!' he yelled, preparing to spring at the ogre. But he was too late. The sound of the gun roared in the empty air, and Carrol looked up in amazement as a red patch spread across his vision. Blood poured from a wound in his head, where the bullet had penetrated his skull. Everything went dark as he fell backwards into the ditch, on top of his semi-conscious daughter.

The police continued to search, and the media were alerted; yet there were no developments for almost two months. Then, on 4 March, two men travelling on a muddy back road near the town of Fredericksburg skidded and got stuck in deep mud. They started to collect brushwood to lay under the wheels to try to get back on the road. It was then that they uncovered the body of a man.

When the police arrived on the scene, the body was

removed, and the corpse of a child was found underneath. Both were badly decomposed. They were the bodies of Carrol Jackson and his daughter Janet. Carrol's hands had been bound in front of him with his tie, and he had been shot in the head. Little Janet had died of suffocation: at only eighteen months, she had not had the strength to crawl from beneath the dead weight of her father.

An abduction had now become a double murder ... possibly worse, as Mildred and Susan Jackson had not yet been found.

The car stopped again. Mildred heard the door slam, and clutched Susan to her. In the darkness, tired and confused, the child had fallen asleep.

The light streamed in as the boot opened.

'Get out,' said the ape-man with a grin. He no longer had the gun on him. Mildred climbed out, pulling Susan with her.

'Where's Carrol?' she said nervously. She already knew the answer. The ape-man smiled again.

'Don't you worry about him, baby. I'm all you got to worry about, right?'

He ordered Mildred to undress in front of him. She was too terrified to resist him: although he was unarmed at the moment, she knew that he had killed her husband, and that he still had a gun somewhere. She prayed death would come soon.

When she was naked, he made her pick up her clothes and follow him to a wooden shack that stood behind some bushes. He dragged Susan along by one arm, casually slapping her with the back of his hand when she tried to resist.

Inside the shack, he tied Mildred to a chair, and made her watch while he stripped the child and raped her before taking an iron rod from the corner of the room and caving in her skull. Then, while the tears rolled down Mildred's face, he untied her. Her spirit was so totally broken that she could hardly fight back. The abductor easily overcame her token resistance by tying one of her stockings around her neck, and throttling her until she complied with his sexual demands. Then he called her a filthy whore and beat her with relish before raping her repeatedly. When he was finally satiated, Mildred lay semi-conscious on the floor.

He dressed and took the gun from his pocket. He pointed it at the weeping and broken Mildred Jackson, and gave her the release she craved; he shot her through the heart. This done, he calmly waddled outside in his strange gait, and opened the boot. He loaded the bodies into the car and drove off, intent on finding a spot to bury them.

Seventeen days later, on 21 March, a group of boys out squirrel hunting came across a mound of freshly dug earth. Poking around to investigate they uncovered some blonde hair.

The police arrived on the scene and organised a full-scale dig: the bodies of Susan and Mildred

Jackson had been found. It was Susan's blonde hair that the boys had uncovered; she had been beaten to death with a blunt instrument. Mildred had been shot, and one of her stockings was tied around her neck. She had been raped; as, too, had five-year-old Susan. The detectives were horrified.

There was a cinder-block building close to the graves and a search of the vicinity revealed a broken-down shack that had relatively fresh tyre marks near it. Inside the shack a red button from Mildred Jackson's dress was found. The police were fairly certain that she and her daughter had been taken there, but probably not murdered in the shack: there was no evidence of violence, and forensic examination yielded no clues.

It seemed as though the police had hit a dead end; yet there was something about the site that made detectives recall a still unsolved murder that had occurred two years earlier.

On 26 June 1957 Margaret Harold was being driven home by her army sergeant boyfriend, who was on a weekend pass. They had pulled into a lonely spot near Annapolis, and didn't at first notice the green Chrysler that overtook them. However, the car returned and screeched to a halt. A man got out: the only description that the police had was that he was tall and thin. He claimed to be the caretaker of the property, just checking up on them. He asked for a cigarette, which the sergeant gave him.

Then the man asked if they could give him a lift, which seemed strange as he had just drawn up in his own vehicle. The sergeant was suspicious and refused. Suddenly the man drew a gun, climbed into the back seat of the car and demanded that they give him all their money and jewellery. When they refused – presumably too shocked to remember the gun – the man wound his fingers into Margaret Harold's hair, and jerked her head back. He repeated his request.

'Don't give it to him,' Margaret snapped. It was a fatal mistake; the man shot her in the head. As she slumped forward, the mysterious killer's hand still entangled in her hair, the sergeant took the opportunity to push open the door of the car and run. He ran until he reached a farmhouse over a mile away where he stopped to use the telephone.

It took the police some time to pick him up and arrive at the scene of the crime. The killer had long since gone. He had left behind a scene that sickened even the hardened detectives of the East Virginia force. Margaret Harold was still in the front seat of the car, but she was now naked. The killer had raped the corpse before taking his leave.

A search of the area revealed a cinder-block building nearby. The police managed to enter through a basement window which was broken. Inside they found the walls covered with shots of dead women in the morgue juxtaposed with pornographic photographs. There was also a photograph of such startling normality among all these that it stood out: from a college yearbook, it showed a beautiful young woman. Subsequent investigation revealed that the college in question was Maryland University, and the girl was Wanda Tipson.

The photograph was only two years old, so it was relatively easy to trace the girl. However, despite a lengthy interrogation by the police, Wanda could not recall ever knowing any man that fitted the hazy description furnished by the sergeant. The investigation into the murder of Margaret Harold ended in failure.

But now there were so many similarities with the Jacksons' murder that the chances were that the same killer was involved in both crimes. But how to find him? There were no clues.

The baffled police called in Peter Hurkos.

Pieter Van Der Hurk was a thirty-year-old Dutch house painter when his whole life was changed by a fall on 10 July 1941. He was up a ladder when he slipped and fell. He broke his shoulder and suffered concussion. Unconscious for four days, he had undergone brain surgery during this time. When he recovered consciousness, he was temporarily blinded; he remembered nothing of the actual fall, only a feeling of his life flashing before him.

When she visited him in hospital his wife used to leave their small son in the care of a neighbour. One afternoon, Pieter suddenly became agitated, and shouted at his wife to go and save the boy as their neighbour's house was on fire. She rushed home, only to find all was well. However, five days later the house was burnt down in a sudden fire.

These strange and disturbing events began to occur more frequently. Pieter warned a nurse to be careful on a train, otherwise she would lose her suitcase, to which she replied she had lost one that morning – how did he know this? He also lectured a patient in the next bed on how his father had worked hard to buy the watch he had left his son when he died, and how wicked the young man was to have sold it. Something Pieter could not have known, as the patient had only just been admitted.

Later Pieter Van Der Hurk joined the Resistance, and his psychic powers proved to be of immense value in determining whether new recruits were genuine or in fact Nazi sympathisers. When the war ended, Van Der Hurk adopted the name by which he had been known in the Resistance – Peter Hurkos.

Hurkos was in the audience at a mind reading show one day when he suddenly stood up and claimed to be a better mind reader than the man on stage. He stated that the man had a letter in his pocket from a woman named Greta, who followed him from town to town, and picked her out in the audience. The mind reader was obviously embarrassed – as well he might have been, for his wife was on stage too, acting as his assistant. Hurkos decided to use his talents to make a living on the stage. He was often asked to help find missing people and criminals and achieved several successes.

In 1948 the Dutch clairvoyant visited the USA for the first time, at the request of Andrija Puharich, a scientist who was planning a two-year study of psychic phenomena and who, after hearing of Hurkos' successes with the police and on the stage decided that Hurkos was perfect for his experiments.

After the two years elapsed, Hurkos decided to remain in the States. He had become self-confident to the point of arrogance about his powers and the press began to look on all his statements as gospel truth.

Hurkos travelled from Florida to East Virginia eager to help in the baffling murder case. By now the police had tentatively fingered some suspects, though there was no evidence to link any of them directly to the killings. They were simply men who had committed sexual offences previously, and had no alibi for the day of the Jackson slaying. One of these men was a garbage collector.

In Falls Church in Virginia – the Baptist church that the Jacksons had attended – Hurkos was given some of their belongings to use for psychometry. Hurkos sat in a church pew holding the Jacksons' belongings, shaking and muttering to himself, with his eyes glazed. It took some time before he was able to relate anything he saw, as the images were jumbled, and much that came to him had little relevance to the killings. The police were growing impatient, but Hurkos refused to be rushed.

He couldn't see the world around him. Instead, there was a jerky series of images: the road, and the Chevrolet. Darkness inside the trunk. The man with the gun. The surrounding countryside. What had happened to Mildred and Susan. The tears streamed down his cheeks as he felt their utter hopelessness in the face of death, and he was determined to do something to help them.

For some time after the visions ended, he was unable to speak – he always found such experiences draining. Eventually, he announced his findings to the police: the man who had committed the murders was tall, with a tattoo on one arm. His arms were long and ape-like, and the man had a beetling brow. He was of quick temper, yet normally appeared placid. And he had a most unusual walk – he waddled like a duck!

Hurkos also claimed that he could lead the police to the scene of the crime, which he believed was also where the murderer lived.

He was bundled into a police car with a map, and told the driver to set off in the direction of the woods. The police were immediately impressed, because that was where the cinder-block bunker was – something Hurkos had not been told about.

Hurkos directed the police from the main road on the edge of the woods, up a muddy trail to a derelict wooden shack. He got out of the car, began to hunt around in the bushes and emerged clutching a torn skirt which had got caught on a bush. The detectives felt great excitement; they were on to something!

Hurkos, however, was quick to disillusion them: he insisted that the skirt had been there some time and belonged to another woman who had been killed in this area. (Subsequently, Hurkos was proved correct: it was Margaret Harold's skirt.)

Hurkos was worried that he was getting impressions from a different crime, but the police asked him to proceed regardless: they believed he was on the right track.

Hurkos and the detectives entered the run-down shack. The faint stains they saw on the walls and floor were later identified as Mildred and Susan Jackson's blood. Hurkos repeated his description of the man he had seen in the church, adding that he had left only recently. But now he added he could see another man on the premises – and the new description fitted perfectly that of the garbage collector who was among the police's list of suspects.

Hurkos then led the police into the woods, along a trail to the cinder-block bunker near where the bodies of Mildred and Susan Jackson had been found. He told the police the killer had been in this vicinity.

The area was subjected to a painstaking search, and an identity bracelet belonging to the garbage collector was uncovered. The officers were sure they had their man.

As Hurkos was driven back to town, he claimed the man had committed nine murders. This shocked the police, but offered them a chance to clear up a backlog of unsolved sex crimes.

Hurkos left town to the trumpeting of the press: 'Psychic Solves Murder', read the headlines. And so he had ... But the police had arrested the wrong man!

A check of renters of the shack revealed that the garbage man had recently left, and there was a new tenant, a man named Melvin Rees. The police arrested the garbage man anyway. He was taken in for questioning, and under intensive interrogation confessed to the murders. All seemed to be over: the evidence was mainly circumstantial, but there was enough to arraign the man.

Peter Hurkos, although loving every second of the publicity, was far from happy with this arrest. The garbage collector didn't fit his initial description in the church, and was the second man he had seen at the shack. Hurkos was convinced that the garbage man was not the killer, but the police refused to listen. They had their man: he was a suspect, and Hurkos had mentioned him. There was also the matter of the identity bracelet found near the burial site.

Hurkos was not the only man with doubts. Two months later the police received an anonymous letter which accused a wandering jazz musician of the murders of both the Jackson family and Margaret Harold. The anonymous writer claimed that he was a salesman who had been travelling with the musician when they passed a town not far from the murders, and that he had asked the musician if he remembered the murders. The musician, high on Benzedrine, had given a rambling answer full of strange details that had made the writer suspicious. There seemed to be things that only the killer would know, details that had not been released to the press.

Later, when the writer had asked the musician about the murders again, the now coherent jazz man had not denied the crimes outright, but had evaded the issue. The name of the musician was Melvin Rees.

This name caused some concern within the police department. Rees had rented the shack after the garbage collector – could it be that they had pulled in the wrong man? A search for Rees began; but Rees was an itinerant musician, drifting from town to town, wherever he could get gigs. They failed to trace him.

It was early in 1960 before the breakthrough finally came: the police received another letter from the anonymous writer. This time he gave his name as Glenn L. Moser, and claimed that he had recently received a letter from Rees, who was keen to get in touch with him again and was now working as a piano and sheet-music salesman in a music shop in West Memphis, Arkansas.

Arrangements were made with the local force, and Rees was tracked down and brought in for questioning by an FBI agent. The sergeant boyfriend of

Margaret Harold was taken to West Memphis to see if he could identify Rees as his assailant. A line-up was organised and the sergeant immediately picked Rees out. The man was remanded in custody pending further investigation.

Armed with a search warrant, detectives travelled to Rees' parents' house in Hyattsville. There was nothing to be found until they searched the attic; there they discovered an old saxophone case – not perhaps an unusual thing in a musician's attic. However, there was nothing in the case that had anything to do with music. Instead, in it the police found a .38 revolver and several diaries and notebooks describing sadistic and sexual activities. There was a description of the Jackson abduction: '...caught on a lonely road ... drove to a selected and secluded area and killed the husband and baby. Now the mother and daughter were all mine...'

The diary went on to describe how he had forced Mildred Jackson to perform fellatio on him by using the stocking to throttle her until she obeyed. He relished the feeling of superiority: 'Now I was her master,' he wrote.

The diaries and notes also revealed links between Rees and four unsolved teenage sex murders. Marie Shomette and Ann Ryan were two teenage schoolgirls who had been shot and raped while walking through College Park near the University of Maryland. The bodies of Mary Fellers and Shelby Venable had been found in rivers around Maryland. Both had been shot and raped.

Rees was a man unashamed of his crimes; in fact, he was proud of his activities, and openly boasted about his power over the women he raped and killed. The taking of life was the ultimate show of power and rape after death gave him the greatest thrill.

Melvin Rees was tried for the murder of the Jackson family and convicted. Strangely enough, many people who had known him found it hard to accept the verdict: to them, he was an intelligent and mild-mannered musician who had been proficient on piano, guitar, saxophone and clarinet. He was an all-round good guy.

Wanda Tipson had known him quite well. When the police approached her after finding her year-book photograph pinned up in the cinder-block house after the murder of Margaret Harold, she had considered Rees among the men the sergeant's description brought to mind, but she had discounted him as being 'too nice' to even consider such a crime. She had had an affair with Rees; however, he was married at the time and unwilling to divorce, so she had terminated the relationship.

If the police had checked back on renters of the cinder-block bunker they would have found that the last tenant prior to the murder of Margaret Harold had been Melvin Rees, just as he had been the last tenant of the wooden shack.

Melvin Rees was executed in late 1961. The final tally of deaths attributed to him was nine: the figure Peter Hurkos had given.

A Fatal Affair

South Africa in the 1950s was a puritanical and
repressive society, particularly in matters of sex.
Pregnancy before marriage was considered the worst
kind of sin, and pregnancy by an already married
man would have ruined the prospects of any young
girl. It was in such an atmosphere that Myrna Joy
Aken was the victim of a vicious sex murder, and a
retired South African headmaster used his skills in
psychometry to try to find her killer and supply a
motive for the crime.

Myrna Joy Aken was eighteen, and worked as a
typist in Durban city centre. On the evening of 2
October 1956, she left work – never to be seen alive
again.

A colleague saw her leave at the usual time, and
get into a light-coloured car that was waiting for her.
She had been quiet and morose all afternoon,
something that was unusual for her, as Myrna was a
pretty and vivacious girl, usually quite chatty and
friendly. She had confided in her colleague that she

had been seeing a man, and that things hadn't been going too well. Her colleague remembered seeing the car meeting her before; it was Ford Anglia, a make not that common in Durban, so it had stuck in her mind. She assumed that it belonged to the man Myrna had spoken about, though the girl had given no indication of her boyfriend's identity.

The couple sat in the car in silence. Occasionally, Myrna Joy would turn her head slightly to look at the man driving. He was about fifteen years older than her, and fairly good-looking in a rugged kind of way. His jaw jutted in concentration as he negotiated the traffic.

'I don't see the point of this,' she snapped, her mouth sulkily pouting. 'We were supposed to be going out, but now I've got nothing to say to you.'

'You've got plenty,' he said easily. 'You know we can't talk at your place. Your mother and father don't even know I exist,' his tone hardened.

'Your wife doesn't know I exist, so that makes it even,' she retorted sharply.

They proceeded in silence until he turned the vehicle into the car park of a hotel. She looked at him questioningly.

'Just a quick drink,' he said, getting out of the car. 'Give us a chance to talk about it properly.'

Myrna Joy snorted as she got out, a sneer distorting her pretty features. They walked up the steps of the hotel and into the bar, where he ordered a beer for himself and gin and tonic for Myrna. They took their drinks to a table and sat down.

They talked. In the harsh, bitter whisper of the suppressed argument she told him again that she was pregnant. He asked her if she was sure. She shook her head: not yet, but it was pretty certain. He brooded on this: what did she expect him to do about it?

She reached across the table and grabbed his hand. She wanted him to get a divorce, marry her. All right, her parents would be against it, and society would frown on them. What did they care about that? They had each other.

He looked away. Suddenly, and with a frightening clarity, Myrna could see it all; she had been just a toy, a diversion. He didn't feel anything for her, and never would. She stood up. 'I'd like to go home, please,' she said, trying to hold back her tears.

Her companion stood up and shuffled out to his car, not daring to look at her. He was sure she would talk now, there was little doubt of that. His marriage would collapse, and he would lose his job. The company he worked for was small, and relied for its income on the neighbourhood where Myrna Joy lived. With full knowledge of what had happened, his boss would certainly lose trade if he didn't sack him.

In the vehicle, they left the car park. But they didn't turn back towards town. To Myrna's bewilderment, they took a road leading out of Durban and into the bush. She turned to her companion, but before she

197

could ask him what was going on, she noticed the gun in his left hand.

'You're not going to ruin my life, you scheming little tart,' he hissed.

Myrna did not return home that evening. Her parents became rapidly worried, as she was a strictly brought-up girl, and always told them if she was going to be late. They knew that Myrna was going to a dance that evening; her dress was laid out on the bed. She had been so excited at the prospect that nothing on earth could have made her miss it. Before evening had turned to night, Myrna's parents had called the police to report her missing.

Sergeant N. J. Grobler looked into the matter. His first call the next day was at the office, where he questioned Myrna's workmates. He discovered that she had been depressed by something on the day of her disappearance – possibly the mysterious boy-friend. Here was a lead worth checking, especially as she had been so excited about the dance before leaving home in the morning. Had she received any phone calls or seen anybody that day who could have changed this? He made a note of the light-coloured Anglia that had been waiting for her at six, and also learnt from another of Myrna's colleagues that she had been visited twice before at work by a man who was several years older than her. He was tall and good-looking, and seemed to know her very well. The second time he visited, Myrna had been upset after his departure. The colleague who had seen them together had tried to get Myrna to talk about it – partly, she confessed, because she wanted to know who he was: she had found him rather attractive – but the girl had been unwilling to disclose anything.

So now Grobler had something else besides the Anglia: a man in his thirties (probably), who was good-looking, and who had visited her twice at the office. Were the Anglia and this man connected? If so, what had upset Myrna, and why had she accepted a lift from him?

Grobler returned to Myrna's parents and asked them if they knew anything about the mysterious older man. They were completely in the dark, and had assumed Myrna had been dating the young man she had planned to go to the dance with.

When Grobler followed this up, he found there was no young man: Myrna had been lying to her parents. Could it be that she was to meet this older man? If so, why was she keeping it a secret? It was certainly frowned upon for a well brought-up young girl to date an older man. Was that why she was keeping quiet about him? Or did he have something to hide? For instance, he might be married. Was this the reason for Myrna Joy Aken's deceit? And was it connected to her disappearance?

The car rolled to a halt on a flat stretch of veldt. The man gestured to Myrna with his gun. She got out in shocked silence. Noticing he was having trouble opening his door, she looked around wildly and ran towards the road trying to escape. A shot rang out, and dust kicked up around her feet.

'Don't try and run – you can't get far out here.'

Myrna's heart pounded, and her mouth went dry as she heard the man approaching. Had she really believed that she loved him? Had she really tried to trap him into divorcing his wife by claiming she was pregnant? She turned as he came upon her. 'Look, I'm not really pregnant. I only said it to try and get you to divorce... Take me home, Clarence, I'm scared! I won't make trouble, I'll never see you again if that's what you want. I –'

She was silenced by his hand whip-cracking across her face. 'Shut up, you filthy little tart,' he sneered. 'I'm going to make sure that you say nothing.'

He seized her by the arm; she was sobbing, imploring him to let her go. She stumbled and fell; he didn't allow her to get up, just kept dragging her across the dusty ground. They came to a steep incline leading down to a small culvert covered by scrub and bush. He pushed her down, and she tumbled head over heels, screaming with pain as the rocks bit into her flesh, grazing and cutting her. She landed in a heap at the bottom, and the man she called Clarence picked his way down the incline, gun still slightly raised in case she should try to get away.

'Take your clothes off, woman,' he yelled at her. With the gun trained on her, Myrna did as she was told.

'What are you going to do with me?' she asked nervously.

'Not what you think, you cheap whore,' he sneered. 'But I want anyone who finds you to think exactly what you're thinking.'

When Myrna Joy stood naked in front of him, he gestured her to put her clothes to one side. When she stood up straight again, he smiled grimly and shot her in the head. Though it was only a small calibre gun, the bullet hit the bridge of her nose, and the bone splintered into her brain killing her instantly. Myrna Joy Aken's lifeless body slumped to the floor of the culvert, the sluggish stream turning a brownish red.

The man she called Clarence put his gun away and calmly walked over to the body. If she was pregnant, he planned to eradicate all traces. He looked around for a sharp rock; finding one with a jagged edge, he hacked at her lifeless body, ripping into the lower abdomen and gouging out great gouts of her intestines. He didn't stop until he had ripped out everything clear to her backbone.

A week went by, and Grobler had turned up nothing of interest. He had set up a check of every light-coloured Ford Anglia in Durban and the surrounding territory, but until this had been done, there were no paths for the policeman to follow. There were no computers then and a relatively large number of drivers to trace and question. All this would take time.

The Aken family were not disposed to wait. The worry was making Myrna's parents ill, and her brother Colin was desperately thinking of ways in which he could assist the search for Myrna when he remembered his old schoolfriend Jack Palmer. Jack's father Nelson had become a minor celebrity in the last three years for the assistance he had been able to give the police in tracing missing people. Perhaps he would be able to help in the search for Myrna?

Colin Aken contacted Jack Palmer and asked for his father's help. He learnt that Nelson Palmer's methods involved holding an object belonging to the missing person, which would then bring on visions which he would describe to the police. Apparently this approach had already yielded impressive results, but Colin felt uneasy. In religious South Africa, such things were looked on by the church as impossible, and to believe in them would be akin to believing in magic and fairies at the bottom of the veldt. It would seem a stupid thing to suggest to his parents when they were under such great strain worrying about Myrna.

However, you had to balance this against the fact that Nelson Palmer was a retired headmaster with a long record of success in his career in education. He was a respectable man with a solid reputation – moreover, the police had turned to him several times for help in finding missing persons.

Jack could tell that Colin was unsure, so he put his

202

father on the line. Nelson Palmer explained to Colin that he didn't know how he was able to see these things when he held objects, but he believed that it worked in the same way that a radio aerial does: he was the receiver, able to see signals beamed from the object or the person it belonged to. He disdained any notion of the supernatural, and told Colin that he felt anyone could do it given time – he himself had been unaware of his talent until a few years before! He also added that he would be glad to help the Akens if Colin felt he could be of some use.

On the eighth day following her disappearance, Myrna's mother Maud called to see Nelson Palmer, accompanied by Colin. With her she carried some of Myrna's underwear. Palmer preferred underwear to outer clothing because it was closer to the body, and therefore more likely to yield results.

Palmer welcomed them to his home and led them into his study. He drew the curtains and laid the clothing out on a table: there were some panties, a bra, and two slips. Palmer sat down at the table, and rested his hands lightly on the pile of clothing. He began to take deep, regular breaths. Apart from the fact that it was now slightly dark in the room, there was nothing to suggest that anything unusual was taking place, and Maud Aken wondered momentarily if she had done the right thing.

There was silence for a few minutes as Palmer concentrated his thoughts and tried to focus on images that were beginning to come to him. The images came not in a succession of brilliant flashes, but rather as a series of snapshots. He could see events with a startling clarity, yet could feel nothing. He closed his eyes to concentrate fully. Eventually he began to speak. He told Maud that he had bad news for her.

'I'm afraid your daughter is dead,' he said. It distressed him to see the tears spring to Maud's eyes. Colin had to look away, in order to hide his pain; he didn't want Jack or his father to see him cry.

Palmer turned back to the pile of clothing and tried to relax himself. He wanted to see as much as possible, render as much help as he could. Gradually, it began to come to him. He could see her body, hidden in a culvert in countryside some miles from the edge of the city. He could see the area quite clearly, and he began to describe it in great detail. It was scrub country, with small rivers criss-crossing it. There was very little here to attract visitors from the city, which was presumably why the killer had chosen it; it might be ages before the body was discovered.

Palmer opened his eyes. His breathing had grown a little heavier. He rose from the table and pulled the curtains, admitting the light. Both Maud and Colin Aken were still upset; they believed Palmer and were sure Myrna was dead. He tried to comfort them as best he could, and then added that he believed he would be able to lead police to the body.

From Palmer's house, they contacted Sergeant Grobler, whose investigation was still at an impasse, and a search party was quickly arranged which included Palmer and Colin Aken.

Led by Palmer, they travelled south out of Durban until they approached the village of Umtwalumi, some sixty miles away. Here there was a valley between two hills. Palmer brought the party to a halt, and got out his jeep. Followed at a distance by the others, Palmer left the road and began climbing down the course of the sluggish stream. Colin Aken stood at the top of the incline, nervously tapping a hand against his leg.

Picking his way carefully down the rock-strewn incline Palmer finally reached the culvert at the bottom, watched intently by Aken and Grobler. They began to follow, but Palmer peered into the culvert and told them both to stop and let the police come down first. There was something in the culvert...

Palmer had found the mutilated corpse of Myrna Joy Aken. She had been shot in the head, and her lower torso was severely battered. The body had been stuffed into the culvert head first, and was invisible from the road. She was naked, and there was no sign of her clothes.

At first it seemed obvious that this was a sex crime, and the police would have to look for a perverted maniac. However, forensic tests revealed that she had not been raped and that her severe injuries had been inflicted after death. Doubts began to creep in: was this a sex crime performed by a madman whose kicks came from mutilation? Or was it that the sex angle was a blind for the murder – was there some other motive to uncover?

Meanwhile, the check on Ford Anglias had yielded a clue. One of the light-coloured cars had been registered to the owner of a radio shop. When police interviewed him, he claimed that on the day in question the car had not been in his possession. He had loaned it to one of his engineers a few days before, and it had not been returned until the day after Myrna Joy Aken had gone missing.

The name of the engineer was Clarence Van Buuren, and the radio-shop owner stated that he hadn't reported for work for some days. When the police were given Van Buuren's address, things began to fall into place. He lived a few hundred yards from the Akens, and a glance at the work records revealed that he had twice visited the house to repair the radio. If he had met Myrna Joy on those occasions, then surely it would have seemed natural to her to accept a lift home from him. He might even be the man who had visited her at the office – the older boyfriend of whom she refused to speak.

Over a hundred officers took part in the search for Van Buuren, who hadn't been seen since 3 October. He couldn't return home, as everyone in the Pinetown district of Durban, where both Van Buuren and the Akens lived, knew that he was wanted for questioning, and the police were keeping his home under surveillance.

Eight days after his disappearance – 11 October – a gardener working nearby spotted a man creeping on all fours in the shrubbery around the house, and immediately alerted the police. Within minutes officers were on the scene and cornered the lurking man. When he was challenged, he tried to run away. The police drew their guns and fired warning shots. Realising the game was up, the man turned to surrender; but not before throwing something into a nearby bush.

He was in full view of the police officers, and although it was early evening, it was still light enough to see clearly, so his act of desperation was in vain. A search of the bushes produced a gun, a .22 – the gun that had killed Myrna Joy Aken was also a .22.

The police approached the mystery man – it was Clarence Van Buuren. He was taken into custody.

Van Buuren had been married three times. His first two wives had divorced him when they found out he had a police record – mostly for petty burglary – and he had drifted from town to town before settling in Durban. He and his third wife seemed to be quite happy; certainly, she had been co-operating fully with the police, convinced that they had the wrong man and that Clarence was on the run purely through fear. She was shocked to hear of his record, but was ready to stand by him.

When he was questioned by the police Van Buuren unveiled a story that was so absurd as almost to have the ring of truth. He admitted he knew Myrna Joy from the times he had repaired the family radio, and was keen to get to know her better. He had been passing by her work when he saw her come out, and had offered her a lift home. In the car, he had invited her for a drink, and she had agreed.

This was the first bone of contention: Myrna had been excited at the prospect of going to a dance that evening. Would she really drop this for a drink with someone who claimed to be merely acquainted with her? The police did not know that the dance date was with Van Buuren, and that he had merely picked her up too early. Van Buuren, aware of this, was playing on it in his tale of innocence.

In the car they had talked of their domestic problems. Van Buuren spun the age-old line about his wife not understanding him any more, and how they no longer got on as they once had (news to his wife, who had been telling police exactly the opposite!). Myrna had talked of her recent arguments with her father. They were no more than the usual clash of the adolescent with parents, but they had been getting her down. These thoughts depressed her and she changed her mind and wanted to go straight home. Van Buuren was not too pleased and pulled up outside a hotel, telling her he was going for a drink anyway. He got out, leaving her in the car.

He spent over an hour in the bar, drinking steadily. When he came out, the vehicle was gone, and he assumed. that Myrna had been annoyed by his attitude and had driven herself home. The police were unconvinced: did he expect them to believe that he would leave the keys in the car while he went off to drink, especially after annoying her?

According to Van Buuren, instead of getting mad at being stranded at the hotel he had merely shrugged his shoulders and returned to the bar, spending some more time getting drunk. He wasn't sure how long, but it was dark when he left.

Walking through the car park, he was surprised to find the vehicle parked at the back of the lot. It was unlocked, and as he went to get in he was shocked to find Myrna Joy Aken in the back seat; she was dead. He realised that he was the obvious suspect, and that he had no real alibi. He believed that someone had taken her off in the car and committed the crime while he was drinking, but of course he couldn't back this up.

He claimed that he did what any drunk would have done: he panicked. He decided the best thing to do would be to dump the body and keep quiet about the whole affair – perhaps go away for a short while.

Grimly he drove out of the city to the village of Umtwalumi, where he knew there was a culvert and here he buried the body. He then drove straight back to town.

The police were completely baffled by this statement: if it was pure fiction, wouldn't he have invented details to cover the mutilations and Myrna's nudity? And wouldn't he have tried to establish some kind of alibi? Surely a murderer would have produced a more plausible story? Was it possible that he really was just a lecherous drunk who found a body and panicked?

But Van Buuren had a pistol the same calibre as the one that shot Myrna; it was sent away for tests. And the results sealed Van Buuren's fate: it was the same weapon as that used on Myrna Joy Aken. Van Buuren was the killer.

Van Buuren continued to be adamant in his denials of being anything more than simply acquainted with the girl. Myrna had been so successful in hiding her shameful affair that her parents were positive that she didn't know him. And the police still had not been able to come up with a motive for the murder. But the .22 revolver and the implausibility of Van Buuren's story were enough and the trial took place in early 1957.

The murder of an innocent young girl by the older, married man with whom she was having an affair was a crime that morally outraged the country, but in the absence of a motive there were still those who thought Van Buuren might be innocent.

If Nelson Palmer had been called to testify at the trial, he could have given the court Van Buuren's motive. During his psychometric reading of Myrna's clothing, Palmer had been able to see that Van Buuren and Myrna had been lovers for some time, and that Myrna believed that Van Buuren would leave his wife and marry her. Palmer also saw that at

210

the time of her disappearance, Myrna believed that she was pregnant, though this was in fact not so. When she told him of her pregnancy, Van Buuren's response was not as she would have desired. The phantom pregnancy would also have made clear to the police that the mutilation that had led them to believe it was a sex crime was, in fact, an attempt by Van Buuren to destroy any evidence of Myrna's pregnancy, and the motive that could be traced to him.

Palmer, however, did not testify; his evidence would have been inadmissible, based as it was on a method of detection that many people in South Africa at that time would have found impossible to accept.

The jury was quick to find Clarence Gordon Van Buuren guilty of murder. He was hanged in Durban prison, still maintaining his innocence up to the end.

Because of the sexual and moral content of the case, it caused a sensation in South Africa and drew the glare of the spotlight on Nelson Palmer. As a result, he was inundated with mail and callers. These ranged from the cranks who called him evil for having such power, to those who were genuinely interested and believed they also shared his gifts.

Then there were the requests for help. Most of them were from people who wanted to find missing pets or things from the home that had been lost. Some people even enclosed objects for him to psychometrise.

Palmer rejected all of these: the only request he

responded to was that of a woman whose husband, a doctor, had gone missing. He was soon able to locate the man, who had committed suicide in a lonely spot. This depressed Palmer even more, and he tried to shut himself away from the requests and questions. He was basically a shy man, and was unhappy with his talent because it brought with it a burden of grief that he found hard to bear.

In finding Myrna Joy Aken, and helping to uncover the reasons behind her death, Palmer had encountered again the feelings that made him despise the dark side of his gift. It was enough: Nelson Palmer never aided the police in another case.

Death of a Hitch-hiker

Pat McAdam sat in the cab of the lorry listening to the driver go on about his job, and how boring it could be, although, he said with a smile, it did have its benefits. He was looking at her in that way again. She had to admit he wasn't bad-looking: young, with plenty of muscles. She could quite fancy him. But she was so tired. She wished she could be like her friend Hazel, and just fall asleep in the cab.

While Hazel snored gently in the corner, and the driver droned on and on, Pat remembered the night before. After spending the day shopping, she and Hazel had gone for a few drinks at the Flamingo in the early evening. There they had heard about the party, and Pat hadn't needed much persuading to go: where they lived there was little to do on a Saturday night – or any night, come to that – and she was in no hurry to get home.

The party had been fine: there was that blond boy who followed Hazel everywhere, and Pat herself had met this guy called Steve who wanted her to – but she didn't. There was no way she was going to get pregnant at seventeen, and caught in a life of drudgery. She wanted more than that.

The driver turned off the main road.

'Where are you going?' asked Pat, suddenly realising that he was travelling away from the route he had been telling her about for the last three miles.

'I'm taking you and sleeping beauty home, aren't I?' he smiled, nodding towards the dozing Hazel.

Pat felt guilty for not listening to him more closely, and started asking him about his job, and the places he'd travelled to. He told her that the plus side of lorry driving was the way in which he got to see so many different places, meet new people and do interesting things. As he said it, he winked suggestively at her. Pat felt herself blush, and was angry about it: he was good-looking, but it was the same as with Steve – no way would she get into trouble and be shackled.

The lorry pulled into Annan town square. A distant church clock chimed two in the afternoon. Pat shook Hazel's shoulder.

'Hey, wake up sleepy!'

Hazel grunted into consciousness and asked where they were. She was pleasantly surprised to find she was in Annan. As she climbed down from the cab, she said to Pat: 'Will you be okay?'

Pat nodded: 'Sure. I'll ring you tomorrow, all right?'

Hazel nodded and walked away across the square. The lorry started up and they drove out of town. 'Just you and me, eh doll?' said the driver, winking.

* * *

Pat McAdam went missing on 19 February 1967. She was seventeen years old. There is nothing remarkable about this in itself: 3,000 people, on average, go missing each year in Great Britain. About 95 per cent turn up sooner or later, either dead or alive.

Pat McAdam was one of the 5 per cent who do not...

She came from Dumfries, and had been in Glasgow on the eighteenth with a friend, Hazel Campbell, who came from Annan. They were on a shopping trip, and in order to save money had hitched from Gretna to Glasgow after catching a bus to take them part of the way. Both the girls had bought black patent leather handbags, and Hazel had bought some clothes, but they hadn't spent all their money, so they met some friends in town, and went drinking at the Flamingo, a small dance hall. Then they went on to a party and spent the night there.

Early the next morning, the girls had washed at the Central Station washrooms in Glasgow, before catching the bus for London Road. From there, they planned to hitch home. In fact, it wasn't long before a lorry offered them a lift.

Pat's last meal was hamburger, egg and beans, at the Star service station at Lesmahagow, about twenty miles from Glasgow on the A74, when the driver of the lorry stopped for a break at half-past eleven. He and Pat drank whisky in the service cafe, while Hazel tried to sleep in the cab.

215

As they set off again the girls realised the driver was going out of his way to drop them home; when Hazel jumped out of the cab at Annan the town clock showed 2 p.m.

To this day, no one has seen anything of Pat McAdam, alive or dead.

She was reported missing by her parents, Mary and Matthew McAdam, on Tuesday 21 February. Her description, issued by the police, read: 'Patricia Mary McAdam, born 25/6/49, medium build, fresh complexion, brown eyes, dark hair cut in a "Mia Farrow" style'. It added that she had last been seen wearing a purple coat over a black and silver low-cut, sleeveless woollen dress, black suede shoes, yellow cardigan, and a green and red head-scarf.

Pat was starting to like the lorry driver; he was cheeky, but nice with it. He didn't come on to her too strong, not like Steve had the night before – maybe he'd realised that she wasn't that easy. She asked him if he was married. He snorted: in his job? He was away from home too often. He had been married, but it hadn't lasted long. Besides, there were too many good women around to tie yourself down to one. He looked at Pat as he said it. She wasn't so sure that she liked that look at all. She started to feel uneasy again.

The lorry driver turned off the main road. They weren't headed towards Dumfries.

'I thought you were taking me home,' she said angrily.

'There's no need to get upset about it! I just thought that maybe a little detour wouldn't go amiss, right?'

They went over a bridge and turned off on to a side road. Just before they turned off, she could remember seeing a run-down cottage, but now there was nothing but forest for miles around: trees and barren scrub leading down to the river.

They were in the middle of nowhere. He turned off the engine. 'Howsabout we get to know each other a bit better, right?'

At first, the police viewed this as just another teenage runaway. Yet there were aspects that didn't add up: Pat had left home without her national insurance card and, though she would be unable to get a job without it, had failed to apply for a replacement. She had left her entire wardrobe and £47 in cash at home: not the behaviour of a girl who loved clothes and was keen on a good time.

So a police enquiry was set up. Mrs McAdam told the police that Pat's friend Hazel had assumed the lorry driver who had given them a lift would drop Pat home before continuing to Hull, which was his eventual destination. The search was on for the lorry driver: who was he, and where was he now?

A nationwide hunt turned him up after three weeks; but he told the police that he had dropped Pat off in Dumfries, and continued on his way.

Establishing the movements of the lorry after it had left Annan was not difficult as the 26-tonne articulated vehicle had been easily noticeable in the narrow roads and lanes it had to take in order to rejoin its regular route, and several witnesses turned up who had seen it take the A75 to Dumfries, then the narrow B7020, heading towards the village of Dalton. It had been spotted near Williamwath Bridge, just to the north of the village, and was probably headed towards the A74, via the Birkshaw Forest.

A police appeal was put out, asking for drivers who could remember seeing such a lorry in the Dalton area in unusual circumstances – stationary in a lay-by or a side road – to come forward. There was no response.

On the same day that the appeal was broadcast – 17 March – the police, using tracker dogs, combed the undergrowth in the area surrounding Dalton. No clues were found.

The Regional Crime Squad, based in Glasgow, joined the hunt on 20 March, and the Glasgow *Daily Record* distributed posters and leaflets throughout the country. In the newspaper Pat's father expressed his fears that something had happened to his daughter and that the police were inclined to agree with him. The lorry driver was interviewed again. Digging continued in the woodlands and around the riverbanks of the search area. In April, Mrs McAdam

218

made a television appeal. There was an enormous response to the *Daily Record* campaign. None of this produced any leads.

'No!' Pat pushed the man away from her. She slapped his face so hard her palm tingled. He sat back behind the wheel, momentarily stunned by the force of her blow. He hadn't expected her not to accede to his demands. Most of the girls he picked up in his cab were only too keen. And those that weren't...

The shock turned to cold rage and he spun around to grab at her. His hands snatched at her dress as she thrust open the door of the cab and slithered down the side of the wheel arch on to the cold turf.

'Come here, you bitch,' he snarled, lunging across the seat and trying to grab her before she had a chance to run away.

He grasped at thin air: Pat had already regained her feet, and was running desperately for the cover of the woods. She felt sick and scared; the whole thing seemed to be like one giant nightmare, and she would awake any minute to find herself back in Glasgow, with Hazel.

But there was to be no awakening from this nightmare. She looked over her shoulder and saw that the driver was out of his cab, and was following her. He was carrying something in his right hand. Through her tears, Pat was unable to make out what it was.

* * *

Detective Inspector Cullinan, in charge of the investigation, was convinced that any clue to Pat's whereabouts – alive or dead – lay in the Dalton area, and he appealed to the locals to think back and try to recall any unusual happenings on the day in question. However, nothing came to light, and as time went on the case slipped from the public eye. The police investigation was scaled down.

Not everyone was ready to forget, though; Frank Ryan, a journalist on the *Daily Record*, finding himself in Holland in 1970, decided to look up Gerald Croiset, the Dutch psychic who had worked with the police in Holland and America on a variety of cases, though he had been involved in the Hosein case in Britain in 1969.

It was almost three years to the day after the disappearance of Pat McAdam that Frank Ryan first approached Gerald Croiset. At that time, the psychic had a small consulting room and office at his home at 21 Willem Zwigerstraat, Utrecht, where he had moved in order to be near Professor W. H. C. Tenhaeff. It was he who had convinced Croiset that his powers could be used in criminal cases and had called on the psychic's help in court cases in which he had been involved.

Ryan was shown into a room where a tall, dapper man with white hair brushed back from his temples was standing by a window. He looked round as Ryan entered and shook hands with him. There was also an interpreter present, as Croiset could not speak English.

Ryan explained why he had come to see Croiset, and showed him one of the police posters that bore a picture of Pat McAdam. He started to tell Croiset about the background to the story when Croiset rather theatrically raised his hand for silence. He then told Ryan: 'I want to know only two things: was the girl happy at home? And where was she seen last?'

This melodramatic way of behaving was typical of Croiset. He was a complex character: half-Jewish and a member of the Dutch Resistance, he had spent the war in and out of internment camps. He had lived with the presentiments of war, and the foreknowledge of the deaths of people he came into contact with. Yet sometimes his flamboyant behaviour made him resemble a caricature medium, the sort that can be seen in countless Hollywood chillers. Jack Harrison Pollack, an author who made a study of Tenhaeff's experiments with Croiset, remarked that the psychic was theatrical in behaviour, and tended to be childlike and insecure; he suffered from stomach disorders, was talkative and tense, and derived much satisfaction from the attention his talents brought him.

Ryan produced a map of south-west Scotland he had brought with him to show Croiset the area that Pat McAdam was believed to have disappeared. After a while Croiset said that he could see a transport cafe.

He knew it was of significance, but was not sure how. Ryan told him of Pat McAdam's last meal. He then indicated on the map the spot where Hazel Campbell had said goodbye to Pat.

Croiset concentrated, and was quiet for some time. Finally he told Ryan that he could see an area with exposed tree roots. They were near the bank of a river, and there were fir trees nearby. He described in great detail how the bank of the river had been eroded and undermined by the flow of water. And there was a bridge nearby. It had grey tubular railings and ran flat across the river. Croiset described how, if he crossed the bridge from where he stood in his mind's eye, he would come to a small cottage, once someone's home, but now used as business premises, as there were advertising hoardings around it, and posters on the actual building. The building and grounds (presumably a garden) were surrounded by a white paling fence.

Taking several large sheets of paper, Croiset rapidly sketched what he could see psychically. He gave the paper to Ryan and made him swear not to publish anything until such time as he had found the site, and had photographed it to verify the 'sighting'.

Ryan returned to Scotland in a state of great excitement, and recruited local photographer Jack Johnstone in order to find the location. At first, he thought that Croiset had been describing the Williamwath Bridge, near Dalton, but when they reached the bridge, Ryan was disappointed. The bridge matched the sketch but the setting was quite different. 'The old man's not all he's cracked up to be,' he muttered.

Jack Johnstone was not to be put off, however. 'I think I recognise it. There's a bridge at Middleshaw that's in an area a bit like that.'

'Where the hell is that, then?'

'About three miles.'

'Then let's have a look!' said Ryan.

They went back to Ryan's car. He knew nothing about this Middleshaw bridge, and there had been no sighting of the lorry there. Still, he mused, there was a chance that Jack could be right.

As their car approached the bridge, Ryan felt the hairs on the back of his neck rise . . .

The bridge lay at the foot of a hill, with grey tubular railings. The surrounding landscape matched Croiset's descriptions and sketches, down to the eroded bank on one side of the river. The cottage lay nearby, with its surrounding hoardings and white fence. There were even fir trees covering the hills.

There was one more test, to make sure that this was the place. In his sketches, Croiset had described one of the bridge railings as having a kink. Ryan examined the bridge, but could find no kink; there was, however, a wire trailing over one railing that described an arc similar to the pattern of the kinked railing in Croiset's drawings . . .

Ryan told the McAdams what had happened and

they requested Croiset's further help. Ryan got in touch with the Dutchman and asked him what he would need to be able to divine more. The psychic informed Ryan that he would need some personal belonging of Pat's.

Ryan travelled to Utrecht again. He showed Croiset the photographs of the area, whereupon the Dutchman exclaimed delightedly that it was exactly as he had seen it. Then Ryan produced Pat McAdam's Bible.

Croiset took the book in his hand, and said bluntly, without a pause: 'She is dead.' And he added that he knew where her body was hidden. It lay in a kind of cave, formed by the tree roots in the river bank. He was unable to see if this was above or below water level. Pressed for further details, he told Ryan that he would try to see some clothing belonging to Pat.

Ryan produced a large-scale map of the area, and laid it in front of the psychic. Croiset examined it and pointed out areas that should be investigated. At a point on the map marked 'Broom Cottage', Croiset told Ryan that he would find a wheelbarrow standing beside a car.

Croiset and Ryan were still speaking through an interpreter, and here the interpreter had to go back and correct himself. Croiset had not said a wheelbarrow against a car, but rather a part of a car.

Ryan returned to Dumfries determined to take witnesses with him on his next search using Croiset's maps and visions. So it was with his wife and another journalist that Frank Ryan set off for the bridge that Croiset had seen in his first vision. It crossed a river called the Water of Milk, which ran west of Middleshaw. The wheelbarrow in the second vision should be three-quarters of a mile downstream.

And there it was: Broom Cottage, complete with the wreck of an old Ford Poplar in the garden. The car had no wheels, and most of the doors were missing. It was being used as a hen house, and the wheelbarrow was propped against its boot. Once again, Ryan felt shivers in his spine.

Ryan wrote up the story for the *Daily Record*, and informed Detective Inspector Cullinan of Croiset's visions. He emphasised that he had never been near Broom Cottage in his life, and hardly knew the area around Middleshaw, so the impressions of the place that Croiset had picked up could not have come from him. He was convinced that Croiset had used paranormal powers to receive impressions from the other sources – either the map or the Bible.

The police investigation, which had lain dormant for some time, was once again stepped up, and on Sunday 15 February 1970, the police, accompanied by Frank Ryan, searched the area for clothing. They found a stocking, part of a handbag, and the remains of a black dress, caught in the undergrowth on the river bank. However, there was no sign of the concealed grave that Croiset had seen.

The discovery of the clothing was front page news,

and the local people waited with impatience for further developments. Everyone's hopes were dashed, though, when no body or grave was found, and the clothing was eliminated from the enquiry. The dress had been long-sleeved whereas Pat's was short, and the other articles were just pieces of the detritus regularly washed on to the banks by the river.

Ryan returned to Utrecht to break the news of this failure to Croiset. The psychic expressed disappointment, but made it clear that when he focused on a scene he could not be sure that all the details in it would help the police. The photos proved he was on to something: after all, he had been able to describe in detail an area he had never seen.

Croiset then described a man to Ryan, the man whom police needed to find and question in relation to the disappearance of Pat McAdam. He was aged between thirty-two and thirty-four, dark-haired and quite short, around 5ft 4in, with one ear larger than the other. Croiset said he could see Pat McAdam with this man shortly before she died, in an area where trees had been felled. Her body was buried nearby. Her death had been horrible: she had been battered about the head with a heavy tool of some kind – a spanner, or a wrench. Her skull was shattered, and her clothes covered with blood. The man had raped her before killing her, and had started to hit her when she fought back. She had been dead when he raped her again. At this point, Croiset was overcome with emotion at what he could see . . .

* * *

Pat tripped and fell yet again. She hauled herself up, and started to run once more. Run! That was rich! It was more of a hobble, as she had already lost one shoe and felt covered in bruises. Each time she fell he gained more ground on her. Sobbing with each breath, she tried to reach the river. What good it would do she didn't know, but it was out in the open: perhaps someone would pass over the bridge and see her in the distance. Perhaps he couldn't swim, and she could evade him that way.

She fell again. She could hear his breathing and the thump of his feet on the ground as he gained on her. She tried to get up, but it was all over: he fell on her, knocking her back down. She tasted the muddy earth as her face hit the ground, and the breath was crushed from her body.

'Right, doll, it's time I had what was mine.'

He turned her over and began to rip her clothes. Pat tried to scream but there was no breath left in her body. Just a dry, wracking sob emerged from her.

As he raped her, she looked away. The river was only a hundred yards from where she lay – only a hundred yards from potential freedom.

'That's better,' he said in a satisfied tone after he had finished. 'That gave you something to think about, right?'

He put his face close to hers, and laughed. She spat into his eye.

'Bitch!' He wiped the spittle from his face. 'You'll

227

pay for that.' He reached out to one side and from the corner of her eye she saw him raise the object he had been carrying with him. It was a wrench, and she tried to scream as she saw it fall towards her.

It was the last thing she would see.

He rained blows on her head, until her skull was pulped into her brain. Then he covered her head and raped her again – just to show her who was in charge.

When he was finished, he wrapped the body in a blanket he took from his lorry, and carried it down to the river. There was small hole under some tree and scrub roots, and the river level being low, he was able to slide the body into it, hidden from view.

A few weeks later, there was heavy rain, and the water level rose. It took the mud and earth from around the tree and scrub roots along the bank. It also took the body, which was washed down the river. Somewhere along the way, the body snagged on river weed. Miles from the scene of the crime, this was Pat McAdam's last resting place.

By 19 February, Ryan had had seven interviews with Croiset, each one adding more detail to the overall picture that the psychic was building up of Pat McAdam's last movements. Croiset was convinced that the dress that had been found was Pat McAdam's, and not just the flotsam that the police claimed. Certainly, Pat's mother recalled giving her money to buy a new dress, so it was a possibility. However, Hazel Campbell could not remember Pat buying a dress on that last shopping trip. Could it have slipped her mind?

Meanwhile, there was a new glimmer of hope: forestry workers confirmed that tree felling had taken place in the area Croiset suggested, and at around the time Pat McAdam disappeared. Would a search reveal new clues?

Alas, the weather took a hand: before the end of February there was heavy snow, and further searches were ruled out until it had thawed. In the meantime, the *Daily Record*'s editor was beginning to realise what a strong story he had on his hands. The stage was set for the arrival of Gerald Croiset in Scotland...

Croiset was flown across at the newspaper's expense. As he toured the areas he had described to Frank Ryan, he was entranced by the fact that it was all exactly as he had described it, something he was keen to point out to the local CID, who accompanied him.

At the spot where he had seen Pat McAdam raped and killed he stood in wonder. It was as he had seen it in his vision. 'This is where it happened,' he said. 'She was buried over here.' He ran to the water's edge, where a few trees bent over in the wind. 'Down here!'

Ryan looked at Cullinan. The officer in charge of the case and the journalist had collaborated to get Croiset this far. Ryan was hopeful of a great discovery. He was disappointed when Cullinan shook his head.

'We've already looked along here. Whatever there was has long gone.'

But Gerald Croiset was convinced that Pat McAdam had been murdered in this spot, her body dumped in a shallow grave around the clusters of tree roots below the water level, and later washed out to sea. If this was so, then the chances of recovering her body were zero. It seemed as though the whole thing was over.

The clairvoyant powers of Croiset were now dismissed by the police as being of no further use. No evidence had been uncovered. Pat McAdam was still missing. The only man who knew what had happened to her on that day in 1967 was the lorry driver...

Ten years after the strange disappearance of Pat McAdam, a farmer at Glenboig, near Glasgow, noticed a sickening smell coming from the undergrowth alongside a track near his farm. Pulling aside the weeds and grasses, he was horrified to find the decomposing body of a young woman. She was naked from the waist down, and her pants had been stuffed into her mouth to act as a gag. Her hands were tied behind her. The body had been mutilated, and her head battered beyond recognition by a blunt instrument.

After the body had been reported, a woman in Glasgow was able to identify it as that of Frances Barker, who had vanished seventeen days before, on 10 June. She had disappeared after taking a taxi home from her brother-in-law's. Part of the way home, she had discovered that her keys were still back at his house, and had begun to walk back through the Maryhill area of Glasgow. Somewhere between the taxi and her brother-in-law's house, she vanished.

Further police investigations revealed that there was a rapist at work in the area. A large number of women had been attacked, many of them prostitutes who were unwilling to go to the police, believing that their stories would not be listened to. Now, however, they talked: many of the rapes took place at knife-point, and most of the girls were also savagely beaten – one girl had her hearing permanently damaged after being hit about the head as the rapist tried to drag her into his car. Only the intervention of a passer-by prevented her from being abducted.

An unexpected lead came the way of the police: a sixteen-year-old girl reported that she had been repeatedly raped by a lorry driver named Thomas Young after calling at 71 Ashley Street in search of a friend on 24 June. A powerfully built man had answered the door, and had dragged her into the house, holding her there for ten hours, and repeatedly raping and beating her.

When officers arrived at the house, Young had fled. They called on his wife but she told them she had not seen him for some time, as they were separated. She seemed to be nervy and on edge, though, and police decided to watch the house. Soon their hunch paid off and they saw Young in the kitchen, although they had no idea how he had entered the house.

A raid on the house led to his arrest, and the discovery that Young had in fact been there all the time – in a carefully built hideout beneath the floorboards! A search of this sanctuary revealed a powder compact that had belonged to Frances Barker, and, later, forensic examination of the cab of Young's lorry yielded hairs that had come from Barker. Faced with the evidence, Young confessed to the rape and murder ...

It transpired that Young had been arrested for theft aged nine, and at thirteen had been sent to an approved school for committing indecent assault. In 1962 he was jailed for housebreaking, and in 1963 he was imprisoned for a short time for failure to maintain his children. In 1967 he was jailed for eighteen months for raping a girl in Shropshire, and in 1970 received eight years for raping a girl of fifteen in the cab of his lorry.

Thomas Young was the lorry driver who picked up Pat McAdam and Hazel Campbell in 1967 ...

Were the Dumfries police aware of Young's violent tendencies and his conviction for rape in the same year as Pat's disappearance? Certainly, he had told police that he and Pat had made love in a lay-by before he had dropped her off near her home. The lay-by was near a bridge like the one Croiset described, and a lorry driver would have had a large wrench – the kind of blunt instrument Gerald Croiset was

(Above) The decomposed body of Carol Jackson is examined by farmer James Beach (left), who discovered the body, and Sheriff B. W. Davis. (*Hulton Deutsch Collection Limited*)

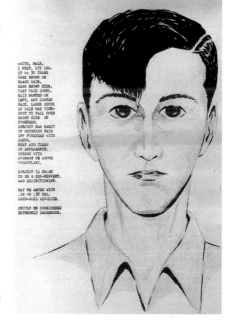

WHITE, MALE,
6 FEET, 175 LBS.
25 to 30 YEARS
DARK BROWN OR
BLACK HAIR,
DARK BROWN EYES,
VERY FAIR COMPL.
HAIR PARTED ON
LEFT, AND COMBED
BACK. LARGE SHOCK
OF HAIR HAS TEND-
ENCY TO FALL OVER
RIGHT SIDE OF
FOREHEAD.
SUBJECT HAS HABIT
OF BRUSHING HAIR
OFF FOREHEAD WITH
HANDS.
NEAT AND CLEAN
IN APPEARANCE.
SPEAKS WITH
AVERAGE OR ABOVE
VOCABULARY.

SUBJECT IS KNOWN
TO BE A SEX-PERVERT.
AND EXHIBITIONIST.

MAY BE ARMED WITH
.32 OR .38 CAL.
SNUB-NOSE REVOLVER.

SHOULD BE CONSIDERED
EXTREMELY DANGEROUS.

(Right) A police artist's sketch of the man seen by psychic Peter Hurkos through psychometry. It almost exactly resembles the murderer Melvin Rees. (*Hulton Deutsch Collection Limited*)

Charles A. Lindbergh Jnr: the kidnapped child. Was it his body that was found? (*Hulton Deutsch Collection Limited*)

The Lindbergh home. The child was abducted from here, but where was he taken? (*Hulton Deutsch Collection Limited*)

(Right) Edgar Cayce, 'The Sleeping Prophet', whose trance statements suggested who the real kidnappers were and the location of the child. (*Topham Picture Source*)

(Below) Charles Lindbergh gives evidence against Bruno Hauptmann, who he erroneously believed had kidnapped his son. (*Hulton Deutsch Collection Limited*)

(Above) Bruno Hauptmann (centre) is led away after being convicted of murder and sentenced to death. If Cayce was correct, Hauptmann was innocent and Lindbergh Jnr was still alive. (*Hulton Deutsch Collection Limited*)

(Left) Andrija Puharich, the psychic researcher who investigated both Uri Geller and Peter Hurkos. He pronounced them genuine after rigorous experiment. (*Topham Picture Source*)

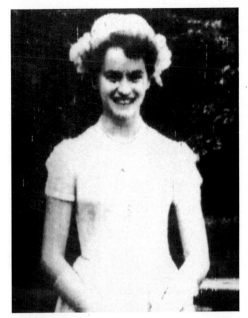

Myrna Joy Aken, the Durban secretary whose disappearance and subsequent murder led to Nelson Palmer being called in to help solve the crime. (*Associated Press*)

Nelson Palmer, the schoolmaster psychic, who traced Myrna's killer, Clarence Van Buuren. (*Psychic News*)

(Right) Peter Hurkos sits opposite the courthouse, waiting to be called during the trial of Norman John Collins. (*Hulton Deutsch Collection Limited*)

(Below) Detective Sergeant Donald Carnahan searches the area where Maralynn Skelton's body was found. (*Hulton Deutsch Collection Limited*)

(Left) Norman John Collins, slayer of six, arrives at the courthouse to be tried. (*Hulton Deutsch Collection Limited*)

(Below) Collins' victims. (Top, left to right): Mary Fleszar, Joan Schell, Jane Louise Mixer; (Bottom, left to right): Maralynn Skelton, Dawn Basom, Alice Kalom. (*Hulton Deutsch Collection Limited*)

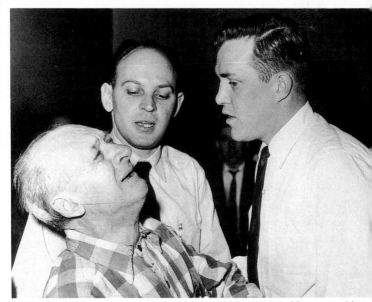

Fred Thompson collapses as he is booked with the murder of four-year-old Edith Kiecorius in New York. (*Hulton Deutsch Collection Limited*)

Edith's body is removed from the tenement room where Thompson kept her for four days after her death. (*Hulton Deutsch Collection Limited*)

certain had been used to kill Pat McAdam. And apart from a couple of inches in height discrepancy, Thomas Young fitted Gerald Croiset's description of the man police should be looking for.

Hazel Campbell had already told detectives that Pat had refused to have sex with a boy at the party they had attended, telling him she was menstruating. So why, then, would she willingly have sex with Thomas Young less than twenty-four hours later? Should his story not have been investigated further after his conviction for rape in 1967?

After his capture Young openly boasted to police that he had had sex with more than two hundred women in the cab of his lorry, and that many of these he had raped after they had initially refused him. Even after he had murdered Frances Barker he had attempted to rape a woman in the same spot. Medical evidence at Young's trial for the murder of Frances Barker revealed that he was a man whose sex urge was so violent and compulsive that it turned him virtually insane.

In 1975 a television team, investigating the disappearance of Pat McAdam – it became the best documented of all the cases involving psychic detection – interviewed Gerald Croiset in Utrecht. He claimed the case a total success for himself, which seemed very strange to the film crew, until it was revealed that Croiset had been told by a friend that Pat McAdam's body had been found. A police search of the area had, in fact, unearthed a body: but it was not Pat McAdam. The remains of a woman had been found in a pond, but she was in her forties, wore a wedding ring, and had in her possession coins minted after the disappearance of Pat McAdam.

Even after being told this, the Dutch psychic was still unwilling to claim anything less than a success. He was hardly the kind of man to admit to a mistake in front of a camera crew! Gerald Croiset clung on to the idea that he had solved the murder of Pat McAdam until the day he died, in 1980.

Only Thomas Young knows what really happened, and he remains silent. The case of Pat McAdam is still an open file.

Slaughter at the Mannville Farmhouse

The case of the quadruple murder at Mannville Farm
·seemed destined to remain unsolved.

Six months after the crime, the psychic Maximillien Langsner was called in and, through the use
of telepathic power, was able to supply information
as to the whereabouts of the missing murder weapon,
the name of the killer, and that of a witness who could
corroborate his evidence. It is one of the most clear-
cut cases on record of psychically supplied evidence
leading to an arrest and a conviction.

Mannville Farm lay eighty miles to the north of
Edmonton, Alberta, in Canada. On 9 July 1928
Vernon Booher returned home to find the farmhouse
turned into a slaughterhouse.

According to his statement, when he arrived home
in the early evening everything was strangely quiet.
Preparation for the evening meal should have been
under way. Two farmhands should have been around
the house, as well as Vernon's mother and father, and
his brother Fred. He wondered where everyone had

gone. He called out, but there was no answer. He was soon to find out why.

Entering the kitchen, he found his mother sprawled across the floor, her body half-hidden under the kitchen table. She had been shot in the back of the neck, and little of her head remained. A bloodied pulp was splattered over the kitchen range.

Vernon stumbled into the next room, where he found his brother Fred. He had been shot through the mouth and was identifiable only by his clothes.

In shock, Booher searched the remainder of the house and found nothing. He then tried the outhouses. In a bunkhouse, he stumbled across the body of Gabriel Cromby, a casual farmhand. He, too, was dead – another bullet to the head. Suppressing the urge to vomit, Vernon ran blindly across the fields, back in the direction he had come from, unable to think straight.

Somehow, Vernon made it to a neighbour's house, where he blurted out what he had discovered. His neighbours tried their best to comfort him, and offered to phone the police for him. Vernon refused. In his confusion, he wanted to get a doctor for his mother and brother and insisted on calling himself. He telephoned the Boohers' family doctor, who after hearing Vernon's story contacted the police before leaving for the farmhouse.

In the meantime, Henry Booher – Vernon's father, and owner of the farm – had returned from the fields, and stumbled upon the carnage in his home. When the doctor and the police arrived, they found him sitting in the kitchen, staring at the corpse of his wife. He looked up at them with a blank, uncomprehending stare. He was in shock and unable to speak, and had to be sedated.

Some time later, detectives questioned Vernon and Henry. Both professed no knowledge of why such a crime should have been perpetrated. The Boohers had no enemies; on the contrary, they were a well-respected family in the area. The only suggestion Vernon could make was that Herman Rosyk, another casual farmhand, could be responsible, a suggestion based on nothing more than the fact that Rosyk had disappeared from the farm.

This theory was shattered when the police combed the area of the farm and found Rosyk in one of the outlying barns. He, too, had been killed – also shot through the head. The killer had wanted to make sure that his victims could not possibly survive long enough to talk.

Forensic examination of the bodies revealed that the same weapon had been used in all four cases. This weapon, a .303 rifle, became the subject of an intensive search, but nothing was found. Rose Booher, Fred Booher, and Herman Rosyk had been killed at the same time – around half-past six in the evening, and people in neighbouring farms told detectives that they had heard shots at that time, but had thought nothing of it because Mannville was a hunting area, and the sound of shooting was not unusual at any time of day or night.

One of the most puzzling things about the case was the fact that Gabriel Cromby had been killed around eight o'clock. Vernon could confirm this, as he had heard two shots at that time. This meant that the killer had probably still been in the vicinity when Vernon made his gruesome discovery. But this also meant that, for some reason they could not yet fathom, the killer had returned to the farm after a ninety-minute period in order to kill again. Either that or he had hung around the buildings for that time – an extraordinarily risky thing for a triple killer to do. Had he been waiting for Vernon or Henry?

Whichever way the police looked at it, the case was full of puzzling dead ends: why had the murders been committed? Where was the rifle? Why had the murderer waited around or returned? How had he fled without being seen?

Nearly six months passed, and the police were still without a weapon, a motive, or a suspect. Mike Gier, who was police chief in Edmonton at this time, decided that desperate measures were called for – or, at least, measures that were distinctly unusual. He telegraphed Dr Maximillien Langsner...

Langsner was a PhD from the University of Calcutta, and had spent most of his life studying telepathy and psi powers. Originally a student of Sigmund Freud in

Vienna, he had turned away from the theories of the pioneer psychologist when Freud had dismissed all talk of psi power (the blanket term at that time for all forms of psychic phenomena believed to emanate from the brain) and telepathy as 'the black tide of occultism'.

Langsner decided to set off in his own direction. After the Great War, he spent some time in India studying the history of psychic activity, particularly telepathy and mind control, and evolved a theory of 'brainwaves', in which the thoughts of the 'controller' were transmitted to the potentially 'controlled' by a process similar to that of radio waves.

Langsner became a celebrity after a remarkable case in Vancouver. Standing in the same room as a suspect in a jewel robbery, he was able to read his mind and describe the room the jewels were hidden in. The police recognised the description as that of a room in the home of the suspect's girlfriend. A search led to the recovery of the jewels, and the suspect was later convicted.

Langsner was on his way to Alaska, where he hoped to study the psi powers of the Eskimos, when he was called in to the case of Mannville Farm. He arrived at Mannville in time for the inquest – a small, elderly man with a heavy Viennese accent, dressed in a neat dark suit, and with a mass of white hair that fought to escape from underneath his hat.

239

Throughout the inquest he sat quietly, listening to all the evidence. The .303 rifle provided the only clue as to any suspect: Charles Stevenson ran a nearby farm, and a rifle of the same calibre as that used to commit the murders had disappeared from his farm at around the time of the slayings. This promoted Stevenson to number one suspect. In truth, he was the only man the police had their eye upon – and only then because of his missing rifle. It was a stab in the dark, but all they had to go on.

After the inquest, Gier took Langsner back to his office, and asked the psychic if he could help in any way. Langsner considered his answer carefully. 'I can tell you the name of the killer,' he said. 'Vernon Booher.'

Gier was obviously taken aback. Vernon had discovered the bodies, and had been in a visible state of shock when the police arrived. He had even put forward Rosyk as the possible killer, before that man too had been found dead. On the other hand, if Vernon Booher had committed the murders, what better way was there of avoiding suspicion than 'discovering' the bodies? But this still left Gier with a problem: what possible motive could Vernon have for the four slayings? Gier couldn't see Vernon Booher as a murderer yet, but he had been impressed by the quiet assurance in Langsner's tone, and decided to give him all the co-operation he required.

'Have you any proof?' he asked Langsner.

The Viennese shook his head. 'No, but I can tell you

where the murder weapon was hidden – in a clump of prairie grass at the back of the house.'

The search took place on the following day. Langsner accompanied the police to the farm, and led the small party – Gier and three officers – around the property. To Gier, it seemed as though he was dowsing in the same manner as a water diviner – except that Langsner didn't use a hazel twig! The policemen carried spades and picks.

Langsner wandered around the farmhouse and outbuildings for twenty minutes apparently getting his bearings and working out the lie of the land. Suddenly he turned to one of the policemen and asked him to step ten paces forward.

On the ninth pace, the policeman tripped over something hidden in the grass. 'What the hell—' he began, stumbling. Then he looked more closely at the mound of earth he had tripped over. It was freshly dug, with a sod of wild grass thrown on top. It looked undisturbed, except when examined closely. 'Hey!' he called. 'There's something over here! C'mon!'

Gier rushed over to where his man crouched, followed by the other officers. Langsner strolled calmly over and was in time to see Gier's spade bite into the earth, and almost with the first downward stroke hit something that reverberated with a metallic clang. Gier looked round at Langsner. The Viennese nodded. 'That will be what you are looking for.'

Gier pulled out the spade and gestured to two of his

men. Carefully, they scooped away the earth with
their bare hands. It took them only a couple of
minutes to uncover the stock and barrel of a rifle.

Dusting them off, the officers handed them to Gier,
who fitted the pieces together. 'Well whaddaya
know,' he grinned. 'It's a three-oh-damn-three rifle.'

Gier was ecstatic at such a find and wanted the rifle
to be taken away and dusted for fingerprints.
Langsner, however, shook his head. 'It is no use
looking for fingerprints,' he said. 'Vernon Booher has
wiped it clean.'

If Gier was confused by the psychic's certainty
of Vernon's guilt, he was even more puzzled by
Langsner's suggestion that Booher be taken into
protective custody 'for his own good'. However, more
than satisfied by the results achieved so far, he
complied with this strange request and when asked,
explained his action on the grounds that Vernon was
a major witness to the case and the killer might wish
to tie up a few loose ends . . .

The cell was a bare-walled room with a wooden bunk
suspended from the wall by two chains. A thin
mattress and dusty pillow were the only comforts. A
bucket stood in the corner. Vernon Booher sat with
his head in his hands. They had told him he was here
for his own good – but what did that mean? He was
trying to work out how long it would take a lawyer to
get him out when he heard the scraping of a chair
outside. A little fat man with a shock of white hair

and a beard sat on the chair, looking in directly at Vernon.

'Well look-a here,' Vernon said slowly. 'What have we got here, then?'

The little man said nothing. Vernon looked back into his hands, and tried to pretend that the stranger wasn't there, that he wasn't bothering him. But he was ... Vernon felt as though the man's eyes were boring into him, sucking something from him that he wanted to keep hidden. He looked up at the little man again. 'Who are you, then? What have they got you here for? Your own protection?' His tone was cheery.

Langsner sat silently, studying Vernon's face. A smile played around the corners of his mouth.

Vernon tried to strike up conversation. He talked about the weather, how he was being kept here for his own good, how the investigation was progressing. 'Must be close to getting someone for it, otherwise they wouldn't be keeping me out of harm's way in here, right?' He smiled brightly.

Still the Viennese failed to respond. Still he looked intently and yet impassively, inviting no comment from Vernon. Still that smile played around the corners of his mouth.

Vernon began to get annoyed. 'Just what the hell are you playing at here, boy? Why don't you speak to me? Can't you speak damn English or something?' His tone got harder with each sentence, as his anger grew.

Still Langsner said nothing.

'Dammit to hell!' screamed Vernon, throwing himself at the bars. 'Why don't you say something! Anything! Just speak to me, for Chrissakes!' He stared at Langsner with hatred in his eyes, chest heaving with fury.

Langsner smiled softly and stood up.

'Thank you, Mr Booher, I have learnt a lot. Goodnight.' He turned and walked away from the cell.

Seated in Gier's office, Langsner outlined the case as he saw it. Vernon Booher was his mother's favourite son, but he had come to despise her. The reason for this was not clear, but it had something to do with the way in which she dominated the entire family. Vernon had stolen the rifle, then after a period of some days had shot his mother from behind. His brother Fred had been killed when Vernon had realised that he was not alone in the house. He was reluctant to do this, but felt compelled. When he had gone to hide the rifle, he had seen Rosyk and so had to kill him in case the farmhand had spotted him.

Gabriel Cromby had been on the farm at the time: Vernon hadn't seen him, but had brooded on the fact that Cromby might say that Vernon had been in the vicinity. So after nearly two hours, he had returned to the farm, recovered the rifle, and shot Cromby before returning the gun to its hiding place.

The police chief was amazed by this story. It made sense, and fitted the facts – tests on the rifle had shown it to be the one that had been stolen, and also the one that had killed the Boohers, Rosyk and Cromby. But how could it be corroborated? The Viennese psychic smiled and told Gier that there was a woman who could supply the police with the link they needed between Booher and the rifle. He could not name her, but was able to describe her: she was a small, ageing woman with a long jaw and small eyes, who was wearing a poke bonnet. Charles Stevenson's rifle had been stolen when he was in church; this woman had also been in church and she had seen Vernon Booher sneak out in order to steal the rifle. What is more, Vernon had noticed her watching him, because it was from Vernon that he had picked up this picture of her.

The priority now was to find this woman before Booher was let out of jail – and the police could not continue to hold him under 'protective custody' for very much longer! If Vernon Booher was released, would he try to tie up this particular loose end? Vernon had no idea that he was the prime suspect and that Langsner had supplied a fully detailed description of events at the farm, so he would feel safe in making such a move.

Fortunately for the forces of law, Mannville was a small town, and they soon came across a woman who fitted the description perfectly ...

Erma Higgins was a spinster, and someone who liked to keep her finger on the pulse of the community. Less kind people may have called her

inquisitive and a gossip, but to Mike Gier she was just
the kind of break he was looking for. When he
interviewed her, it was clear that she knew everyone's activities in the community, be they legitimate
or illicit: there was little that escaped her small,
sharp eyes – and her long jaw seemed to be set in a
perpetual scowl of indignation.

She was pleased to be part of the investigation –
and such an important part! It didn't take long for
Gier to elicit from her the information he needed: she
had seen Vernon Booher sneak out of church that
Sunday, and then sneak back again. And she knew
that he had seen her watching him, as he had seemed
shifty and uncomfortable, and had avoided greeting
her ever since.

There was a danger that Erma could be just
another sour old gossip with a grudge against Vernon
for some unknown reason, but her story tied in with
what Langsner had said. Erma could not have known
the rifle had been stolen during that particular
Sunday service, yet she had put Vernon Booher at the
right place at the right time to steal the rifle.

Gier sat Erma in his office and told her that he
wanted her to confront Vernon with the truth, what
she had seen that Sunday, no more than that. She
nodded nervously. She had worked out that Gier
believed Booher to be the murderer, and the thought
of confronting him frightened her.

'You okay to see him?' asked Gier, when Vernon
had been brought up from the cells, and was waiting

outside his office, handcuffed to one of Gier's men.

Erma nodded, and Gier opened the door, motioning his man to bring Booher in. Vernon stopped dead at the sight of Erma. Gier rejoiced as he saw Vernon's face harden in an attempt to stop the look of shock, and watched Vernon look everywhere but directly at the old woman.

Erma took a deep breath. 'Vernon, I saw you leave church the day Charlie's rifle was stolen,' she said, as briefed by Gier.

'I know you did,' Vernon replied quietly. There was a long pause fraught with tension. Would Booher break down and confess? This was Gier's best chance to wind up the case tidily.

'Let me confess,' Vernon whispered, 'I killed them all . . .'

The confession fleshed out some of the details. Rose Booher ran her family with the proverbial rod of iron, and Vernon was her favourite son. But then Vernon had started to see a girl that Rose didn't approve of: she wasn't good enough for a boy like Vernon. So Rose had tried to break the romance, even going so far as to throw the girl out of the farmhouse when she had been visiting Vernon.

Vernon had been unable to stand up to his mother. Like the rest of the family, he was cowed by this formidable matriarch, and had bent to her will. The romance died, but his resentment of his mother grew as she constantly told him what she thought of the girl. Rose Booher did not realise she was writing her

247

own death warrant. Vernon's feelings stayed hidden and festered into a desire to kill her, a desire that he had decided to act upon by stealing his neighbour Charles Stevenson's rifle and sneaking back to the farmhouse at a time when he knew his mother would be alone to shoot her.

Langsner had been right about the other murders; they were merely the chain of events spiralling out of Vernon's control. For some reason Vernon's brother Fred had been in the house when he should have been out working and stumbled upon the murder scene after hearing the first shot. Vernon had been forced to shoot him. A rattled and paranoid Vernon had been convinced that the farmhand Herman Rosyk had seen him as he tried to escape across the farmyard to hide the gun. He had shot him too: Rosyk had probably never known why he died.

But Vernon was still brooding on who else might have seen him. Gabriel Cromby had been working near the farm, and though it's highly unlikely that he would have seen or heard anything, he, too, had to go. Vernon had returned to the farm when he knew Cromby would be in the bunkhouse, and had shot him. Then he had hidden the rifle and gone over to his neighbour's farm with his story of returning home to find the bodies. His shocked state at the time was unlikely to be an act: Vernon was mentally unbalanced and the fact that he had committed three more murders than he had planned no doubt added to his distress. If the old man had been unfortunate enough to return early, Vernon would have killed his father as well: it was fortunate for Henry Booher that he had been working that day on the far side of the farm.

Vernon Booher was formally arrested and charged with the killings. The result of his trial was inevitable: presented with Vernon's confession, the jury found him guilty on four counts of murder. On 26 April 1929 Vernon Booher was executed: hanged by the neck until dead.

The Severed Foot
and the Letter 'S'

When Mary Lou Cousett left the small town of Alton, Illinois, on 14 April 1983, those who knew her had no idea that it was the last time she would be seen alive. The fact that her murderer eventually stood trial was due to Greta Alexander, a psychic from nearby Delarvan.

Mary Lou was an upright citizen: she worked as a secretary, and at the age of twenty-eight was buying her own home. She was a pretty girl with friends who cared about her so much that they couldn't help but speak out when she started to hang around with Stanley Holliday Jnr, a man the small-town people said had 'bad ways'. Stanley was a drifter, who had recently returned to the town, and was only a little younger than Mary Lou. He had a long police record for petty offences all over the state – robbery, drugs, illegal firearms – and was thought to be trouble.

Mary Lou liked him, though, and believed that he couldn't be as bad as people painted him. As the disquiet voiced by her friends grew louder, so Mary

Lou spent more and more time in his company. She was determined to prove them wrong, and her own judgement right. What began as a casual relationship developed into something more serious, and Mary Lou became increasingly influenced by Holliday.

Slowly her friends began to drift away, though their concern was unabated. Stanley had a drink problem, and Mary Lou also began to drink heavily. Her behaviour changed; she lost her job and her home, and moved in with Stanley, into his twilight world of drink and drugs.

Finally, things got so bad for the couple that Stanley decided they should leave town and make a fresh start somewhere else, somewhere that they wouldn't be picked on for Stanley's reputation and record.

On 14 April, they were gone: suddenly and without warning. There were fears that something had happened to them, and Mary Lou's friends contacted the police, reporting her as a missing person, even though she had announced her intention to leave town. It was, perhaps, just as well that they took this action. As the police traced the couple's movements they discovered that Stanley Holliday Jnr had turned up in New Jersey ... alone!

They had been on the road for almost two days. Stanley had only a few grammes of cocaine left, and was beginning to fret about where his next line was going to come from. He was also drunk again. The car weaved across the highway, and Mary Lou grabbed at the wheel.

'Why the hell don't you look where you're going,' she screamed at him. He mumbled, laughed, and dismissed her with a wave of the hand. He was in his own little universe.

Mary Lou took the bottle wedged between the seat and the gear box, twisted the screw-top, and took a big swig of bourbon. Hell, if he could get drunk, so could she.

She was beginning to wonder why she had agreed to leave with him: he was bleary and unshaven, with a blank stare in his addled eyes. But then she figured she probably didn't look that much better herself.

The car veered across the road again, narrowly missing a truck whose horn blared at them.

'Gimme the bottle,' he said, grabbing it and drinking some more.

The road seemed to go on forever. They had no idea where they were headed, and Stanley had told her that he didn't really care: they'd keep driving until they reached a town he didn't know.

A roadside cafe loomed in the distance.

'I'm hungry,' she said blankly. 'Let's stop and eat, eh?'

He didn't say anything, but pulled into the car park of the cafe with a squeal of brakes, throwing her forward against the windscreen.

'Watch it,' she yelled. He sneered.

They went in and ordered food. He had whisky, and Mary Lou made do with beer. She felt awful, and he looked awful. The waitress seemed to be looking at them with disdain as she delivered their order. Stanley tried to pinch her bottom as she walked away from the table, and was rewarded with a hard stare from the diner owner, who was probably the waitress's husband.

'Why the hell can't you keep your hands to yourself?' Mary Lou said bitterly.

'You never complained when I did it to you,' he sneered. He looked around, laughing, trying to find someone to share his joke. The few people in the cafe ignored him.

Mary Lou had had enough. 'I'm sick of you, you know that? You treat me like shit, and you treat yourself the same way.'

'Why don't you just shut your Goddamn mouth?' he snarled.

Before she knew what was happening, they started to argue. They yelled and screamed at each other, and she threw the contents of her glass over him. He picked up his plate and tried to throw it at her; but he was too stoned, and the plate shattered on the polished linoleum on the floor.

'That's it! Out, the pair of you,' said the owner, dragging them from their table. He was a big man, and Stanley was in no fit state to argue.

Outside, he simmered in silence as they got in the car and drove off.

* * *

The police could turn up no sign of Mary Lou: they couldn't tell at what point in the journey she and Holliday had parted company, nor where she had gone afterwards. There was little they could do to try to find her: the long stretches of road were punctuated by numerous small towns. Where in all of these could they begin to look?

Given Holliday's character, and his lack of explanations or concern for Mary Lou, the police began to fear that he had murdered her after an argument. All they had to go on was a hearsay report of the couple arguing in a cafe. None the less, they decided to bring Holliday back from New Jersey for questioning.

During the interview Holliday was hazy about detail, claiming that he had been drunk when they argued, and that he couldn't recall where she said she was going – if, indeed, she had said anything. He came across as belligerent and forceful in his assertion that she had left of her own accord, and vehemently denied any suggestion that he had murdered her. This attitude left detectives unconvinced, and they instituted a search for Mary Lou – alive or dead.

Since they had left the cafe they had travelled in silence; the tension in the car was making Mary Lou feel ill: she wished she had never left home. Suddenly, Stanley turned off the road, and the car skidded to halt in the undergrowth – a wooded area with scrub and a few trees. Stanley slammed the door as he got out of the vehicle. Mary Lou sat trembling as he stormed into the woods. There was silence.

After a few minutes, she got out of the car and followed him. He was sitting on a fallen tree, smoking.

'So are we going on or what?' she asked tentatively. He ignored her. She reached out and touched him on the shoulder.

He reacted so explosively that she didn't know what was happening: he spun around and grabbed her arm, pulling her down on to the tree stump. 'Why don't you just shut up for once, eh, instead of telling me what to do? Why don't you just shut up?'

'You're hurting me!' Her voice was coming in sobbing gasps as his grip twisted her arm. She had fallen awkwardly, and a dull pain tore at her shoulder.

'I'll show you hurt,' he said, standing up. He pulled her to her feet, and punched her in the jaw. Her head snapped back and her senses reeled. His grip loosened on her arm, and she slumped to the cold earth. As she lay there, he kicked her in the head: her neck snapped, and Mary Lou Cousett felt no more pain.

He kept on kicking her. He picked up a fallen branch and in a senseless rage, hit her body with the hard wood, hardly hearing the snap of bone. In blind fury, he picked up rocks and threw them at her, pounding her corpse. Finally, his rage spent, he sank to the ground and fell into a drunken sleep.

The next morning when he awoke and saw her lifeless body lying almost beside him on the ground, he had no clear recollection of what had occurred the night before.

'Mary Lou?' He reached across and poked tentatively at her still, cold body. 'Oh shit, what have I done?' he whispered to himself.

He sat for a short while considering what to do: one thing was sure, he couldn't leave her like this. Using his bare hands, he dug a shallow grave near the fallen tree and buried Mary Lou. Then he returned to the car, and drove towards New Jersey. He could always say that she had left him: who would ever know? Come to that, who would ever ask?

It was now 17 April, three days after the couple had left town. Holliday was arrested on suspicion of murder, with a variety of smaller charges concerning illegal possession of both a firearm and drugs used to keep him in custody. The search for Mary Lou continued. If she was alive, she had succeeded in disappearing from the face of the earth leaving absolutely no trace.

The search would go on throughout the summer, as the police left no stone unturned – quite literally – in their efforts to find the woman they were convinced was dead. The search was now for a corpse: every piece of waste ground around Alton was turned over again and again. It was impossible to look everywhere between Illinois and New Jersey, but from the edge of town to the diner, where she had last been seen, and along the highway for a few miles in every direction, officers searched any brush or wooded area where a body could have been concealed.

Unfortunately, the ground around the fallen tree where Stanley had buried Mary Lou was missed. The police did not find a body – and they had little hope of getting anything from Stanley.

Holliday was keeping quiet and sitting tight in his cell. He stuck to his story of Mary Lou running out on him, and claimed that his drunkenness prevented a total recall of events. He knew that if a body wasn't found, he would have to be set free. The detectives had scraped together enough circumstantial evidence to use as a holding charge, but, unless some evidence was unearthed, they would have to let him go.

Time dragged on and the investigation was no nearer a solution. Officers were beginning to contemplate desperate measures. One officer in particular – Detective William Fitzgerald – was ready to take unorthodox action: he placed a call to Delarvan, Illinois, and asked to speak to Greta Alexander.

Greta Alexander was a psychic who had in the past helped to find missing children. She had what she described as second sight, and was quite shy about her gifts. None the less, Dixie Yetelerian had mentioned her in one of her own books, and Greta had become something of a local celebrity. Despite this, she rarely worked with the police and then strictly on request. A middle-aged housewife, Greta had first developed her powers after being struck by lightning and a less likely looking psychic is hard to imagine: a small, chubby woman with spectacles, her hair in a bun, she resembled the psychic portrayed by Zelda Rubinstein in Steven Spielberg's film *Poltergeist* – though with none of that character's flamboyance.

She had no real theories about her powers, accepting them as part of herself. She was never tested scientifically, and had no wish to be. She made no claims, and wasn't interested in fame or fortune, but was pleased to try and help families who came to her for assistance.

Although Detective Fitzgerald persuaded her to travel to Alton, Greta Alexander had made it clear to him that she could not control what came to her, and that she might be unable to help. The police were willing to take that chance.

Greta asked for maps of the area around Alton, and also of other areas the police had already searched for the body. There was some puzzlement over this: the whole of each area had been thoroughly turned over, and there was no possibility in the officers' minds that the body could have remained undiscovered. However, with nothing to lose, they complied with the request. Greta Alexander spread the maps out over a table, and began to pore over them. The atmosphere in the small room at Alton police headquarters grew tense: there were several detectives clustered around the table, moving only to make room for Greta as her hands ranged over the maps. The air was thick with cigarette smoke.

She took a long time over each map, and some of the detectives present became restless: many of them had had experiences with psychics that had left them sceptical. As Alexander studied each map intently, some members of the team made it clear that they doubted Fitzgerald's wisdom in bringing her in to the case.

Greta Alexander took no notice. In her mind's eye she could see each area as she touched it on the map: the woods, the scrub, and the surrounding country. Eventually, she came to a map for an area to the east of the town. It was a heavily wooded area which had been thoroughly searched several times during the course of investigation. She could see another search, and this time there was a body. She could see it in minute detail: it was almost as though her mind zeroed in on the discovery of the corpse, like a camera in close-up. Everything was clear in her mind. She noted every detail.

As she removed her hand from the map, the vision faded. She turned to the officers in the room, and began to speak. To those detectives present – even Fitzgerald – what she said was almost laughable. Pointing to a small area in the wooded section, she told the police that the body could be found there. She also told them that the letter 'S' would be important. Most of the detectives present were less than impressed with this statement: it had been common knowledge for the last six months that Stanley Holliday Jnr was the prime suspect. In fact, the name had been featured in several local newspapers and on the radio and television. It seemed a spurious attempt at credibility.

What came next was treated as a leap into the realms of pure fiction. Greta Alexander told the officers that the head and left foot of the remains would be separated from the body. One of the arms would be broken. The skull would have a three-inch split in it. One of the ribs would be broken, and the right leg would have a fracture in it. One final thing she added was the observation that the man who found the body would have a bad hand. When asked what she meant she replied that she wasn't sure, only that his hand would be injured in some way.

Throughout the whole of her statement, Greta Alexander was quite calm: there was no sign of her entering a trance, and she didn't use any objects for psychometry. All she had was the map of the area. This impressed Fitzgerald, who was otherwise as sceptical as the other policemen in the room. Alexander's calm assurance convinced him they must search the area again. Now all he had to do was convince the other detectives!

Greta Alexander went home, not knowing if the police intended to follow her advice or not. As far as she was concerned, she had done all that was asked of her, and what came next was down to the detectives on the case. Back at the station, Fitzgerald was trying to convince his colleagues that they had nothing to lose in the search. The press would find out that they had brought in a psychic, and if nothing was seen to be done about her evidence, the papers would be severely critical, claiming the police were failing to pursue all leads. All right, the area had already been searched many times: what harm could one more search do? And if she was right, then praise would be heaped on the police – a change from the critical brickbats they had been getting on the Cousett case so far.

His argument convinced his colleagues: another search would take place. Fitzgerald organised it personally the next morning.

In the section of the wooded area singled out by Alexander, the officers and volunteers selected for the search were sceptical about their chances of obtaining any result, but at the same time hopeful.

The dig went on in tense silence, painfully slowly, as earth was sifted more painstakingly than ever before. It was the middle of the afternoon before there was a breakthrough. Auxiliary police officer Steve Trew called out that he had found something. There was a hushed air of expectation as he carefully extracted a bone from the ground. Further digging revealed that it was part of a human foot. How come it had been missed before?

Amazed excitement followed as Trew reported that he had not only unearthed a foot, but that the bones of a leg were attached. With luck, there would be a complete skeleton.

Any thought of it being Mary Lou Cousett was pushed to the back of the officers' minds as they joined Trew in the delicate task of unearthing the skeleton. It was complete, although the skull and left foot were separated from the body. The remains were photographed from every angle and each individual bone catalogued before being placed in sealed bags to be taken to a forensic laboratory.

Greta Alexander had already been proved right in three respects: the body was in the position she had claimed; secondly, the skull had been separated from the body; and thirdly, the left foot was separated from the rest of the leg. Forensic examination also proved her right in other ways: one of the ribs was broken, and the skull was fractured, as was the right leg. The right arm was broken at the elbow.

The matter of the letter 'S' was also cleared up: the name of the auxiliary officer who first uncovered the body was Steve Trew. And finally something that made Fitzgerald gasp: Trew had a deformed left hand which had been injured in an accident some years before – the 'bad hand' Alexander had predicted.

Of course, Greta Alexander had not named the killer, but, faced with the overwhelming evidence, Stanley Holliday Jnr confessed: he had murdered

Mary Lou in a drunken, drug-fuelled rage after an argument.

Holliday was duly charged with murder. On 23 March 1981 he received a life sentence.

Too Many Cooks...

Peter Sutcliffe terrorised the north of England for a period of six years, beginning in October 1975. Women in the larger Yorkshire cities, particularly Leeds and Bradford, didn't feel safe until the trial of this modern-day Ripper began on 5 May 1981.

The hunt for the man who became infamous as the Yorkshire Ripper proved beyond all doubt that the police need technology in order to collate correctly all information received. Because of the jumbled state of the system for filing and storing information, Sutcliffe was twice questioned by police and twice allowed to go free. In the end he was captured by chance: he was stopped by police in connection with a motoring offence.

Like the mysterious Jack the Ripper after whom he was named by the popular press, the case attracted a string of psychics who claimed to have information that could lead to an arrest. Robert Lees, the famous American medium resident in London, had sold his revelations to the newspapers in Victorian times; likewise, in the twentieth century, Doris Stokes and

Gerald Croiset were also approached.

The 'I'm Jack' series of tapes and letters by a hoaxer were submitted by the police to the psychics Stokes and Croiset, but, of course, were no use in identifying the killer. Meanwhile, with the genuine psychics being led up a blind alley, and the fakes and self-deluded casting about in the dark, the psychic Nella Jones was receiving information that could have led to an earlier capture – information that was also lost in the pre-computer chaos of the police operation.

Peter Sutcliffe was, in fact, a highly suitable subject for psychics to trace because the psychic is attracted to the personality whose emotions and emanations of the mind are strongest, as often seems to happen when a person is disturbed.

At his trial Sutcliffe claimed to be a schizophrenic, and had a carefully worked out defence that included all the textbook symptoms, such as the hearing of voices that told him to commit the crimes. Unfortunately for the defendant, he had been overheard whilst on remand discussing the possibility of such a defence, and boasting how he could fool the courts, so his spurious claims of schizophrenia were rightly disregarded by the jury.

However, it is highly likely that Sutcliffe was suffering from an obsessive mania. The almost ritualistic overtones in the way the women were killed, and the consistent pattern of returning to the area of a previous murder to kill again show a disregard for his own freedom that is almost breath-taking. He had an irresistible compulsion to kill and believed the police would never catch him.

Peter Sutcliffe had a relatively normal upbringing. He was born in 1946, the son of a policeman, and his mother's favourite of her five children. His school years were undistinguished, and he left at fifteen to pursue a number of dead-end jobs – including that of grave digger, during which, he claimed at his trial, he heard voices from God telling him to kill prostitutes.

At twenty-one he met Sonia Szurma in a pub. She was sixteen, and like Sutcliffe was introverted and shy. It was seven years before they were to wed, and during this time the relationship seems to have been stormy. At one point Sonia started to date an ice-cream salesman and Sutcliffe picked up a prostitute to 'get even', but proved to be impotent with her. He paid the five-pound fee with a ten-pound note but while he waited in a pub bar for the change she absconded with the money.

Two weeks later he saw her in the same pub, and asked for his change. She jeered at him, and the rest of the punters in the bar joined in. It was this embarrassment that he claimed was the source of his hatred of prostitutes.

He began to brood obsessively over the matter of prostitution, and to haunt the red-light districts of Bradford. His first attack was in 1969, when he hit a prostitute from behind with a gravel-filled sock; and in October of that year he was arrested and charged with being equipped for theft after being caught with a hammer. He received a fine.

Two years later he was driving with Trevor Birdsall, a friend, when he asked him to stop the car. Sutcliffe disappeared, and returned breathless a few minutes later, urging Birdsall to drive off at speed. When they were safely away he revealed that he had hit a prostitute on the head with a brick wrapped in a sock.

The following year – 1972 – Sonia entered teacher-training college. She suffered a nervous breakdown and was diagnosed as schizophrenic, which might have given Sutcliffe the idea for his defence later. When she was sufficiently recovered, the couple married. But the marriage was not a happy one, being punctuated by violent rows during which Sutcliffe claimed to be embarrassed that the neighbours could hear them shouting.

Once again, Sutcliffe turned to prostitutes to 'get even' with his wife. He told Olive Reivers, the prostitute that he was with when eventually captured, that he was unable to 'go with' his wife. She took this as a clear indication that they were having sexual problems. By now it was obvious that Sutcliffe was suffering from a strange obsession with prostitution – at the same time as he was paying prostitutes for sex, he was also intermittently attacking them.

The marriage must have deteriorated rapidly, for a series of attacks on Yorkshire women began on 5 July

1975, when Anna Rogulskyj was battered about the head with a hammer. Just over a month later, on 15 August, Olive Smelt was struck down from behind by another vicious blow to the head. Both women also had their buttocks slashed, and other cuts inflicted on their bodies. Fortunately, both survived after brain surgery.

Wilma stumbled out of the pub. Her four children were at home, and she had the rent to pay. She was going to earn the money in the only way she was able, although she wasn't too sure if she would get any punters tonight; she'd been on a pub crawl since opening time, and it was now nearly closing time. She could hardly stand, let alone ply her trade.

As she stumbled down the street she didn't have to go far before a car drew up beside her. 'Looking for business, love?' she managed to slur as the window on the near side wound down. Squinting in the half light, she could see a bearded man. She recognised him from the red-light district; he was always hanging around, trying to pick up prostitutes.

After a brief conversation she got into the car beside him, and they drove to a quiet piece of waste ground, where he could park undisturbed. All the while, he talked about his wife and how they didn't get on. It went in one ear and straight out the other as Wilma, feeling sick, thought she was going to throw up over his car.

He asked her to get in the back seat so they could

have sex. She began to climb over the seat, but saw something out of the corner of her eye that made her uneasy. She turned to say something, but was cut short as a hammer crashed into her skull. Repeated blows rained pain into her mind as her vision blurred, went red, and finally black ...

It was the first murder, on 29 October – the victim a prostitute called Wilma McCann, a Scot who had left her husband and turned to the Leeds red-light district in order to support herself and her four children.

The killer dragged the body into a playing field, pulled her dress up and inflicted horrendous injuries on her chest, stomach and genitals with a sharp instrument – possibly a screwdriver.

The second victim was killed in January of the following year. She was Emily Jackson, a housewife with three children. Her husband Sydney was a roofing specialist, and she used to drive him to work in their small van. What Sydney didn't know was that, while he worked on people's roofs, his wife would drive to the red-light district of Leeds and solicit customers, using the back of the van to have sex, before picking him up from work. On the evening of 20 January, she failed to arrive to collect him, and Sydney took a taxi home.

The body of Emily Jackson was discovered the next morning, in a narrow alleyway. Her head was battered beyond recognition and her body was a mass of stab wounds – over fifty, all inflicted with a weapon that was similar to a screwdriver. It had been a frenzied attack, with little regard for the attacker's safety as a main road ran nearby and the killer risked being seen. But despite repeated requests for assistance by the police no witnesses came forward.

Detectives feared they had a maniac serial killer on their hands, but investigations drew a blank as the killer went quiet. It was over a year before the next murder occurred, on 5 February 1977.

The victim this time was Irene Richardson. She was separated from her husband and her children had been fostered. She wasn't a professional prostitute, but rather a woman who had fallen on hard times, and had taken to hanging around street corners, trying to pick up passing trade. Because her patch was far from the city centre she was unaware of the police warnings to the prostitutes of Leeds, and when a bearded man picked her up one night, she had no idea that she was on a one-way trip. He took her to Roundhay Park in Leeds, where a jogger found her body the next morning as it lay near a sports pavilion. Once again, there were horrific wounds to her abdomen and genital area, where the frenzied attacker had carved gouges from her flesh with a tool of some kind, and her skull had been smashed.

Sutcliffe lived in Bradford, and had so far perpetrated his crimes in Leeds. However, he was now getting bolder, as his next killing took place in his hometown. Tina Atkinson was a well-known prostitute in the Bradford red-light area, and she picked up Sutcliffe on 23 April, taking him to her flat in Oak Avenue.

Her body was discovered the next morning by a friend, who found the door of her flat open when he called. Tina was lying on the bed: once again, her skull had been smashed, and she had been the victim of a vicious sexual assault with a sharp instrument, though she hadn't been raped.

Two months later, Sutcliffe struck again. After an evening dancing at a club in the centre of Leeds, Jayne MacDonald was on her way home when the Ripper attacked her as she passed Roundhay Park. He hit her from behind, and dragged her into the park, where once again he subjected the victim to a frenzied sexual attack.

Jayne was only sixteen and was not a prostitute. It is possible that Sutcliffe mistook her for a prostitute as she lived only six doors from Wilma McCann, in the heart of the red-light district. After his capture, he had the audacity to apologise for this killing, as if he considered it a mistake in his mission to kill prostitutes.

A month later, the Ripper tried to strike again in Bradford. On 27 July, Maureen Long was walking through the centre of town when Sutcliffe drew up alongside her, and propositioned her. As she tried to get in the car, he hit her. But something must have disturbed him as he was dragging her unconscious form from the glare of the street lamps, and he left her in the road and drove away. After a brain operation, Maureen Long was able to describe her attacker as driving a white Ford Cortina, and having blond hair – a fact which misled police for a long time.

As police activity stepped up in Yorkshire, Sutcliffe broke with his previous pattern and crossed the Pennines to Lancashire in order to perpetrate his next crime.

During the early morning of 1 October he encountered Jean Jordan, a twenty-year-old Scots prostitute. She had run away from Motherwell at the age of fifteen, and had been picked up by a chef – Alan Royle – who worked in Manchester. They had lived together since then and had two children, but the relationship had been deteriorating, and nights that she had claimed were spent with friends were in fact nights working as a prostitute to earn some money.

Now Jean took her punter to Southern Cemetery to have sex. There he partially stripped her and killed her with a force described by police as 'exceptional'. Once again, there were lacerations consistent with the use of a screwdriver. There was an assault of a sexual nature, yet once again no rape. Her clothes were scattered around the site of the killing. The coroner's examination later revealed that she had been hit on the head eleven times, and had received twenty-four stab wounds. Horrifically, she hadn't been naked at the time of her death. About eight days after her death, the killer had returned to the body and ripped the remaining clothes off before slashing the corpse: the abdomen had been torn open, and a long wound ran from her left shoulder across the entire body, ending at her right knee.

It was obviously the work of the same killer as the Yorkshire murders.

Jean Jordan gave police their first concrete clue. In the dead woman's handbag was a new £5 note, which was traceable to a batch issued in Shipley, Yorkshire, only five days before the murder. Further investigation revealed that the note was part of the batch used for the payroll of T & W H Clark (Holdings) Ltd. All the drivers working for this firm were interviewed. One of those drivers was Peter Sutcliffe.

However, despite intense questioning, nothing was uncovered to link any of the drivers with the note, and the hunt switched elsewhere. Sutcliffe's incredible self-belief had enabled him to brazen out a police interrogation that had unnerved many of his workmates. So much so that one policeman remarked that if there was any chance of it being one of the drivers, it certainly wouldn't be Sutcliffe!

Sutcliffe would later be questioned a second time by detectives after his car was logged as one which had visited the red-light district of Bradford more than seven times in a few weeks. His explanation that he had to pass through the district on his way to work sometimes was accepted. The link between the car and the man previously interviewed over the five-pound note found on a victim was not established. During that interview Sutcliffe had been wearing the same boots that he had worn when killing Josephine

Whitaker – an impression of which had been moulded in plaster at the scene of the crime!

At the beginning of 1978, the hunt for the Ripper had become the largest police operation ever to be mounted in the north of England. It was headed by George Oldfield, who began to take each new outrage as a personal affront, and treated the case as if it was a personal challenge between himself and the Ripper. Oldfield was an old-school type of copper: he had worked his way up from uniform, pounding the beat, and had strong Yorkshire morals and attitudes. Catching the killer would become an obsession and would even lead to him having a heart attack.

Meanwhile, the police were following up any lead, and floundering under mountains of paper work.

On the last day of January 1978, Sutcliffe struck again. This time his victim was Helen Rytka, an eighteen-year-old prostitute who worked out of Huddersfield.

Helen and her twin Rita had spent most of their short lives in care, and had decided at the age of seventeen that prostitution was an easier way of earning money than working in the factories that seemed to be their destiny. They began by hanging around on street corners, waiting to be picked up by passing cars. On the evening of the 31st, Helen got a customer around nine in the evening, and Rita shortly afterwards. When Rita returned, Helen was still absent. This in itself was no cause for concern, so

Rita went home and thought no more of it. But when Helen was still missing the following day, she began to worry.

That morning, a lorry driver passing a timber yard noticed a pair of lacy black briefs on the ground. He handed them in to the foreman, who thought it would be fun to hang them on a nail in the yard. Not so funny when, two days later, Rita Rytka reported her missing sister to the police. Given their known profession, the police immediately launched a hunt for what they presumed to be another Ripper victim.

The timber yard was situated near the Rytkas' flat, and was one of the first places searched by the police. Helen's body was found beneath a sheet of corrugated asbestos in an archway, shielded by a pile of timber. She was naked, and her body had been subjected to numerous stab wounds. She had been hit over the head to render her unconscious, probably with a hammer. This time, the killer had had sex with her, but she had been dead by the time the killer had achieved orgasm.

Ten days before, a prostitute called Yvonne Pearson had disappeared. Leaving her children with a babysitter, she had set out for the centre of Bradford to ply her trade, and had not returned home. It was two months before her body was found. A man crossing a piece of waste ground noticed something protruding from underneath an overturned settee. Looking more closely the man was horrified to see it was a human arm.

Medical evidence showed that her head had been battered so violently that her skull had shattered into twenty-one separate pieces. The killer had rammed stuffing from the settee down her throat to keep her quiet. However, there were no stab wounds. This left police in doubt as to whether or not this was a victim of the Ripper. (After his capture, Sutcliffe confessed that he had been disturbed that night during his grisly ritual by a car pulling up on the waste ground.)

It was 16 May and the Ripper was back in Manchester. Vera Millward was a forty-year-old prostitute whose regular client failed to turn up on time. So she left her two children in the care of her common-law husband and set off for the city centre in the early evening to find a replacement.

At 1.15 the next morning a man visiting the Royal Infirmary heard three screams and a cry for help. Alerted, he waited for another sound to give him direction, but nothing was forthcoming. When it was light, Vera Millward's body was found near a flower bed in the Infirmary grounds. This was a favoured site among the prostitutes, and so was obviously the place for which she had headed. She had been stabbed numerous times, and her skull had virtually disintegrated under the rain of violent blows.

It was now the first letters arrived. They were written in an illiterate and scrawling hand, gloating on the murders and the fact that the police had so far failed to find any clues. Because they purported to be from the Ripper himself, an effort was made to trace the stationery on which they were written. But there are always hoax letters from sick minds during murder investigations, so what made this worthy of such an effort? The police claimed that there were details in the letters about the mutilations – details the police had withheld and that they presumed no one but the killer could know.

The killings continued as the press splashed the letters over their front pages, as they arrived. The country was convinced that the Ripper was contacting the police, and goading them on. He even referred to himself as 'Jack' and seemed to be enjoying his infamous celebrity.

By June 1979 there had been three letters. There had also been another killing.

Up to this point the victims had all been prostitutes, except for the case of Jayne MacDonald who seemed to have been cruelly unlucky simply because she lived in a red-light district. But now the whole focus of the Ripper's operations changed. The next two murders were women who in no way could have been mistaken for prostitutes: they were not in red-light areas, and were snatched from the streets rather than being propositioned. To detectives, this represented an even more dangerous development in the Ripper saga: from a killer obsessed with prostitution, he was now a random serial killer. Trying to increase security, in Leeds and Bradford particularly, would be well-nigh impossible. Before they had increased patrols in the red-light districts, now they had the whole cities to cover with a depleted force.

Josephine Whitaker was nineteen, and had spent the evening of 4 April watching television at her grandparents' house in Halifax. Towards midnight, she left to walk home, and it was as she crossed Saville Park that the Ripper struck. He hit her so hard that her skull was fractured from ear to ear, and then pulled up her dress and stabbed her several times in the genitals as a bizarre parody of sexual intercourse in a manic attack with a specially sharpened screwdriver. Forensic evidence showed that the screwdriver was covered in rust.

This time the killer left behind one important clue – traces of machine oil were found on the body. The police inferred that the killer worked for an engineering firm – as indeed Sutcliffe did, but he had already been questioned and eliminated from the inquiries...

The next murder took place in September. On the first of the month Barbara Leach, a student at Bradford University, spent the evening at the Mannville Arms, a pub near the university. She left at about one in the morning, having told friends that she wanted to get a breath of fresh air before returning home to her flat in nearby Grove Terrace.

She never reached it, and her body was found a day later, hidden behind a dustbin in a back alley, crudely covered with a carpet held down by broken bricks. The modus operandi of the Ripper was obvious, and forensic evidence confirmed that the multiple stab wounds on the body had been inflicted with the same rusty screwdriver that had been used on Josephine Whitaker. This was the first concrete proof that the same man was responsible.

The police were now convinced that the man they were after was a Geordie. On 26 June a cassette had arrived at operational headquarters, addressed in the same scrawling hand as the letters. The tape, later released to the press and played repeatedly on radio and television, made for chilling listening. The speaker was a man with a Geordie accent, who spoke slowly and seemed to be reading his message from a prepared statement. He spoke of the murders, introducing himself with the words 'I'm Jack'. He claimed he would go on committing the crimes, and taunted George Oldfield, vowing the police would never find him. It was more likely that he would get sick of the crimes, and 'top' himself.

It was at this point that the psychics Doris Stokes and Gerald Croiset were consulted by the press. Croiset was already known to the police through his involvement with investigations in Europe and the USA, and Doris Stokes was a celebrity, the most famous psychic in the country at that time. Although she was sometimes clairvoyant, she was more famous as a clairaudiant and gave recitals at large concert halls where she would contact the dead, and pass on messages to those in the hall who hoped to hear from

deceased loved ones. She was often accused of
trickery, yet despite the controversy surrounding
her, Doris Stokes had a wealth of psychic experience
that was undoubtedly genuine, and was happy to co-
operate when the *Sunday People* approached her. The
results of her psychometric readings on the 'I'm Jack'
tape were published in the edition dated 1 July 1979.

As the reporter, a photographer and a sketch artist
sat with her in her sitting room, Doris held the tapes
and letters that the newspaper had obtained from the
police. Doris did not operate in the traditional way,
there was no darkened room; instead, she made tea
for the newspaper delegation, and sat chatting with
them about their jobs as she handled the tapes and
letters. She would only break off when an impression
struck her. Doris received a clear vision of the man
she thought was the Ripper, and was able to help the
artist hired by the newspaper to produce a sketch of
the man she saw.

He was clean-shaven, with a scar on one cheek, and
a twitching eye – presumably a nervous tic. She then
claimed that the man's dead mother had appeared to
her in order to give her more information about him.
His name was Ronnie or Johnnie, and he lived in the
Sunderland area. He was a long-distance lorry driver
who was still based in the area of his birth, and his job
enabled him to travel about unnoticed. She also
named a street in the town. This was not published,
but the information was passed on to the police.

This was all deeply embarrassing to a lorry driver

named Ronnie Metcalf, who lived in a street simi-
larly named to the one Doris mentioned, and also had
a scar on his face. In fact, he bore such a resemblance
to the published identikit picture that he went to the
police voluntarily for questioning, as he was being
harassed by neighbours, workmates, and even people
in the streets! It was soon obvious that this unfortunate man had nothing whatsoever to do with the
case and the police made a statement exonerating
him from any involvement with the letters, the tape,
and the murders. Of course, at the time detectives
still thought all three were linked.

The *Sun*, not a newspaper to be outdone by the
Sunday People, sought out their own psychic, and
sent one of their journalists to Holland to interview
Gerald Croiset in his Utrecht home.

Without being aware of Doris' revelations, Croiset
psychometrised the tape and described a man who
looked remarkably similar to the identikit picture,
with the addition that the man had long, straight
hair. Croiset pored over aerial photographs of the
Sunderland area until finally settling on one particular district. Concentrating further, he was able to
pinpoint a block of flats in which he claimed the man
lived.

Doris, meanwhile, had given the matter more
thought and had decided that the man's name was
not Ronnie or Johnnie – she was now sure that it was
Peter. Ironically, she was correct in this.

The police, however, were unwilling to pursue

these findings further. They had already had to apologise to the harassed Ronnie Metcalf and presumably felt that the evidence of a psychic was of no use to them. So Doris Stokes and Gerald Croiset proved to be useless in capturing Peter Sutcliffe, which is not surprising since they were psychometrising hoax material. Any impressions they picked up would have nothing to do with Sutcliffe; instead, they would refer entirely to the hoaxer.

The killings continued.

Before the murder of Barbara Leach in September, there was a killing that wasn't initially attributed to the Ripper, and was only solved when he later confessed in full to his crimes. It happened on 20 August when Marguerite Walls, a Department of Education official in Pudsey, was returning home to Farsley at 10.45 at night after working late when the Ripper attacked her. He knocked her unconscious, then dragged her into a garden, ripping off most of her clothes. He broke three of her ribs by kneeling on her as he strangled her with a piece of rope before attempting to hide the body under grass cuttings. He later told police that he didn't have his knife or screwdriver with him that night.

In October 1979 he attacked a student from Singapore, Dr Uphadya Bandara, on her way home from a course at the Leeds Nuffield Centre. He pulled her to him by looping a rope around her neck before knocking her unconscious and dragging her down the street. For some reason he changed his mind – he even claimed later that he had apologised to her! – and ran away, leaving her. A few weeks later, on 5 November, he attacked again and was almost caught.

Theresa Sykes walked to the bottom of the garden with her boyfriend to say goodnight. He left her standing at the gate as he made his way home. Theresa was sixteen and in love: she stood looking at the moonlit sky, thinking about her future together with her boyfriend. It was an idyll from which she was suddenly rudely awakened. A man moved towards her from the shadows. She had no idea how long he had been waiting there, and was too shocked to cry out. In the half-light she saw him raise his arm up in the air, and heard a whistling sound as something came towards her. She managed to drag herself, almost paralysed by fear, to one side, so he only caught her a glancing blow. There had been something heavy in his fist, and the pain made her scream as blood ran down her face.

The man raised his arm again, but was stayed by the sound of footsteps, and the yelling of her name. Theresa's boyfriend, only just around the corner, had heard the scream and was racing back as fast as he could. He found Theresa unconscious on the ground, and a man disappearing into the night.

Seeing Theresa's father come out of the house to help, the young man didn't hesitate: he raced after the vanishing attacker. He was younger and fitter, and was gaining ground but the attacker dived into his car and screeched off just as he reached it, a half-yard too slow to make the difference. He returned to Theresa: she was more important now. Meanwhile, in his car, Peter Sutcliffe was shaking at such a narrow escape. He wouldn't return to Huddersfield in a hurry.

It was over a year before he attempted any more attacks – and committed his final murder.

In the meantime, another psychic had entered the fray, and she was able to offer evidence that would have successfully led to Sutcliffe's arrest – if it had been heeded.

Nella Jones was well known as a medium and psychic from her concert hall appearances, though she had not yet had any dealings with the police. She was working on her autobiography, ghost-written by journalist Shirley Davenport, and it was to Ms Davenport that she initially confided what she had experienced.

Watching a news report on television about the Ripper, she began to get impressions of the man who had been committing the crimes. A series of images had appeared like a second skin on the screen that had no relation to the report she could still hear. To anyone else this would be frightening and strange, but Nella had received visions for as long as she could remember.

She was sure that his name was Peter, and also that he was a long-distance lorry driver. She was positive that he came from Bradford itself – scene of so many of the crimes – and that he lived in an elevated house numbered six. Ms Davenport asked her what she meant by an elevated house, and Nella explained that she was sure that the house was raised in some way, possibly because it was in a road built upon a steep hill. And she was certain of the number. She could also see the truck he drove for a living. It had the letter C on the cab door as part of the company's name. She was absolutely certain of these things.

The most chilling of her insights she left until last: the Ripper would kill once more, and the date she could see was 17 November.

Shirley Davenport urged her to go to the police; but after the way in which Doris Stokes and Gerald Croiset had been dismissed, Nella Jones was unwilling to set herself up for the same sort of treatment. None the less, Nella did go to the police after some persuasion, and they took down her statement. Unfortunately, it was not followed up. Yet the name of the firm Sutcliffe worked for was T & W H Clark (Holdings) Ltd – the name which is emblazoned on the cab of all their lorries. And Peter Sutcliffe lived at no. 6 Garden Lanes, Bradford – a road which is built on a hill – with several steps up to the front door.

Tragically, Nella's last prediction came true: there was one more murder, and it took place on 17 November.

Jacqueline Hill was a twenty-year-old student at

Leeds University who had attended a meeting of voluntary probation officers, and had left to catch a bus home at approximately nine in the evening. Just an hour later her handbag was found by an Iraqi student as he passed near a patch of waste ground, and he took the bag to the police. There was a search, but it was a foul night with howling wind and driving rain, and nothing was found.

Next morning when the search was resumed, Jacqueline's body was found. The usual trademarks of the Ripper were there: she had been beaten unconscious from behind, and her body stripped and stabbed numerous times. One of the wounds was in her eye, and after his capture Sutcliffe stated that she seemed to be looking at him reproachfully, so he drove the blade of the screwdriver into her eye to stop it...

On 2 January 1981, a prostitute was approached by a bearded man in a Rover who asked her how much she charged for full sex. She replied £10 and got into the front of the car. He talked to her for a while about his troubled home life before asking her to get in the back of the car. She refused, which may well have saved her, as the man was Sutcliffe, whose habit was to strike his victims from behind. He attempted to have sex with her, but was impotent.

It was at this point that a police car drove up, and the officers stopped to question him. He told the prostitute to say that she was his girlfriend, and gave his name as Peter Williams.

The two policemen – Sergeant Robert Ring and PC Robert Hydes – were carrying out random checks on cars. Sergeant Ring took down the licence number, and radioed in to have it checked on the police computer. PC Hydes sat in the back of the Rover.

'Look, mate, I'm dying for a piss. All right if I go over there?' asked the man claiming to be Williams, pointing to an oil tank a few feet away from the car.

Hydes tutted. 'If you hurry. And don't try anything clever, son, 'cause we've got the car, and I'll be after you.'

'Cheers,' said 'Williams', trotting off. He pretended to urinate, while Hydes tried to keep an eye on him without appearing to be staring. His eye caught that of the prostitute.

'Like watching men piss, do you?' she giggled, pleased at his obvious embarrassment.

Sergeant Ring came over to the car. 'We've got a right one here,' he said to Hydes. 'The number doesn't belong to this.' He banged the roof of the Rover. 'We'd better take this bastard in. More bloody paperwork!'

He returned to the patrol car. Williams/Sutcliffe sat back in the driver's seat, and Hydes told him to follow them to the station.

'You're in the shit, son.'

When they arrived at the station, Sutcliffe again asked for permission to urinate, which was granted with sarcastic comments about his weak bladder. Then he was ordered to turn out his pockets. Among the assorted belongings was a length of clothes line.

'That's a funny thing to carry around, ain't it?' asked the duty sergeant. Sutcliffe shrugged. When he had been booked in and taken to the cells, the duty sergeant began to book in his companion. Realising she was a prostitute, he stopped writing and looked up at her. 'I think you may have had a lucky escape, love,' he said quietly. He turned to Hydes. 'Get CID down here, son. This bloke might be that bastard Jack.'

Once CID officers came to question Sutcliffe, word spread like wildfire through the station. It was possible that public enemy number one was sitting in their cells.

During his initial questioning, Sutcliffe lied consistently about the prostitute and his reasons for carrying the clothes line. Sergeant Ring decided to check out the place where Sutcliffe was supposed to have relieved himself the night before.

The next morning he returned to the site of the arrest. He remembered the oil storage tank, and began to search the area for anything Sutcliffe might have thrown away or dumped. In leaves near the oil storage tank he found a ball-headed hammer and a knife.

When he returned to the station he searched the cistern in the station lavatory, where he found a second knife.

Faced with the evidence, Sutcliffe must have realised that he couldn't explain away the weapons, so he confessed. Initially he confessed to eleven murders instead of thirteen – perhaps he had genuinely lost count of the true total.

In the cab of his lorry there was a card that had these words written on it: 'In this truck is a man whose latent genius, if unleashed, would rock the nation, whose dynamic energy would overpower those around him. Better let him sleep?' He later claimed that the devil drove him in his crimes, but it was more likely that he had simply found a sexual thrill in the killings that had become like a drug – a substitute for sex. It had become almost normal to him to commit such atrocities.

The trial of Peter Sutcliffe began on 5 May 1981. He pleaded not guilty on grounds of diminished responsibility. However, the Attorney General, Sir Michael Havers, stressed that Sutcliffe had behaved quite normally in the early stages of interrogation, laughing at the idea of mental illness or abnormality, and had introduced the notion of hearing voices only when it became obvious that there was no escape.

The jury agreed with the Attorney General, and on 22 May Peter Sutcliffe was found guilty on all charges and jailed for life, with the recommendation that he serve at least thirty years.

In the summer of 1992 the *Sunday People* revealed that since his imprisonment, Sutcliffe has become a regular correspondent of several women – one of them the elderly woman who used to run a cafe in

Sunderland that was frequented by Sutcliffe. Her name is Olive Curry and she claims that Sutcliffe had a friend who frequented the cafe with him. He was a twitchy man, named Ronnie, a local with a Geordie accent. This fits not only the voice on the 'I'm Jack' tape, but also the clairvoyant readings of Doris Stokes and Gerald Croiset and could account for his in-depth knowledge of the killings which had made the police take his communications seriously. Olive Curry also says that Sutcliffe has been hinting to her in his letters that he had an accomplice on some of the crimes, and that this man could possibly have been that accomplice.

Is this just Sutcliffe playing some twisted game with an old woman foolish enough to correspond with him? Or is he revelling in having in some small way defeated the police?

After the story appeared Sutcliffe was asked if he had been lying to Olive Curry. He claims he was. Perhaps someone should take into account that this man has lied consistently before. Every story he tells needs checking if the bottom of this mystery is ever to be reached.

Although both Doris Stokes and Gerald Croiset are dead, their evidence is still on record, and it is still possible to use that to try to trace the man who made the hoax tape and wrote the letters. It is possible that he is the same man as this friend of Sutcliffe's named Ronnie, and also possible that he may have witnessed, if not taken part in, some of the atrocities.

Could it be that Doris Stokes and Gerald Croiset could yet reach out from beyond the grave and help to catch a hoaxer and possible accomplice to murder?

From Russia with Terror

It was a cold and frosty day in Fryazino, in the USSR. Inessa Tchurina, nine years old and keen on ice skating, looked out of the window to the streets below. She would have to wrap up warm.

Inessa dressed and hurried from her tiny bedroom to the small kitchen, where her father was drinking tea before leaving for his factory shift. She begged her father to let her go skating as it was not a school day. All her friends were bound to be at the open-air rink in the town and she would make sure she stayed with them. Would he let her go?

Inessa's father turned to her mother, standing over the stove. She said nothing. He knew that she didn't like the girl to go out on her own. Inessa was an only child, and her mother always feared that something would happen to her. They had waited so long, almost losing hope of children, before she had arrived. Their little miracle, she always said.

'Why not let her go? She'll be all right. It's broad daylight, and the rink will be full of children.'

Inessa watched her mother carefully; still she stood

with her back to them. She gave the slightest shrug.

'As long as she is careful. What harm can it do?'

Inessa leapt up and down with joy, hugging her father, running to her mother and hugging her too. She thanked them profusely, and rushed to her room to get her skates.

'You come back here and have something warm inside you first!' called her mother. She glanced at her husband, who was smiling indulgently at her. 'Can't have her getting cold,' she said brusquely.

What could possibly be the connection between a murder in Russia and an English housewife? The story begins in December 1979 . . .

Inessa Tchurina, a pretty nine-year-old who lived with her family just outside Moscow, had been allowed by her parents to go ice skating at a rink near her home because she was going in a party of friends, and they thought she would be safe.

And so she probably would have been, if not for the fact that some of her friends got bored easily and it was not long before there were only a few children, and then just Inessa. She was relishing the skating, and didn't want to leave when the others did. Her friends said goodbye and left – never to see her again.

It was late in the afternoon when Yuri Tchurina returned home from his shift at the factory. He was tired and bored. All he wanted was to eat and then watch television before falling asleep. If he could get a better job, better money, then he could do more for his family. But there were no other jobs.

When he opened his front door, he was greeted by the sight of his wife staring at him.

'What's wrong?' he asked, every muscle in his body tensing up. He had never seen her look so worried.

'I thought you were Inessa.' Her voice was reduced to a harsh whisper by her worry and fear.

'She isn't home yet?' Even as he asked, he knew it was a stupid question; he could see it in his wife's haggard expression. 'Then we must look for her.'

Despite his tiredness, Yuri went out into town, headed for the ice rink. It was virtually empty with just a few desultory skaters making the most of the failing light. He stopped them and asked if they had seen his daughter. They shrugged as he described her; they hadn't seen any little girl answering to that description.

He trudged home under the yellow sodium glare of the street lighting. He took the route he knew Inessa must take to get home, hoping that he would see her, that she had gone to friend's house, that something had delayed her. But there was nothing.

Slowly and wearily he climbed the stairs to his apartment, hoping against hope that Inessa would have come home while he was out looking for her. He knew that this was not so when he opened the door to his wife's desolate glare.

The Tchurinas contacted the police. And so began the usual process of searching for a missing person:

people were questioned, any suspicious characters in the vicinity of the rink checked out. The police spent several days on the streets, asking if anyone even just passing by the rink had seen Inessa or any man or woman hanging about, watching. One or two remembered the party of giggling young children but no one could recall Inessa on her own.

Searches were made of rivers, streams and rubbish dumps: if the worst had happened, there would be a corpse to be discovered. Again, the search yielded nothing. It was as if Inessa had vanished from the face of the earth. It was a lonely and sad Christmas for Inessa's parents.

In the new year, Inessa's father, desperate to try anything, including the paranormal, approached Viktor Adamenko, one of the country's leading parapsychologists, with an impassioned plea for help.

'I'm not saying that the police are no good, don't misunderstand me, comrade. It's just that they have tried everything they know. They have questioned everyone, they have searched everywhere, but there is nothing.' Tears came into Yuri Tchurina's eyes, and his tone softened almost to a whisper, 'My wife, she no longer leaves the house. At Christmas she had the presents we had bought for our Inessa, and she stared at them for two days. Not one word did she speak to me. She's a broken woman. I don't think our baby is alive any more, but even so I think it would help my wife if she was found, and we could say goodbye to her.'

Adamenko, sitting behind his desk, shrugged. 'But what do you expect me to do about it? I am not a policeman, neither am I a magician.'

Tchurina leant forward over the desk. His tone was quiet. 'I know that. But I am not a stupid man. I only work in a factory, but I always try to improve myself. I know that there are powers that some people possess, and I know that you study them. I have heard of such people helping to find those who are missing. I appeal to you, if not for me then for my wife – let one of these people look for my daughter.'

Adamenko sat in silence for some time after Yuri Tchurina had left his office. It would be irregular for him to step into a police case. However, his thoughts turned towards England, and a man called Benson Herbert. Viktor and Herbert were long-time correspondents on the subject of psychic phenomena and both men had made studies of the paranormal. Adamenko knew that Herbert had studied a psychic who would be perfect for such a case. She was a housewife living near the New Forest in England, one of the best practising psychics in the world and one of the most thoroughly researched. Her name was Suzanne Padfield.

This would give him the opportunity to study her findings – it had been a long time since he had had such an opportunity. He picked up the red telephone on his desk. 'I want to place a call to England. Get me a line.'

* * *

Suzanne Padfield had been aware of her powers from an early age and was not scared by them. As a child she lived in Wells, Somerset, in a house that had a reputation as haunted, and where strange things happened. On one occasion a clothes horse – complete with clothes – quite simply vanished; several other objects disappeared. And things happened around young Suzanne, such as the ghost that appeared to visit her at night. She would hear footsteps approaching her bed and feel a hand touch her, but she could see nothing. When she told her parents about it, they were dismissive and told her not to make things up. Eventually they bowed to the inevitable, and moved house to escape the hauntings.

But the hauntings followed Suzanne. At the new house, she and her sister would lie awake at night watching an array of coloured lights dance across the ceiling. Frequently, as she tried to sleep, she would find herself flung out of bed. Her parents put this down to earth tremors – until they were told that this house, too, had a reputation for being haunted.

Suzanne seemed to attract these phenomena; her psychic powers magnified anything that lurked within the house, and made it manifest itself.

As she grew older, she began to take her powers for granted, and was not disturbed by anything that occurred around her. She hadn't thought of subjecting her powers to investigation, and only came into contact with Benson Herbert through the long arm of fate.

When she was eighteen, Suzanne was indulging in one of her favourite hobbies, archaeology. She was involved in a dig at Cadbury Castle, and found herself in a trench next to a man who started talking about his interest in the paranormal. She confessed to her own interest in the subject, and told him how she could see pictures when she held things.

The man gave her a locket that had been around his neck. As she held it, she was able to tell him that it was Viking, and that it had been dug up from under water. When she handed it back, the man confirmed that she had been right in everything she'd said. He introduced himself as Mervyn Hinge, and told her about the Paraphysical Laboratory, which had only just opened. It was to be run by a man named Benson Herbert, with whom he had been associated in the past. He invited Suzanne to take part in experiments there. He told her that her expenses would be paid, and she would be able to live in as she was tested.

It seems to have been this offer of accommodation that swung Suzanne into accepting Hinge's offer, as she was living in a run-down cottage at this time. She was existing on very little money, and the opportunity to improve her finances could not have come at a more opportune moment.

However, Benson Herbert was not exactly what she was expecting. Here was a man held in distaste and suspicion by some of his fellow scientists because he attended seances. He had also gone into a trance and spoken with a voice claiming to be the spirit of a thousand-year-old Chinese. And there was the time when he had succeeded in levitating a table with the medium R. G. Medhurst, and had nearly broken his own jaw when the table had flown towards him and he had failed to duck! However, despite his dabblings in the world of Spiritualism, he was still a scientist at heart and was convinced that the levitating table and the Chinese spirit were products of his own mind.

Suzanne stayed with him, and they produced some remarkable results – the most extraordinary of which have much in common with the tricks that made Uri Geller a household name. As Geller was adept at halting cable cars and escalators, so Padfield could affect the motion of clocks – she could make them 'clunk' at regular intervals; in fact she was able to say out loud that the clock would clunk a set number of times after she had counted to three, and this the clock would do, as if to order.

After twelve years Padfield severed her links with the laboratory in 1978. Her interest in her work had waned since she had been called in by the police to help locate a missing girl, Alison Chadwick, in 1974. It had been a particularly distressing case as the little ten-year-old had been sexually assaulted and strangled. Suzanne's visions during psychometry had been so traumatic that she felt as though she wanted to cut herself off from her power. And her marriage to physicist Ted Bastin in 1975 had led to her also spending less time in research.

Suzanne hadn't spoken to Benson Herbert for

almost two years when the phone call came one morning in January 1980. As she and Herbert indulged in idle chatter, she wondered about the real reason for his call. He asked her if she was still using her powers.

'Depends what you mean,' she said warily. 'Things come, things go, you know?'

There was a pause. Then: 'So you wouldn't be interested in doing something for me?'

Suzanne hesitated; she knew what he was going to say, not from precognition, but because she was only too well aware of the way in which he had tried to persuade her to do things in the past.

'Suzanne? Are you still there?'

She replied in the affirmative, her voice flat.

'I've had a call from Russia. You remember Viktor Adamenko, my colleague in the USSR?' She didn't reply, so he continued: 'He's been approached by someone to help find a missing schoolgirl. He hasn't anyone under study who could do such a thing ... he remembered what you did with the Alison Chadwick thing.'

As she stood in her hall, Suzanne's mind went back to the Alison Chadwick case, and she remembered the fear and revulsion that had wracked her body during psychometry, how she had nearly fainted as she relived the terror and pain of Alison's last moments. She didn't want to go through that again.

She began to say no, then stopped as she thought of the parents of this missing girl. She knew nothing of them, but she could recall Alison's parents and their anguish. If there was anything she could do to stop anyone from feeling that way ever again...

'Okay, I'll do it. No promises, though,' Suzanne said. She didn't want to be told anything about the case, in order to have no preconceived ideas. 'Get him to send me something of hers, and I'll see what I can do.'

A few weeks passed. Suzanne had heard nothing more from Benson Herbert, and assumed that either things were taking a long time, or the case had been resolved.

One day a small package with a Hampshire postmark arrived. Suzanne carried it into the kitchen and turned it over: there was no return address. Using a knife, she slit along one end of the package, and took the contents out...

The shock hit her like a wave of nausea and fear. It jolted her physically, and she dropped the knife. Everything seemed to swim around her.

The package was from Herbert. In it was a sample of the girl's handwriting – some of her school work – and a few objects spared by her grieving family – a couple of pencils and a hairbrush. These clattered to the floor. A photograph of a pretty little dark-haired girl floated down to join them. Suzanne held the sheets of lined paper covered with Russian characters in her hand, and these acted as a gateway into the world of Inessa Tchurina.

Suzanne Padfield was no longer in England, but in the town of Fryazino, outside Moscow; she now inhabited the body of Inessa Tchurina. She was skating at the rink, alone: all her friends had gone, but she wanted to stay a bit longer. A large, thick-set man with a bushy beard was observing her. He appeared to be watching only her, and smiled as she skated around. Although she knew she mustn't talk to strangers, she liked the fact that he was looking at her and tried to skate better, executing moves that she had often practised. She wanted him to like her skating.

When she had finished, and had left the rink, the man came up to her. He started telling her how good she was, and that she should practise more – perhaps she would make the Olympic team. She liked the man a lot, and when he asked her to go home with him, she said that she would. She knew she shouldn't, but he was obviously such a nice man she couldn't come to any harm. He told her he had some new skates that he wanted her to see; they were the latest kind, just on the market. With skates like these she would soon be a champion. No one had paid this kind of attention to her skating before, and she was flattered. Her mother and father loved her, but they didn't like her to skate, as it meant going out on her own, and they feared for her safety. But all Inessa wanted to do was skate. And if it meant that she met nice people like this bearded giant, then what harm could befall her?

When they got to the man's house, he only wanted to sit and talk to Inessa. She became impatient and asked him where the skates were. He said he would get them in a little while but just wanted to talk a little first. He came and sat next to her and began to stroke her hair. Inessa became worried and said she wanted to go. The man asked her to stay, but she became more and more vehement about leaving. Suzanne realised that though Inessa knew what the man looked like and how to get to his house from the rink, she didn't know his name. As Inessa became more and more frightened, Suzanne could feel the terror rising in herself, she was feeling Inessa's fear.

The little girl begged the man to let her go, but he was worried: would she say anything to her parents? She became more distressed, refusing to answer him. She tried to run for the front door, and the man grabbed hold of her. Inessa struggled to be free, and the man held her firmly, his hands went around her throat, and his grip became tighter. He begged Inessa not to struggle and make a noise, but in her panic she tried to scream. The man's grip grew stronger, and Inessa began to black out. Suzanne Padfield believed that she, too, would black out.

But suddenly the whole picture changed. It was as though Suzanne was now on the outside, watching a film – or perhaps, even, she was seeing things as the disembodied spirit of Inessa would have seen them.

Inessa was blacking out, but still she struggled. The man panicked, and hit her on the side of the head with such a strong blow that it broke her neck. She was dead. Her murderer was shocked: he hadn't meant to kill her, he only wanted to have sex with her. In his twisted mind, he had never considered that she would object provided he was nice to her. Her terror had spread to him, and he had acted in haste, and now she was dead. He felt a great sorrow that communicated itself to Suzanne Padfield. This was soon overtaken by a feeling of panic and a desire to hide his crime. To be caught would mean death. He must act now to save himself.

He wrapped the corpse in a blue sheet or blanket. Things began to get hazy at this point, possibly because the link with Inessa was fading as her spirit departed further from her body. The killer then carried it from the house in a sack, and caught a bus into the country. He travelled far out of town before leaving the bus, and dumping the body in a river. He returned to his house and shaved off his beard...

At this point the vision faded, and Suzanne found herself returning to the present, and to her kitchen. Though she felt drained by the experience, she tried to rally her thoughts and write down everything she could remember. Her description of the man was particularly good: in his mid-thirties, thick-set and burly, with dark brown hair and bushy eyebrows. She was able to describe him both bearded and clean-shaven.

Suzanne sent her descriptions to Benson Herbert

who forwarded the material to Viktor Adamenko. Adamenko took it to the police. He was a respected scientist, and the Soviet police were more inclined than their western counterparts to listen to the evidence of psychics.

Detectives set up a search for the body within a fifty-mile radius of Fryazino, along the bus routes. It was not long before a corpse was found – wrapped in a blue blanket. It was so badly decomposed as to be unidentifiable.

At the same time, a list of suspects was being drawn up from the names collated at the time of the original investigation. Included among them was a labourer in his mid-thirties, who corresponded to Suzanne Padfield's description and only had a shaky alibi for the day in question. When detectives discovered from neighbours that he had only recently shaved off a beard, they brought him in for questioning again. The burly policemen who collected him noticed that the route from his house to the ice rink was almost exactly as that described by the British psychic – who had never been to Russia in her life.

Faced with the discovery of the body and detectives who seemed to know so much about what had happened, the man broke down and confessed. His story was just as Suzanne had seen it: the only difference was that he had caught an electric tram from the town to the country, not a bus.

Some time afterwards Suzanne Padfield heard through Herbert that the killer had confessed, been sentenced to death and executed – but she never knew his name.

Subsequent attempts to find out the murderer's name were obstructed. When Benson Herbert asked Viktor Adamenko, the Russian apologetically told him that such information was not easily obtained, as the official line was that such crimes did not exist.

Suzanne considered her agonies had been worthwhile and she felt satisfied that she had helped to find not only the body, but the man responsible. Inessa Tchurina could rest in peace.

In a small cemetery on the outskirts of Fryazino, Yuri Tchurina watched with sadness as his wife placed a small bunch of wild flowers on their daughter's grave. Nothing could bring her back, but at least he had the satisfaction of knowing that justice had been done – all thanks to a woman he would never meet, and whose name he did not even know.

Panic on Campus

In June 1969 the psychic Peter Hurkos travelled to the town of Ypsilanti, in the state of Michigan. For two years, the area had been terrorised by a sex killer who, so far, had six known victims – perhaps more as yet undiscovered. Hurkos was called in by a local residents' group concerned at the lack of progress in the police investigation. He was recommended to the group by a local journalist who had heard of Hurkos' part in trapping sex killer Melvin Rees (see 'The Killer Played Jazz', pp. 175–94).

Hurkos had recently fallen on hard times – his stock was low with the police and audiences were tired of his stage performances – but the citizens' defence league of Ypsilanti were ready to try anything in their anxiety to rid themselves of the maniac who was killing off the town's female teenage population. They were only too happy to call for Hurkos' help.

Hurkos, for his part, was pleased to be getting the money for travel and expenses that they offered him –

it meant a little time without worries about finances. He agreed instantly to journey to Ypsilanti.

The story begins with the discovery of a body on 7 August 1967. The summer of love was in full swing, but it hadn't arrived for one young girl...

Two teenage boys were playing in a field on the outskirts of Superior Township, two miles north of Ypsilanti, when they heard a car pull up behind the ruined farmhouse that stood on the field. A door of the car slammed, and it screeched away. Curious, the boys crept up to the house and explored around the back.

They were greeted by the sight of a corpse, lying in the weeds around a rubbish heap. There was the sickly stench of decomposing flesh, and as they looked more closely they could see that the hands and feet had been hacked off the body. From the appalling state of the corpse – bloated and rotten in the sun – it must have been lying there for some time. Was the car connected to it, or just a coincidence that had drawn the boys to the spot? An answer to this question was never found.

A search of the area led police to the naked corpse's clothing, hidden under some boards – a dress and underwear, obviously ripped off the girl, who was naked when she was killed. She had been raped, then stabbed around the chest and neck at least twenty times, and the feet and hands had been hacked off after death. They were never found. Perhaps this was to delay identification, but it didn't work, as it wasn't long before the body gained a name.

The dead girl was eighteen-year-old Mary Fleszar, an Eastern Michigan University student who had gone missing on 10 July. There were no clues to her disappearance, which occurred as she was returning from classes. She seemed to have vanished into thin air.

Two days after the body had been identified, and while it was lying in a funeral home awaiting burial, a blue Chevrolet driven by a dark-haired young man stopped by. Claiming to be a friend of the family, he asked the mortician if he could take some photographs of the body and was upset and angry when he was told this would be impossible. After he had gone, the mortician reported the matter to the police. They found it interesting as a blue Chevrolet had been seen in the area where they suspected that Mary Fleszar had disappeared. Yet appeals for witnesses and an attempt to trace the car yielded nothing – it was as if their killer had come from nowhere, and had returned there.

A year passed, and Mary's killer was never found. Things seemed to quieten down in the town, when suddenly another teenage death caused panic.

Joan Schell was also a student at Eastern Michigan University, and she disappeared in similar circumstances to Mary Fleszar. She had been returning home on a Sunday evening – 1 July 1968 – when she was seen accepting a lift from three young men in a red car. Joan was reported missing by her roommate the next day. The car could not be traced, nor could the three young men.

On 6 July, a body was found by construction workers repairing a storm drain in north-east Ann Arbor. The body was clothed, but the clothes were all pushed up around the corpse's neck. She had been raped, and stabbed forty-seven times – again, mostly around the chest. Her genital area had also been frenziedly attacked with some kind of instrument. The body was in two different states of decomposition: the lower half was better preserved than the top half which was virtually rotten, because the corpse had been left near the lip of the storm drain, and the sun had only reached the torso. It was Joan Schell.

Meanwhile, the police had been conducting enquiries at the university regarding Joan's disappearance. It was not an easy time to be a policeman on campus, as 1968 was the year of student unrest, but there were still some who responded to the police pleas for assistance. Two male students who didn't know Joan Schell reported seeing a girl answering her description in the company of Norman Collins on the evening of 1 July.

Collins was a twenty-one-year-old student at the university, just over a year older than Joan. When the police interviewed him he denied being with her that evening, claiming that he had been out with her on a date a few days before, but that weekend he

312

hadn't even been in Ypsilanti – he had spent it in the town of Center Line with his mother and family, and hadn't left until late Sunday evening, only arriving in Ypsilanti in the early hours of Monday morning. Detectives checked this alibi and found it was watertight. Police investigations ground to a halt as leads petered to nothing.

Again there was a long period of quiet when it seemed as though the murderer had gone away; yet it was a tense silence, as the killer had been quiet for a year between the murders before. And there was no doubt in police minds that they were dealing with only one man; the modus operandi was far too similar for it to be otherwise.

It was, in fact, less than a year before the killer struck again. Another student at Eastern Michigan University, Jane Mixer, was the victim.

On 21 March 1969, a young child came across a shopping bag outside a cemetery in the village of Denton, four miles from Ypsilanti. He took it home to his mother, who found it was full of gift-wrapped parcels. She asked the child to show her where he had found it, and he took her to the cemetery. As she looked through the gates, she could see a yellow raincoat lying in the grass, but the raincoat wasn't flat, and looked as though it had something underneath. She asked her son if he had been in the cemetery. He replied that he hadn't, and that the bag had been outside. The mother said a silent prayer of thanks for what her son had been spared. She sent him home, and called the police from a phone box, waiting until they arrived.

It took them only a matter of seconds to uncover a body.

The corpse was that of Jane Mixer. She had been shot in the chest with a gun that forensic tests showed to be a .22 – a small calibre, usually a handgun – and the bullet hole was small and hadn't killed her. She had actually been strangled with one of her own stockings, which was found nearby. The body was fully clothed, and the girl hadn't been sexually assaulted, possibly because she was menstruating.

At first, there was some doubt as to whether or not this could be the same killer as in the cases of Joan Schell and Mary Fleszar. There was no sexual assault, and the murder was clean compared to the previous two – no multiple stab wounds or amputations. Maybe this simply indicated the absence of sexual frenzy given that the killer hadn't had sex with his victim. He might have been repulsed by Jane's period and might have wanted to kill her quickly.

The body was in a relatively good condition as Jane had only gone missing a few days before. She had intended to return home to Muskegon on Thursday evening, and had put a notice on the college noticeboard asking if anyone could offer her a ride. She had later rung her parents to say that a man would be giving her a lift that evening. From this, the police presumed that the killer was a fellow-student at the college, which also tied in with the earlier disappearance of Joan Schell. However, Norman Collins had been eliminated as a suspect in the Schell case, so he was not questioned again.

Forensic examination of Jane Mixer's body produced no clues. Three murders, all probably the work of the same killer, and no suspect – the pressure was on for the police.

Then, another body was found...

On 25 March a construction crew working near the storm drain where Joan Schell had been found nearly a year earlier were shocked to discover a naked body at the entrance to the drain. The corpse had been covered with wet leaves in an effort to hide it, and had not been there the previous day.

The victim was a sixteen-year-old girl called Maralynn Skelton. Unlike the previous victims, she was not a student, but was a known juvenile delinquent with a police record. She was a heroin addict and also an occasional pusher and prostitute. From the condition of the corpse it was obvious that her death was the work of the man who had killed Joan Schell and Mary Fleszar. She had been raped, and there were strap marks across her breasts consistent with her being tied up. Across her torso, front and back, were heavy welts and cuts which suggested that she had been flogged with a belt with a heavy metal buckle. Her skull had been crushed with great violence by a blunt object – her head was unidentifiable. A piece of cloth had been stuffed down her throat to prevent her screaming. In a final outrage a tree branch had been forced into her vagina, with the leaves sticking out between the corpse's legs, as if in some kind of macabre joke.

No one had reported Maralynn missing, few people care about or mourn street kids like her. But the fact that the body had seemingly appeared overnight, and was in a very early state of decomposition, told detectives that she hadn't been missing for long.

The police began to put together a picture of the man they were looking for: he was young, probably a student, or had easy access to the campus of the college; he was possibly dark-haired (from the descriptions of the young man seen in the company of Joan Schell, and the young man who had called at the funeral parlour to photograph Mary Fleszar). He was certainly psychotic and sexually disturbed. Obviously, he had no fear of being caught, and seemed to believe implicitly that the police would never discover him. How else could you explain the way in which he had abducted, raped and murdered, then disposed of Maralynn Skelton in the midst of the police investigation into the death of Jane Mixer?

At the beginning of April, Maralynn's family were located. She was on bad terms with them, and had left to return to Ypsilanti from the family home in Flint on 24 March after a visit to beg for money. Her father had initially agreed to take her back to town, but they had argued yet again and she had left him just outside town, saying she would get a lift the rest of the way.

Maralynn was young and pretty, and dressed in a provocative manner – this was the beginning of the age of the mini-skirt. It wasn't long before she was picked up. But who had picked her up? Attempts to trace any driver who had given her a lift were under way when the next corpse was discovered...

On 15 April, thirteen-year-old Dawn Basom had vanished on her way home from school in Superior Township. Her body was found in a field the next morning by a farmhand on his way to work. She had been strangled, like Jane Mixer. The weapon this time was a piece of black electrical cord which was still around her neck. She had been raped, and her stomach and genital area had been slashed to ribbons with a sharp instrument – possibly an ice-pick.

The police were greatly alarmed at the increasing frequency of the attacks: obviously the killer was becoming more and more confident of his invulnerability.

In the ensuing search, a routine inspection of a deserted and wrecked farmhouse a short way from where the body was found revealed a new lock had been installed on one of the doors. Breaking in to the ruin, the police discovered the sweater Dawn Basom had been wearing on the fateful day lying in a corner of one room. Officers suspected that this house had been used in other killings, as it was only a mile from the site where Mary Fleszar's body had been found, and they were proved right when careful forensic examination of the building came up with fibres belonging to the clothes of Joan Schell.

Unbeknown to the detectives, a mystery motor-cyclist was watching them: a tall, powerfully built young man dressed in black leathers. He had always been watching when the police were at the scene of a murder. He had a particular interest in these murders, and noted the discovery of the farmhouse.

The building was kept under regular, though not daily, surveillance. Looking through the main room one day, a patrolman found a gold earring and a piece of nylon belonging to Dawn's blouse which had not been there before. It seemed as though the killer was playing a game with the police. A few days after the discovery of the earring and blouse, a barn near the property was set on fire. When the blaze was dowsed, officers found a roll of black electrical cord left nearby, to taunt them. It was the same type of wire used to strangle Dawn Basom.

The motorcyclist returned to the house several times – he knew it well. Each time he waited until the police patrol was changing over, or the patrolman was relieving himself. If you had patience, it was easy to get past them. He enjoyed planting the items: it was a cat and mouse game. The police thought he was the mouse, but he knew he was the cat. The last time he called, he brought them a gift of flowers, five lilac blossoms with their heads severed, one blossom for every murder.

It was soon to become six murders.

On 9 June, in Northfield Township, a few miles from the farmhouse, three teenage boys took a shortcut across a field and stumbled upon a woman's body. This was Alice Elizabeth Kalom. Another student at Eastern Michigan University – although she had graduated the previous year – she hadn't even been reported missing yet. The corpse was in a mess: although the actual cause of death was a bullet to the brain (a .22 again), her throat had been cut and she had been stabbed over forty times, particularly around the breasts and genital area. The body was covered in blood, and the ground surrounding it was also soaked. It was obviously another frenzied attack by the same killer. The corpse was partially clothed: her dress was up around her neck, and her pants and pantihose were found lying nearby. She had been raped, probably after she was killed.

An extensive search of the field turned up no clues. By now the police did know, however, that the killer was keen to revisit the scene of his crimes so they were prepared to sit it out and wait to see if he returned. They needed to prevent news of the discovery from getting out. Unfortunately, one of the boys who found the body had decided to earn a few dollars by selling his story to a local radio station, and the news was broadcast later in the day. The police packed up and went home, aware that the killer – however confident he was of evading capture – would not risk returning with a squad of police on hand.

* * *

Later that month, Peter Hurkos arrived in town. As was his usual practice, he asked to be given only the most basic facts of the case. He was told by the citizens' group who had hired him that six young women had been raped and killed in horrible circumstances, and that the police had no suspects. A member of the detective team investigating the case was present. He told Hurkos that the police could not officially endorse his use by the group, but they would be only too glad to assist him with anything he required.

Hurkos asked the detective if he could have maps of the areas where the murders were believed to have taken place, and where the bodies had been found.

When these were supplied, he sat in a quiet room with a representative of the citizens' group, the detective who had brought the maps, and the journalist who had acted as the link man (and obviously believed there was a story in the offing!). He pored over the maps in silence for some time before beginning to speak. His voice was low and quiet – almost as though he was in a trance. There was none of the theatrical flourish of his earlier successes. Subdued in every way, he spoke slowly in broken sentences, his accent becoming heavy at times.

Inside his head a whirl of thoughts spun around. There were flashes of pictures and emotions as each place name on the map triggered off a small sequence, like running loops of film that he had to grasp quickly before they were gone.

'He is not an old man ... at most around twenty-five or six. He is brilliant, with quite a bit of education. He has a young face, like a student ... it is quite a baby face. He is not a stupid man, but very intelligent. I think he goes to school at night – a university that has night classes. I see a small school ... He isn't a heavy person, around one hundred and thirty-six pounds, maybe, but not thin ... he has muscle. He drives a motorbike.

'There is a farm – I see it here, and behind the house, further up ... I see water, a dry well ...'

The detective was stunned at this. No mention had been made of the fact that most of the victims had Eastern Michigan University as a link, or that the police suspected a student as the possible killer. No mention had been made of the farmhouse, and the killer's connection to it. It seemed as though Hurkos was on to something... Especially when he mentioned the dry well. This was something that had been discovered quite by accident during a routine search when a police officer had nearly fallen down the covered hole but no one thought it was important.

Feeling sure that Hurkos was on the right track, the detective produced a photograph of the farmhouse and surrounding buildings. Hurkos focused on the farmhouse, and began to speak again. His tone was firmer as he began to receive a better impression of events.

'He operated in this house. But not now – there is
no clue that the girl was in the house. In this house
was a chair with broken legs, a chair and beer bottles,
cases. And I see a lot of newspapers in the house. He
didn't kill the girl in the house – that isn't true ... but
it was his headquarters. He watched her here for a
long time. He is still active around there. In other
words, he is not in the house any more, but he drives
around the area, on a motorbike...'

This seemed to be all that he could offer for
the present. It was more than enough! For the
detective had to admit that the farmhouse had been
full of discarded beer bottles, and one room was
piled high with old newspapers. There had also
been a chair with a broken leg. Hurkos could not
have merely guessed these details. And even if
a sceptic argued that he could have picked things
up from the mind of the detective, that would not
account for Hurkos' description of the killer and the
motorcycle.

As the detective rose to leave, Hurkos put out his
hand. 'Wait. There is one thing more. This man – you
have already spoken to him.'

'Questioned him?'

Hurkos nodded. 'Look in your files. I am sure you
will find him in there. You have spoken to him about
these killings.' His tone became harder and tinged
with regret. 'There is something else. There will be
another murder. I wish I could do something to stop
it, but I know it will be.'

322

The officer looked at him. 'Not if I can help it,' he said softly.

As the detective left the room, Hurkos looked after him with sorrow. He had seen it: it would be.

And sure enough, there *was* one more murder . . .

Karen Sue Beineman was an eighteen-year-old Eastern Michigan University student who went missing from her dormitory on campus on 23 July. Her roommates, who called the police, told them that she had planned to go to a wig shop that lunchtime, and that she had failed to return. The shop proprietress was interviewed and disclosed that the girl had come to collect her wig, and had left saying that there were two foolish things she had done that day: the first was to buy a wig, and the second was to accept a lift from a stranger.

The shop owner had seen the stranger in question. He was a handsome, well-built young man with dark hair. He wore leathers, and a candy-striped shirt. He was waiting outside with his motorcycle – a new model by the look of it, in chromium and blue.

The police feared that Hurkos' final prediction had come true; they were sure that Karen Sue was dead. However, they now had an eyewitness description of the man with the motorcycle. They decided to ask questions on campus again – with surprising results. Several students identified the stranger wearing a candy-stripe shirt and riding a motorbike as Norman Collins.

Collins' alibi for the murder of Joan Schell depended solely on his mother's word; could it be that she had got the times wrong, or could she be lying to protect her son?

Before detectives had a chance to question Collins, a body was found in a wooded gully just outside Ypsilanti. A young couple out walking had stumbled across it, and had reported their horrific find: the corpse was disfigured with a corrosive fluid, creating burn marks on the breasts. Her genital area was scarred by tooth marks where the killer had bitten her repeatedly. One of her front teeth had been knocked out. And there were marks on her wrists and ankles consistent with being tied up. Cause of death was strangulation, but there was no sign of what she had been strangled with. In fact, the body had been lying naked and face down in the gully, and a search of the area uncovered no discarded clothing.

The police decided to bide their time before questioning Collins. They imposed a news blackout on the discovery of the body, replaced the corpse with a mannequin and sat tight, hoping the killer would return to the scene of the crime.

Two nights later a man was seen approaching the mannequin. When the officers challenged him he managed to give them the slip and fled into the woods.

Meanwhile, forensic tests revealed that Karen Sue's pants had been stuffed deep into her vagina. Adhering to the material of the pants were a number of minute hairs. This discovery rang alarm bells in State Police Corporal David Leik's head. He had recently been on holiday and left his wife's nephew in charge of feeding the dogs. When Leik returned, he went down to his basement where he was surprised to see that black spray paint had been used to cover some old red varnish stains. This made him look more closely at the floor, and there he saw what appeared to be small splashes of blood.

His wife's nephew was a student. His name was Norman Collins.

When he got to the police station, he told his superior what he had found and that his wife's nephew was Norman Collins. He was horrified to learn that Collins was the prime suspect in the sex murders. A forensic team set to work in Leik's basement but there was little they could detect from the stains. However, they found the floor of the basement covered in hair clippings as he had cut his sons' hair there before going on holiday. When tested, the clippings matched the hairs found in Karen Sue's pants. In order for the hairs to be on her body, she must have been in the basement! There was now a definite link between the last victim and the prime suspect.

The plan now was to keep Collins under close observation, and pull him in as soon as he moved on another girl. But Collins was put on his guard when two detectives blundered and pulled him in for questioning too soon. This gave Collins a chance to provide himself with an alibi for the time when he had supposedly been giving Karen Sue a lift. Collins claimed that he had been with a roommate, a story partially substantiated by the roommate who, however, wasn't sure of the exact time involved.

The roommate remembered Collins returning in his car rather than on the motorcycle, and after more thought he concluded that the time may have been up to a couple of hours later than Collins had claimed. He also recalled that Collins had carried a cardboard box into the house, and had burnt its contents in the furnace in the basement. As far as the contents of the box were concerned, the roommate had only glimpsed rolled-up jeans and a shoe – a woman's shoe...

The police now had enough to hold Collins for questioning. At first he was silent, and when he spoke claimed to know nothing about the murders. But when detectives told him that he had sprayed black paint over varnish – not blood – and this was what led them to the discovery of the hair clippings that linked him with Karen Sue Beineman, Collins broke down in a paroxysm of self-pity. It was obvious now that the police had the right man: all they had to do was collate enough evidence, or wait for a confession.

Meanwhile, detectives were delving into Norman Collins' past and a picture began to emerge that was far from edifying: he had made a habit of petty theft and burglary, and had gone on several burglaries with former roommate Andrew Manuel. Together they had worked a credit card scam to take a hired caravan trailer from Ypsilanti to Salinas, California – using a card stolen from another student. The trailer was recovered by local police, who reported to Ypsilanti police that they had an unsolved murder on their books. Roxie Ann Phillips had been murdered at the time of Collins' and Manuel's stay in Salinas. Her body was covered in marks consistent with being tied, multiple stab wounds and genital mutilation – it was Collins' handiwork.

When Manuel was questioned, he admitted the burglaries, but denied all knowledge of the rape and murder. A polygraph test showed he was telling the truth. He confessed to the police that he and Collins had been two of the youths who had picked Joan Schell up the night she disappeared. Collins had told her he would take her home in his car, and had complained the next day that he had had to kick her out on the way home because she wouldn't 'come across'.

Collins was good-looking and successful with girls: he would often bring two or three back to his rooms in a week. So why did he feel the need to go out and commit sex murders? A clue may lie in the way he treated women. His roommate remembered Collins chasing one girl from the house, snarling that he didn't like 'prick teasers', and a number of girls came forward to tell how he had tried to tie them up and beat them during sex. He also had a strange relationship with his sister: they were very close until he caught her having sex with a man. Collins beat both of them up, and refused to have anything more to do with his sister after that.

He considered himself above other mortals. Once he wrote that 'if a person wants something, he alone is the deciding factor of whether or not to take it – regardless of what society believes to be right or wrong'. Society decided that Collins did not have that right. At his trial he was found guilty of murder and sentenced to at least twenty years in prison.

Peter Hurkos had provided that quantum leap in logic that is seen time and time again in psychic detection. Had he not done so, how many more women would Norman Collins have killed before being caught? How many lives did Peter Hurkos save?

It proved to be his last great success.

Gerald Croiset
and Edith Kiecorius

The small, middle-aged man in the shabby suit had been walking the streets for some time. Every day he pounded the pavements of New York, hoping to find what he was looking for: something that would slake his thirst. Maybe today would be the day. Perhaps 21 February would be the lucky date he had been waiting for. Inside his tortured mind there was no doubt that his day must come soon: the voices had told him as much.

As he turned the corner, he could see a small child walking towards him. A serious-faced girl of about four or five, in a warm coat. She looked up at him.

'Hello, little one,' he said, crouching down to her eye level. 'What are you doing?' His voice was soft, and he smiled warmly at her. If she had been older, she might have seen that the smile stopped at his eyes.

'Nothing,' she said. 'I mustn't talk to strangers. That's what my mommy says.'

'And where is your mommy?' he asked.

'At home.' The child looked around. 'I was playing, but I got bored.'

He licked his dry lips. 'Do you want to come with me?'

'I've got to go home.'

'But if you come with me, I'll take you home. You can't be too careful, you know.'

The child seemed to think hard about this. 'Okay,' she said finally. 'As long as we go straight home.' She held out her hand; he took it, and led her further down the street, away from where he presumed her friends had been playing.

'I've got some nice new toys at my place: do you want to see them?'

In February 1961, four-year-old Edith Kiecorius was snatched from the streets of Manhattan, where she had been playing with friends. There was no apparent reason why Edith should have been chosen: she was an average four-year-old, and her parents had no enemies. The only thing that singled her out from the crowd of friends she was with was that she wandered down a side street on her own for a couple of minutes. When she failed to return, her friends, peevish at the fact that they couldn't continue their game without her to make up the numbers, went to find her.

As some of them walked down the side streets, they called out her name, but received no reply. Most of the children were the same age or a little older, so they didn't become worried or concerned by her disappearance. Instead they shrugged, thinking that she had gone home because of some tantrum concerning the game, and went about the important task of re-arranging themselves so that they could continue with one less player.

It was only much later, when Edith failed to return home, and her parents went around her circle of playmates to find out if Edith was with any of them, that they realised that something was wrong. They hadn't seen Edith since that time when she wandered down the side street – and they couldn't remember anyone else being around then.

It was a seedy boarding-house-cum-hotel. The walls were peeling and there were rats in some of the rooms – but not in this one. Behind the door, little piles of rat poison stood in each corner. He had a hatred of rodents and insects and tried to keep them away. This wasn't easy when the rest of the one-room apartment was such a rubbish tip: old cartons and tin cans littered the floor, and the bed was stained and sagging. One solitary naked light bulb lit the room and threw its dim beam across the rancid ceiling, stained and crumbling.

Edith screwed up her nose as the man led her into the room and closed the door behind them. She heard him throw the bolts. He was breathing heavily.

'This is horrible. I thought I was going home.'

'You will be,' he said softly. 'But I wanted to play with you first.'

'But I don't want to play,' she said petulantly. 'I want to go home. And where are the toys? I want to see them.'

'You'll do what I say,' he snarled. The sudden and violent change in his tone made her start. She began to cry. 'Shaddup!' he shouted, and picked her up off the floor, throwing her on to the bed. For such a small man, he had astounding strength. 'You'll do what I want from now on.'

Edith's parents called in the police, but they held out little hope of quick results: New York is a large city with a good public transport system and children of all ages went missing every day. Edith could have wandered off and got lost, or she might have been abducted. There was no clue as to what had happened. But when routine patrols reported no lost children wandering the streets, and a check of other police stations failed to turn up a child answering Edith's description, it became obvious that something nastier had happened to Edith.

Mr and Mrs Kiecorius were first-generation immigrants, used to the safety of ethnic New York. In areas where one group of immigrants had formed a community, small children could, at that time, play fairly safely. There was usually someone around who would keep an eye on the kids. How had Edith slipped through this net?

As they sat in the station, they were disheartened by what the detective in charge of the hunt for Edith had to say: 'It's not that we're not looking – we are. But you've got to see it from our point of view. Kids go missing every day in a city this big. It takes time to cover every option. That's what we need: time.' Time to make a thorough investigation – time they might not have.

The police questioned her playmates but, as you would expect with very young children, each one told a different story, centring mostly around what they had been doing in the game at that time. Concrete evidence was hard to come by. However, a few things in a couple of stories, when added up, seemed to give something resembling a lead. Some of the children thought they recalled an old woman – well, a woman who was older than their mother – leading a small child around the corner at the end of the street when they looked for Edith. It might have been Edith, they couldn't remember – anyway, she never answered their shouts, and Edith would have!

This was a definite lead, and could tie in with reports that a middle-aged woman had been trying to abduct children in the area. Patrolling officers had been told to keep a look-out at schools and places where children played. If this was the same woman, then it was a distinct possibility that she had abducted Edith Kiecorius. It took the police several hours – and much patience! – to piece together details from the various descriptions given by the group of young children of the woman seen with the little girl – whom they weren't even sure was Edith!

This composite picture fitted the unknown woman the police had been aware of for some time, so a search began for this woman and the missing child. The trail led them to Chicago because someone remembered a woman resembling the one they were searching for at the airport, and boarding a flight for Chicago. Someone recalled seeing a girl that looked like Edith in the city. It was all half-truth and speculation, but the police – keen to track down this woman and find Edith before something happened to her – had to follow every lead however tenuous.

The Chicago police tried to assist and made enquiries of airport staff, but all they had to go on was a vague description of the woman, and a description of Edith. Already several days had passed, and airport staff dealing with thousands of people in the course of one work shift tend not to remember faces unless something really stands out. A study of flight and passenger records also drew a blank. There was no woman and child booked on a flight that didn't check out: grannies and grandchildren, mothers and offspring – those they had on their lists were legitimate guardians.

It seemed as though there was no record of the woman and Edith. There was very good reason for this: the police were following a false trail of their own partial invention.

* * *

The man's name was Fred. He was in his early fifties, and felt that things had passed him by all his life. All his desires and his needs had been ignored. He had worked and tried to make his way, but always something dragged him down, until he was here in this crummy apartment, watching the cockroaches nibble at the poison in the corners of the room.

The smell was awful, but he didn't really notice it any more. It came from the corpse on the bed where he was sitting. He hadn't wanted to kill her, and the voices had told him that it was wrong. What he wanted was right, but it would have been better if ... he remembered how it had happened. He had wanted to touch her, and she had screamed as he took off her clothes. He didn't want her to be heard, so he had tried to silence her by putting his hand over her mouth.

She had bitten his hand, drawing blood. It was too much for him to bear: another rejection. He couldn't remember much after that. He knew that he had hit her: that had made her shut up. And he remembered hitting her again ... and again. And then he knew that she was dead, and there was nothing more he could do.

He stood up. Time to move on.

The problem for the New York police department was that the leads ran out in Chicago, and they found themselves at a dead end. Not knowing where to turn in the search for Edith, the NYPD decided to call in a psychic whose results were, to their mind, impeccable – Gerald Croiset.

Why would the police officially call in a psychic, when usually it's only a lone officer who is prepared to take the plunge? The answer lies in the high regard that the Dutch legal authorities had for Croiset – a regard that gave him a seal of approval as far as the NYPD were concerned. His reputation as genuine was unimpeachable, and it was a controlled risk the NYPD hierarchy were prepared to take when faced with press interest in the disappearance of Edith, and the pleas of Mr and Mrs Kiecorius. The public wanted a result – the mayor had promised one. Now the police had to deliver.

Everything rested on Gerald Croiset.

Croiset had always been aware of his powers, which came from his mother who was also psychic. He came to the attention of the parapsychologist and researcher Professor W. H. C. Tenhaeff of Utrecht after attending one of his lectures. Croiset made his home in the town, and was the subject of many studies by Tenhaeff. One of these involved the reopening by the Dutch authorities in 1949 of the case of the suspicious death of two young children out riding their bicycles in woods near Utrecht nine years earlier. Croiset was able to provide vital information that led to the solution of the case – and it made his reputation.

Since then, he had been treated with respect by the

authorities, and was sometimes consulted. This satisfied his ego and he enjoyed the official sanction he received as a kind of 'state psychic'.

When the New York police contacted him to help them in the search for Edith Kiecorius, Gerald Croiset agreed immediately, and one airline went so far as to offer him a free trip to Chicago so he would be near the area where Edith was believed to have been taken. Croiset declined the offer, preferring to stay in his Utrecht home, away from any pressures that might have been put on him. Unlike some other psychics, Croiset was never a publicity seeker. He just asked the police to send him maps of the areas where Edith lived and where she disappeared and he would try to divine her whereabouts from these. He felt that being close to the area of the crime could also confuse him, as there might be too many impressions for him to assimilate.

The maps arrived with great speed, courtesy of the American embassy, because pressure from the mayor of New York and the press had spurred the State Department into sending the maps of Chicago and New York to Croiset by diplomatic bag, on an overnight flight.

Over two weeks had elapsed since Edith had gone missing.

Gerald Croiset opened the bag, and spread the maps out on a table in his sparsely furnished study. In the quiet of the morning, with nothing but the distant traffic noise, Croiset could hear the sound of his own breathing reverberate through his body. His concentration was intense. Yet, even as he had taken the first map out of the bag, he could tell that it would reveal nothing to him. He had spread it out, and could feel nothing unusual. It was dead. He unfolded the map: it was of Chicago. He raised an eyebrow: this was where the child was supposed to have been taken.

The next map was of New York. As he unfolded it, he could feel something beginning to happen. As he studied the map, the depth of his breathing increased, and images began to crowd his mind. He could still see the study around him, but at the same time he could see Edith meeting a small man in his late forties or early fifties. He was speaking to her, then took her back to his hotel room. It was filthy and sordid. He tried to assault the child, and she resisted. He hit her repeatedly, then raped her. She was already dead, Croiset was sure of that. The tears rolled down his face as he saw the man return to the body again and again, over a period of days.

He closed his eyes, and the impressions faded away. When he looked at his watch, he could see that it had only been a matter of minutes since he had unfurled the map. He looked at the map again. He was certain he could trace on it the route the man had taken. If he could pinpoint the hotel, then the police would find the child and her murderer.

Croiset phoned the NYPD and told the detectives that Edith was dead, and that she had never left the area in which she was abducted. Her abductor was not a woman at all, but a small, sharp-faced man of around fifty who had taken her to an apartment near her home. He described the area where she had been playing in great detail – even down to street signs – which led a shocked police team to change the focus of their investigations from Chicago back to Manhattan.

The police were so certain that Edith was in Chicago that they would have been disinclined to believe the psychic, had it not been for the small details he supplied: the existence of a bent street sign on the corner, and the names of shops along the route that he had seen in his vision.

Croiset had told the detectives that Edith would be found in a rooming house near the street where she had disappeared. Within hours of beginning their investigation in the area, they came across a locked room in a run-down rooming house and hotel. The previous occupant was a man named Fred Thompson, who fitted the description Croiset had supplied: he was a small, thin man with a weasel-like face, and was aged fifty-three. He had vacated the room a few days before.

'We want to look in there,' said one of the police officers to the fat landlord, who stood chewing a cigar behind the desk.

'I ain't got a key,' he shrugged.

'Whaddaya mean, you ain't got a key?'

'This guy Thompson, he changed the lock without

telling me. I tried to get in there when he left, but my key wouldn't fit.'

'So why didn't ya call a locksmith?' exclaimed the exasperated officer.

The fat man looked at the empty hotel register. 'So business is booming?' he said sarcastically.

The sighing policeman asked him if they could break down the door, rather than call in a locksmith or get a search warrant.

'You pay for a new door, you do what the hell you like,' he shrugged.

It was all the permission they needed.

An appalling stench hit them as they entered the room. On the bed lay a badly decomposed body – it had lain there for some time. Thompson must have slept beside it, as Edith had been missing for over a fortnight now, and Thompson had only vacated the room in the last two or three days. Having been led to it by Croiset's visions, the police were convinced that the corpse of this young child was Edith Kiecorius, although the body wasn't formally identified until later. She was naked, and had been repeatedly raped and beaten to death – probably with Thompson's bare hands, as the marks were consistent with punching rather than a blunt instrument. Her neck was broken, and it seemed likely that the killer had continued to have intercourse with the child after she was dead – an impression later confirmed by forensic evidence.

The imperative now was to catch Thompson before

he abducted another child. Someone capable of doing this was more than capable of doing it again.

A search was mounted for Fred Thompson, and he was picked up three days later in another rooming house in New York. He didn't seem to be unduly worried about his arrest, and when questioned talked quite freely of how he had picked up Edith as she wandered away from her friends, tempting her to his room with the promise of new toys. He described how he had stripped her and raped her, hitting her when she cried out. He couldn't remember when she had died, as she had ceased to cry after a short while. (Forensic evidence later proved that she had died the day she was abducted.)

Fred Thompson stood trial and was found guilty but insane. He spent the rest of his life in an institution.

Kill the Messenger

When a thirty-one-year-old nurse disappeared from Los Angeles in December 1980, the last thing anyone following the case would have expected was the arrest of a thirty-two-year-old office worker and mother who had never even met the nurse! And on a charge of murder, at that! But this is what Etta Smith endured, and this is why she fought the Los Angeles Police Department for seven years before gaining some kind of compensation for her ordeal.

Mel was late – for the third time this week! Grabbing a quick cup of coffee, she ran out of the front door and down the steps of her apartment house. Jumping into her car, she headed towards the junction. She hadn't thought to lock her car doors.

There was a red light, and she screeched to a halt. Three teenage boys were crossing, and they yelled and jeered at her braking. She smiled at them – but the smile vanished as they came towards her car. She locked the door on her side, and lunged across towards the passenger door. Her fingertips brushed the locking catch as the door was pulled open.

'Well hello,' said one of the youths, sitting down next to her. He was tall and heavily built, with long hair and a bad case of acne. 'You gonna take us for a little ride, baby?'

The other youths had got into the back of the car. There were too many of them for her to try anything. She looked around the junction – it was virtually deserted, and those people that were around were either in cars themselves, or too far away for her to call to.

She was trapped.

Melanie Uribe was a nurse in Los Angeles, building her career at a hospital on the outer fringe of the city. She was a pretty thirty-one-year-old, who was popular at her work place, and lived alone in an apartment near the hospital. Every day she would drive to work, skirting the edges of the canyons that surround the city.

On 15 December 1980, she failed to arrive at work. Her supervisor rang her home, but there was no reply. It was unlike Melanie not to call in if sick. If she wasn't ill, and she wasn't answering her phone, then perhaps she was just taking the day off? This, her supervisor felt, could not be the case: Melanie was dedicated to her job, and was always careful to book time off in advance. The whole thing would be out of character for her. There was immediate concern

344

about what might have happened to Melanie.

So, when her shift finished, the supervisor decided to drop in on Melanie on her way home. There was no one around, and Melanie's car was missing. The supervisor became even more worried, and called in at the police station. The officers were polite, and made a note of what they were told, but explained there was little they could do, and that such missing person cases were plentiful. The supervisor was not happy with this attitude, and went home unsatisfied.

On 16 December, the police began to check Melanie's movements in a cursory fashion: they questioned her neighbours and tried to trace her movements that previous morning, but there was little else they could do. For all they knew, she might have decided to ride off into the sunset with a boyfriend to start a new life!

While this was going on, in an office not too far away worked Etta Smith, a thirty-two-year-old administrative assistant at the Lockheed Aircraft Corporation. She was a single mother with two children, who worked hard to make ends meet, though things weren't easy for someone like her. But she was relatively happy in her untroubled suburban life: she liked her job, her kids were good and rarely in any kind of trouble – she was the average Mrs America. Etta had no interest in the paranormal and had never exhibited any powers or tendencies to such abilities.

Etta was discussing with a workmate the problems

of a woman alone in the city. It seemed to her that LA was getting more dangerous – even out here on the fringes of the desert and the canyons. Like everyone else, she was concerned about the crime rate and the possibility of becoming a statistic.

Her workmate was a friend of the hospital supervisor and told Etta about Melanie Uribe's disappearance. She explained that Melanie had simply vanished into thin air, and that the police weren't interested. (This, of course, was not strictly true, but it was the impression she had received from her friend.) The two women shook their heads and bemoaned the state of the city. No one was safe.

On 17 December, the story broke on local radio and television. The initial investigation had led nowhere: Melanie had literally vanished after driving off from her home. The trail came to a dead end somewhere between the apartment and the hospital – as though she had been plucked from the road by an unseen hand.

Melanie drove out into the canyons. She could feel something hard in the small of her back, pressed against the seat of the car. One of the youths had told her it was a gun. She was in no mood to question this.

'Turn off here,' the one in the passenger seat said to her as they reached a deserted stretch of road. Her car bumped over the rocky sand, and into the cover of some boulders. The youth reached across and switched off the ignition.

346

They had been talking between them all the way out of town about what they wanted to do to her. She felt sick, and trembled as they ushered her out of the car, and pushed her into a small gully. She stumbled and fell. They laughed, and one of them threw himself on her, ripping at her clothes. The other two cheered and clapped. They shouted encouragement as he raped her repeatedly. They all took turns forcing her to have sex with them.

When they had finished, they stood discussing among themselves what to do with her. Melanie lay on the cold sand, staring at the sky. She didn't care what happened any more. The long-haired youth argued that they couldn't let her get away now. She had to be silenced once and for all. The others nodded in agreement.

Picking up a small boulder, he turned and walked towards her. Melanie watched him, feeling as though she was distanced from events: they meant nothing to her. She saw him raise the boulder above his head, then bring it down on her. Everything went black . . .

He smashed the boulder again and again on her head. Then the other two joined in, until her head was unrecognisable. The flies were already gathering as they walked, laughing and joking, back to her car. The long-haired one had thought to take her keys from her purse before leaving the body.

Police investigations now stepped up a gear, which included contacting the media. They had to know if anybody had seen Melanie on her way to work, and if anyone had been with her. Meanwhile, they continued to dig into her background in the hope of finding some clue.

Etta was at work when she heard the story on the radio, but thought no more of it until she was relaxing at home that night. It was late, and her children (aged ten and twelve) were in bed. She was watching television in her bedroom when a strange feeling began to sweep over her. It was like nothing she had ever experienced before; yet instead of being scared she felt warm and happy that it was happening.

From the way that Etta subsequently described what happened, it's hard to pin down what kind of psychic experience it was, all the more so since no two people ever experience anything the same way, which makes an attempted analysis difficult. Strangely Etta didn't have a vision of any kind – she described it as a feeling rather than a vision. But she knew that Melanie Uribe was dead, and that she was in one of the canyons not far from their suburb.

The feeling subsided and left Etta wondering what to do. She didn't feel disturbed in any way. There had been no big revelation; the feeling had crept up on her while she was almost dozing, and had seemed to wash over her before she had a chance to worry. Part of her thought that she should be scared – yet another part of her said that there was nothing to worry about.

It was while she was pondering this that the feeling

returned again. This time she received a vision with her feelings: so perhaps, she later assumed, her first wave of feeling was like a transmission to a faulty TV set. She was not tuned in properly the first time, and so received only part of the transmission. But now that she was aware of the phenomena happening to her, her brain was able to tune in to the signal and receive it fully.

Once again, Etta received the impression that Melanie Uribe was dead, and in a canyon near the suburb. This time, however, she could see the body hidden in a particular part of the canyon, and she was able to note the exact area from the scrub vegetation and the rock formation. It was as though her mind was making a detailed sketch of the impressions it was receiving.

When the vision had receded, Etta made up her mind to do something about it. Despite her qualms, she left the house and her sleeping children, and drove to her nearest police station. She was worried that they would think her a crank, perhaps even charge her with wasting police time. None the less, she had a belief in what she had just experienced that was unshakable. She was sure that what she had seen was true, and a search of that area would reveal the body of Melanie Uribe.

At the station she spoke to the desk sergeant, and was then taken into a room to await the arrival of Detective Lee Ryan, who was assigned to the case. As she waited, her nerves began to get the better of her,

349

and she thought about leaving quickly. But she didn't
have to wait for very long, and when Ryan entered
and asked her to repeat her story she took a deep
breath and plunged in. She finished by telling him
that she fully realised how cranky she must sound,
but she was merely telling it the way it happened.
Ryan said nothing; he tried to size up this ordinary
housewife and mother who sat in front of him, telling
him about dreams that weren't quite dreams. He had
heard of other departments using psychics – but they
always came with some kind of recommendation,
didn't they? He was unsure what to do.

Finally, he rose from his chair and left the office.
When he returned a few minutes later, he had maps
of the canyons around the suburbs of Los Angeles. He
gave them to Etta, and asked her to show him where
she had seen the body.

Almost instantly, she picked out one small area on
one of the maps. It was only afterwards that she
wondered: how had she known where to point? It was
as if instinct guided her, and she indicated the spot
without thinking. She told Ryan that was where he
would find the body and that Melanie was wearing a
white t-shirt and jeans. He then asked her if she had
any idea who had committed the crime. She replied
that she had only seen the body. A thought then
struck Ryan, and he asked her if Melanie's car had
been in her vision. Etta shook her head: no car, she
would definitely remember that.

Ryan thanked Etta, and she left the station with no

idea as to whether or not her findings would be used. She was still a little bemused at the sudden appearance of psychic abilities she didn't know she had.

Back home, she tried to sleep, but it was a troubled night, full of strange dreams.

Lee Ryan took Etta Smith's statement to his superiors, but they were frankly sceptical and, though there were no other real lines of enquiry to pursue, they dismissed Etta as a crank and did not investigate her claims.

Meanwhile, the next day – a Saturday – was going badly for Etta. She had a weight on her mind and was preoccupied. Her children noticed this and wanted to know why their mother was behaving so oddly. At first she was unwilling to let them know what had been going on: she still felt strangely about her experience, but before long she decided to tell the children what had happened.

The kids were very excited by this: their mother was involved in a murder case, and had had a psychic experience! They nagged at her to take them out to the area where she had 'seen' the body; they wanted to know what was going on and to feel part of the whole thing. Etta wasn't keen on the idea, and at first tried to refuse them: but the more she thought of it, the more exciting it seemed. Finally, she agreed.

Etta and her two children drove out of Los Angeles to the Lopez canyon – a distance of only a few miles.

351

When they arrived and turned off the road, the area was deserted and undisturbed – it was obvious that the police hadn't bothered to search in spite of her evidence. The children were not disappointed, although Etta was, realising the police had dismissed her as yet another crank.

Spurred on by her kids, Etta pointed out the area of the canyon in which she believed the body was hidden. The children wanted to search the place – even if the police didn't believe their mother, they were convinced that they would find something. Etta didn't want them to: she was afraid. On the one hand, she was terrified of finding a corpse, and on the other she was scared that there would be nothing there. If this was the case, then surely she must be going mad.

However, her children were not to be denied, and trailing their reluctant mother behind them they set off for the part of the canyon she had seen in her vision. It was some way away, but finally they arrived in that corner of Lopez canyon that was at the centre of Etta's dilemma. The kids were quick to start hunting among the rocks, though Etta had refrained from telling them the exact location.

She gingerly approached the area and became anxious as she saw a flash of white in among the scrub. Moving nearer, she could see it was a body. She didn't want to look any closer for fear of it being Melanie Uribe. Gathering the children, she rushed to the car and drove back to the road. Her intention was to stop the first police patrol she could find. As they were leaving Lopez, she saw a motorcycle patrol and stopped the patrolman. Breathlessly she reported finding something in the canyon – she was sure it was a body.

She was panicky and anxious, and the patrolman found it difficult to understand at first what exactly she wanted. He calmed her down, and made her repeat what she had said. She told him about the flash of white, but did not mention her previous visit to the police, in case it put the patrolman off following her.

With the patrolman following behind her, she drove back into the canyon and off the road to the point where she had previously stopped. She left the car and took him to the spot where she had seen what she assumed to be the body of Melanie Uribe. The patrolman walked into the small cluster of rocks and examined the white bundle. It was, indeed, a dead body. It had been in the sun and air for too long, and the flies were clustered around the pulped head. The patrolman had to stop to vomit before returning to his cycle to radio in his find.

Before too long the canyon was swarming with officers, and Etta Smith was taken to police head-quarters where she told the whole story, including her visit the previous evening when she had made a statement to Lee Ryan. Despite this, Ryan was not called in to speak to her, and after making her statement she was allowed home.

Her problems began an hour or two after she got

home. There was a knock at the door, and when she answered she was confronted with two uniformed policemen. They asked her if she would come to the station with them, as there were a few questions that the detectives on the case would like to ask her. She asked them what it was all about: surely her statement covered everything? The policemen replied that if she didn't go with them now, someone else would return with a warrant for her arrest. Reluctantly, she left her sleeping children and got into the waiting police car.

Etta Smith was pitched into a nightmare.

At the station, she was put into a dimly lit, bare room with two hard-faced detectives. She could feel their hostile attitude radiate from them. They told her that there were a few things in her statements of that evening and the night before that they were not happy about – her vision was troubling them greatly. If she had said that Melanie (the body had by now been formally identified) was wearing a uniform, this they would have been able to accept – after all, Melanie was a nurse, so you would expect her to be in a uniform. But she hadn't been wearing a uniform at all: the body had a white T-shirt on, and a pair of jeans were found nearby. How did Etta know what Melanie had been wearing? They were also disturbed by the way in which she had been able to pinpoint the exact location of the body. Lopez canyon is not small, and for Etta to manage to mark the exact spot on a map and then take a patrolman there was something quite remarkable – too remarkable for it to be mere coincidence.

They then changed the course of the interrogation: had Etta ever known Melanie Uribe? When she replied that she hadn't, the detectives asked her to think carefully before answering as they would be checking out her story. At this, Etta became suspicious. Why would they want to check out her story? Where was the interrogation leading?

One of the detectives told her he would be straight with her: there were no leads in the case, and they had to consider the fact that Etta had not only found the body, but had been able to say the night before where it was hidden and how it was dressed. This was suspicious. There was a possibility that Etta may have committed the murder, and they were asking her if she knew Melanie in order to eliminate her from their investigations.

Etta was horrified. She reminded them that she had been to the police the night before of her own free will, and asked if she could see Detective Ryan, but was told that Ryan was busy, and that her previous visit proved nothing – if anything, it was a good attempt at an alibi.

This terrified Etta: everything she said was being twisted against her. For lack of another suspect, they seemed prepared to pin the murder on her!

She was asked to undergo a polygraph test. These can be unreliable at the best of times, and it was now the early hours of the morning, with Etta tired, hungry and extremely anxious. None the less, the detectives on the Uribe case were adamant: she must take the test, and take it now. A polygraph operator was called for. He was not happy at the situation and, taking into account Etta's condition and the length of time she had been in the station, advised her to refuse to take the test then and offer to undertake one when she had rested. He warned her that the results could be misleading, even detrimental, if she went ahead then.

But Etta wasn't thinking straight: tired, hungry, upset – she merely wanted to get home to her children, and hopefully forget this nightmare. She told the polygraph operator that she wanted to take the test right there and then. He shrugged, and got on with it...

It was a bad decision on Etta's part, perfectly understandable in her stressed condition, but nevertheless potentially disastrous. Because of her anxiety and tiredness, the readings on the polygraph were distorted. According to the graph spilled out by the machine, Etta was lying about her vision, and about not knowing Melanie Uribe. It was exactly the result the detectives were waiting for.

They became even more aggressive and told Etta they had every intention of charging her with murder. She was detained in custody pending further interrogation, but not charged. Why? Because there was a problem with charging her alone for the murder since medical evidence had shown that

Melanie Uribe had been raped before she was killed. If Etta was involved, there had to be an accomplice.

Etta was questioned for four days. Who was with her? How had she known Melanie Uribe? Every time she referred to the vision she had experienced, she was told that the polygraph test had proved her a liar. Most of the detectives on the case were convinced they were close to cracking it. But there was one exception...

Detective Lee Ryan believed that Etta had had nothing to do with the killing, and that her clairvoyant vision had been genuine, even though he had nothing concrete to work on, only his feeling that Etta had been sincere when she made her initial statement. He spoke to the polygraph operator, who told Ryan that he was far from happy with the conditions under which the test was taken. And then there was the matter of this accomplice: an investigation into Etta Smith's background and associates produced no one who could be a likely suspect. Lee Ryan was convinced that his colleagues had jumped to a wrong conclusion, but had nothing to put forward that would back up his suspicions.

Meanwhile, the hunt for the real killers was non-existent. It seemed as though Etta Smith was to be treated by the LAPD as the medieval church treated witches. She was to be a sacrifice, in this case for the sake of a quick and clean result.

Then two things occurred that can be put down to fate or synchronicity. The first was in response to a police plea for witnesses who might have seen Melanie Uribe on her way to work the morning she was killed. Someone called in with the information that they had seen her driving towards Lopez canyon with three young men in the car. This alerted Ryan's suspicion, as he had been worried from the start about the fact that Melanie's car did not appear in Etta's vision. Could this be the reason? Had it, in fact, been used to transport her killers from the scene of the crime? If so, did they still have it? This seemed likely to him, but he was one officer alone, and there was the whole city to search for this vehicle.

The second fortunate event proved that some kind of natural justice was on Etta Smith's side. Melanie Uribe's car was stopped by a patrolman on a motoring offence, and the driver was detained when it was discovered it wasn't his vehicle. The youth was eighteen, and panicked when arrested. Taken into custody for being in possession of a motor vehicle that was registered to someone else, he feared that the police were on to him; he didn't know that the police had not made the connection between the stolen car and Melanie Uribe's missing vehicle. Instead of a possible theft charge, he believed that he was being brought in for murder. He wasn't going to face that alone. He told the police everything ... and pointed the finger at his two accomplices, like himself bored college students out for some fun that had gone horribly wrong.

The other two were rounded up and placed under

arrest. Etta Smith was released without an apology. She was badly shaken when all she had wanted to do was help the police.

Though Etta had managed to keep her children from catching a glimpse of Melanie Uribe's battered and decomposing, fly-infested body, she herself had seen it and the horrible sight had left her traumatised. She was reduced to a wreck when the detectives accused her of being complicit in the crime, and bullied her into taking a polygraph test, which had only led to further bullying. If it had not been for the trust Lee Ryan had in her sincerity, goodness knows what might have happened to her. And Etta felt afraid of the unknown forces that had led her to dream of the body's hiding place. She found herself unable to return to work, and suffered a nervous breakdown.

At the trial of the three youths, she was not called on to give evidence. The confession of the young man arrested in possession of Melanie Uribe's car was enough and the youths (Kenneth Newman, Andrew Keel and John Holland – all college students under twenty) received a thirty-year sentence each.

For Etta Smith, the sentence was shorter, but just as dramatic. She had no more visions, and her psychic powers – so recently awakened – never returned. The trauma she had suffered was enough to dissuade her subconscious from breaking through again.

In March 1987, Etta Smith's case against the police

for wrongful arrest and harassment finally came to court. It had taken over five years to reach this stage as there was no precedent: never before had a psychic sued the police for such a reason. The court had trouble understanding the case and the tabloid press didn't help. As is usual, they either took the view that Etta was a saint who was being persecuted, or else she was a fraud who was trying to screw money from the beleaguered LA police department.

The case, heard before the Supreme Court, dragged up dreadful memories for Etta and she broke down in the box when reliving the finding of the body, but the judge was sceptical suspecting she was exaggerating her turmoil to strengthen her claim for reimbursement for the years off work and the mental anguish caused by her wrongful detainment. Throughout the hearing he was openly hostile towards the idea of a psychic experience and tried to influence the jury in his summing up.

However, the jury were more impressed with the evidence of the polygraph operator and of Detective Lee Ryan, who described the fact that Etta was almost charged with murder as a 'gross miscarriage of justice', and added that it was unlikely that the body of Melanie Uribe would have been found without Etta's help.

Despite the bias of the judge, the jury found in favour of Etta Smith. However, they were not without their reservations. Etta's lawyers had asked for damages of $750,000, but the jury awarded her a total of only $26,184, which did not even cover her costs. It can only be assumed that they believed that she had been wrongfully detained, but also thought that she had been wasting police time. The judge had convinced them that the idea of a psychic vision was absurd.

The police attitude to the use of psychics needs to be reviewed. If they decide, on the basis of evidence, that psychics are worth using, then a system must be established whereby a psychic can be recorded in a data base. Because it is a fact that some psychics are able to get results. This is an avenue that the police can no longer afford to ignore. Of course, those who are consistently fraudulent must be excluded, but the true psychic should be treated with respect.

It's a shame that it would come too late for Etta Smith.

Bibliography

Much of the criminal detail in this book was obtained through old press cuttings, particularly from the tabloid press, including back issues of the *People*, the *News of the World*, the *Daily Mail*, the *Daily Express* and the American *National Enquirer* (thank you to Sue, my US friend!). I also raided back bulletins of the SPR, back numbers of *Psychic News* and various issues of *The Unexplained* for initial detail.

The following books were referred to for theory and detail, although some of them were barely used for the finished text. All of them had some use, however large or small.

Sylvia Barbanell: *Some Discern Spirits* (Psychic Press Ltd, 1944)

Michael Bentine: *The Doors of the Mind* (Grafton, 1983)

J. W. Dunne: *An Experiment with Time* (Faber & Faber, 1927)

Christopher Evans: *Landscapes of the Night* (Victor Gollancz, 1983)

Peter Hurkos: *The Story of Peter Hurkos* (Arthur Barker, 1961)

T. C. Lethbridge: *The Power of the Pendulum* (Routledge, Kegan & Paul, 1976)

Norma Lee Browning: *The Psychic World of Peter Hurkos* (Muller, 1972)

Arthur Lyons and Marshall Truzzi PhD: *The Blue Sense* (Mysterious Press, 1991)

Guy Lyon Playfair: *This House Is Haunted* (Souvenir Press, 1980)

Guy Lyon Playfair and Uri Geller: *The Geller Effect* (Grafton, 1987)

Maurice Maeterlinck: *The Unknown Guest* (Methuen, 1914)

Jenny Randles and Peter Hough: *Death By Unnatural Causes* (Grafton, 1989)

Estelle Roberts: *Fifty Years a Medium* (Corgi, Revised Edition, 1974)

Alex Tanous (with Harvey Ardman): *Beyond Coincidence* (Doubleday, 1976)

Colin Wilson: *Beyond the Occult* (Bantam, 1988)

Colin Wilson: *The Psychic Detectives* (Pan, 1984)

Colin Wilson and Donald Seaman: *The Serial Killers* (True Crime, 1992)

Theon Wright: *In Search of the Lindbergh Baby* (Tower, 1980)

Index

A selection of non-fiction from Headline

THE *INDEPENDENT* BOOK OF ANNIVERSARIES	George Beal	£8.99 ☐
MEAN BEANS	Cas Clarke	£5.99 ☐
ENCYCLOPEDIA OF FORENSIC SCIENCE	Brian Lane	£7.99 ☐
JUST THE ONE: The Wives and Times of Jeffrey Bernard	Graham Lord	£6.99 ☐
MALE SEXUAL AWARENESS	Barry McCarthy	£5.99 ☐
BURNS: A Biography of Robert Burns	James Mackay	£8.99 ☐
WORLD ENCYCLOPEDIA OF 20TH CENTURY MURDER	Jay Robert Nash	£8.99 ☐
PLAYFAIR FOOTBALL ANNUAL 1993-94	Jack Rollin (Ed)	£3.99 ☐
HEART AND SOLE	David Sole with Derek Douglas	£5.99 ☐

All Headline books are available at your local bookshop or newsagent, or can be ordered direct from the publisher. Just tick the titles you want and fill in the form below. Prices and availability subject to change without notice.

Headline Book Publishing PLC, Cash Sales Department, Bookpoint, 39 Milton Park, Abingdon, OXON, OX14 4TD, UK. If you have a credit card you may order by telephone – 0235 831700.

Please enclose a cheque or postal order made payable to Bookpoint Ltd to the value of the cover price and allow the following for postage and packing:
UK & BFPO: £1.00 for the first book, 50p for the second book and 30p for each additional book ordered up to a maximum charge of £3.00.
OVERSEAS & EIRE: £2.00 for the first book, £1.00 for the second book and 50p for each additional book.

Name ....

Address ....

....

....

If you would prefer to pay by credit card, please complete:
Please debit my Visa/Access/Diner's Card/American Express (delete as applicable) card no:

Signature .... Expiry Date ....